Extradition law

a practitioner's guide

Rebecca Niblock is an associate at Kingsley Napley LLP. As a leading extradition lawyer she specialises in matters involving extradition and cross-jurisdictional elements, both within and outside the EU at all levels from the magistrates' court to the Supreme Court. She is the extradition law specialist member of the Law Society's Criminal Law Committee. Rebecca is ranked Band 1 in Chambers UK 2015 for crime: extradition and is described as 'an urbane and thoughtful lawyer with an impressive intellect'.

Edward Grange is a partner at Corker Binning. He is recognised as a leader in the field of extradition law and has extensive experience in defending requested persons in extradition proceedings. Edward is the vice-chair of the Extradition Lawyers' Association and a member of the Legal Experts Advisory Panel that was established by Fair Trials. Edward has provided advice and representation to individuals facing extradition to a wide range of jurisdictions such as the Republic of the Gambia, United Arab Emirates, the Ukraine, the Russian Federation, the USA, Canada, Australia, New Zealand, Peru and India. Edward has had conduct of hundreds of European Arrest Warrant cases from almost every EU state.

In recognition of their expertise in matters relating to extradition law, Rebecca and Edward were called upon by the House of Lords Select Committee on Extradition to give live evidence in October 2014. Their evidence featured prominently in the Committee's report that was published in March 2015.

Available as an ebook at www.lag.org.uk/ebooks

The purpose of the Legal Action Group is to promote equal access to justice for all members of society who are socially, economically or otherwise disadvantaged. To this end, it seeks to improve law and practice, the administration of justice and legal services.

Extradition law

a practitioner's guide

SECOND EDITION

Edward Grange and Rebecca Niblock

 Legal Action Group
2015

This edition published in Great Britain 2015
by LAG Education and Service Trust Limited
3rd floor, Universal House, 88–94 Wentworth Street, London E1 7SA
www.lag.org.uk

First edition published 2013

While every effort has been made to ensure that the details in this text are correct, readers must be aware that the law changes and that the accuracy of the material cannot be guaranteed and the author and the publisher accept no responsibility for any loss or damage sustained.

British Library Cataloguing in Publication Data
a CIP catalogue record for this book is available from the British Library.

This book has been produced using Forest Stewardship Council (FSC) certified paper. The wood used to produce FSC certified products with a 'Mixed Sources' label comes from FSC certified well-managed forests, controlled sources and/or recycled material.

Print ISBN   978 1 908407 60 3
ebook ISBN   978 1 908407 61 0

Typeset by Regent Typesetting, London
Printed in Great Britain by Hobbs the Printers, Totton, Hampshire

Foreword

At the book launch of the previous edition of *Extradition law* I said that the book was already out of date. This was not a criticism. On the contrary, Edward Grange and Rebecca Niblock had done everything then, as they have now, to ensure that the book is completely up to the minute. However the reality is that extradition law continues to evolve rapidly. Some of this change is highlighted by decisions of the higher courts, or more particularly by the interpretations put on those judgments. In addition we have had some significant changes to the Act itself. To meet perceived concern about the workings of the Act, there is a new forum bar, a new proportionality bar, and new protections for those accused of offences abroad but against whom no decision has so far been taken to charge or try. Undoubtedly arguments on these new provisions are currently taking the time of the courts, and it remains to be seen the extent to which, in the long term, they are seen to provide helpful extra protection.

Since the last edition of this book there have been many challenges to extradition based on Article 8 (the right to private and family life) and prison conditions in the receiving country. These are almost always argued persuasively and with considerable skill by the parties on both sides. Have these arguments reached their high-water mark?

Those facing extradition are generally well served by their legal representatives. This is as well, because a person arrested on an extradition warrant needs help. Extradition is stressful, usually more stressful than domestic criminal proceedings. The law is complicated and, as mentioned, constantly developing. It can all happen rather suddenly: one day you are at work, and the next day you are at Westminster Magistrates' Court being asked whether you consent to extradition.

Important decisions need to be made at that first hearing. The lawyer giving advice needs to be well-informed and up-to-date. Often it is unhelpful to adjourn for a few days to consider the position.

Apart from anything else, this may be the only occasion when the defendant has access to free legal advice. So the lawyer needs to get it right first time.

That is where this book comes in. It provides an excellent introduction to the law of extradition in England and Wales (and indeed to other jurisdictions within the United Kingdom). The lawyer who practises in this area, or who intends to practise in this area, will find the book very readable. It gives valuable practical advice on how the court works and what the judges expect. It covers the main arguments that can be raised against extradition. Even experienced lawyers will find they have something to learn, because the law is constantly developing.

Before the Extradition Act 2003 came into force in January 2004 there were fewer than 100 new cases a year at Bow Street Magistrates' Court (the only court at that time dealing with extradition cases). Now there are over 2,100 cases each year at Westminster Magistrates' Court, where all first instance extradition decisions in England and Wales are taken today. The workload of the judges is increasing. We have moved from using one court occasionally to five courts every day plus one or two on Saturday. Moreover, a significant 'spike' of new work is anticipated as a result of Schengen II.

Defendants, and frankly the extradition judges, rely heavily on the specialist lawyers. We recognise that we have the advantage of many excellent extradition lawyers, instructed by the CPS and by the defence. They already have access to specialist practitioners' books and to a significant volume of jurisprudence. Nevertheless this book has filled a gap.

Howard Riddle
Senior District Judge (Chief Magistrate)
Westminster Magistrates' Court

June 2015

Preface

Since the first edition of this book was published in May 2013, the Extradition Act 2003 has been substantially amended by the Crime and Courts Act 2013 and the Anti-social Behaviour, Crime and Policing Act 2014. The forum bar has been in force for two years and the proportionality bar for a little over a year. Practitioners (as well as the judiciary) are still feeling their way around the amendments. Following the recommendation in the Sir Scott Baker review on extradition, a leave to appeal stage was finally brought into force earlier this year in April 2015. This book covers all of the amendments.

Extradition remains a complex and rapidly developing area of law. Although those with a background in criminal law will be familiar with some of the concepts and procedure, there are a number of conventions which differ in extradition proceedings and which are not apparent from the legislation. This book, written by practising solicitors, aims to provide a practical guide to extradition law for those representing requested persons. It is written with the duty solicitor in mind, but should also be of assistance to solicitors and barristers acting for requested persons, from the magistrates' courts to the Supreme Court. The book is one that will fit handsomely into the busy lawyer's bag and prove invaluable as a tool to tackle the minefield of extradition law and procedure.

The following chapters will provide a solid foundation for the extradition duty solicitor to competently represent those facing extradition and to provide the necessary advice. The book begins by looking at practical considerations in chapter 2. Chapter 3 goes on to examine the European Arrest Warrant in detail. A guide to the areas which should be covered when meeting the client for the first time is provided in chapter 4. The book then gives an overview of ways in which extradition can be challenged, looking first at the bars to extradition and then at human rights considerations in chapters 5 and 6. The initial hearing is covered in chapter 7 and chapter 8 deals with requests from outside the European Union.

The preparation required for the contested extradition hearing is considered in chapter 9. An explanation of the steps which will be taken in the full contested extradition hearing is dealt with in chapter 10. The book then goes on to provide a guide to the new appeals process in chapter 11. The final chapter looks at various ancillary matters, such as compromising a warrant, temporary surrender, funding and transfer of sentenced prisoners.

Edward Grange
Rebecca Niblock

July 2015

Acknowledgments

As with the first edition, the meticulous Myles Grandison has been our first, and in many ways our most important, reader. We must thank him for applying the same carefulness to his scrutiny of our book that he applies to his opponents' skeleton arguments. Esther Pilger at LAG has once again been very patient and encouraging throughout; we thank her and Nim Moorthy for all of their help throughout the process. We also thank Danielle Reece-Greenhalgh at Corker Binning and the army of readers at Kingsley Napley for their scrupulous attention to the manuscript.

Those who have been around us will know that it has taken as long to amend the second edition as it did to write the first. Among those who have supported us personally, we thank Natalie Smith, Jasper Jarmain, Sidney Johnston and Rob Blair.

Contents

Table of cases

Table of statutes

Table of statutory instruments

Table of European and international material

Abbreviations

ACO	Administrative Court Office
CLAS	Criminal Law Accreditation Scheme
CJEU	Court of Justice of the European Union
CPS	Crown Prosecution Service
Crim PD	Criminal Practice Directions
Crim PR	Criminal Procedure Rules 2015
DPP	Director of Public Prosecutions
EA 2003	Extradition Act 2003
EAW	European Arrest Warrant
ECHR	European Convention on Human Rights and Fundamental Freedoms
ECRIS	Exchange of information on criminal records
ECtHR	European Court of Human Rights
EU	European Union
Evie	Evidence via the internet hearings
IJO	International Jurisdiction Office
LAA	Legal Aid Agency
NCA	National Crime Agency
SCCO	Senior Courts Cost Office
SIS II	Schengen Information System II
SSHD	Secretary of State for the Home Department
WMC	Westminster Magistrates' Court

Introduction

1.1 Since the Extradition Act (EA) 2003 came into force in 2004, the United Kingdom has seen a vast increase in the number of persons who are the subject of an extradition request. For the period 1997–2003, 781 requests for extradition were made to the United Kingdom. By contrast, in just one year in 2013-2014, the number of requests received by England, Wales and Northern Ireland under the European Arrest Warrant (EAW) scheme alone (ie, requests emanating from EU countries only) was 7,881. Poland made the majority of these requests.

1.2 In October 2012 the Legal Services Commission (now the Legal Aid Agency) created a separate extradition rota for Westminster Magistrates' Court. Each day, two duty solicitors are allocated to the extradition court. The extradition duty solicitors are expected to represent those produced at court following arrest. The extradition courts currently span five courtrooms with the majority of work being heard on the first floor. An increase in the workload of the court is expected as a result of the implementation in the United Kingdom of the Schengen Information System II (SIS II), an EU-wide governmental database that came into effect on 13 April 2015. Although there is no formal requirement for the extradition duty solicitor to have had any extradition training,[1] the courts will expect the duty solicitor to be competent to undertake the work.

Extradition controversy and review

1.3 The EA 2003 has not been without its controversies. In particular, the EAW scheme has been criticised for overuse. It is also said to have been abused, with instances of EAWs being issued for 'trivial' offences, such as theft of a chicken, stealing a garage gate and riding a bicycle while drunk. The government attempted to address these criticisms by implementing a number of amendments under the Anti-social Behaviour, Crime and Policing Act 2014, although whether these amendments will be effective remains to be seen.

1.4 The US–UK extradition arrangements have also come under attack from opponents who maintain that they are one-sided and do not afford British citizens sufficient protection.

1.5 On 8 September 2010, the new coalition government announced plans to review the UK's extradition arrangements. On 14 October

---

1 The Criminal Law Accreditation Scheme (CLAS) does not contain any assessment of extradition law.

2010, Sir Scott Baker, David Perry QC and Anand Doobay were tasked with the challenge of conducting a review. On 18 October 2011, the review panel's report was published.[2] The report concluded that 'apart from the problem of proportionality, we believe that the European arrest warrant scheme has worked reasonably well'.

1.6   Despite the review panel concluding that a forum bar was not necessary, in October 2012 the Secretary of State for the Home Department (SSHD) announced that she would proceed to introduce a forum bar into the EA 2003 to allow a UK court to determine where a person should be tried. The SSHD also announced that her duty to consider human rights issues arising after a person's appeal rights have been exhausted should be transferred to the High Court rather than remain with her. These amendments have now been brought into force.

1.7   A further review was carried out by the House of Lords Select Committee on Extradition which commenced work in March 2014 and published its findings in March 2015. The Committee's remit was to conduct post-legislative scrutiny of the law and practice relating to extradition. It found that although many of the UK's existing arrangements are satisfactory, the system of accepting assurances from countries with a dubious record of compliance with human rights[3] is such that it could not guarantee that the United Kingdom is meeting its human rights obligations. It also called for the government to look again at the decision to require a means test for legal aid in extradition cases.

What is extradition?

1.8   Extradition is the formal process whereby the *requesting state* asks the *requested state* to return an individual that is in the requested state in order to stand trial or to serve a custodial sentence imposed in the requesting state. The EA 2003 governs extradition proceedings in the United Kingdom.

---

2 *A Review of the United Kingdom's Extradition Arrangements* available from www.gov.uk/government/uploads/system/uploads/attachment_data/file/117673/extradition-review.pdf.

3 See paragraph 6.9ff.

Extradition Act 2003

1.9   The EA 2003 came into force on 1 January 2004. Extradition requests received after this date are dealt with under the EA 2003. Requests received on or before 31 December 2003 are dealt with under the Extradition Act 1989.

1.10   The EA 2003 is split into five parts:

Part 1 – Extradition to category 1 territories (known as 'EAW cases');
Part 2 – Extradition to category 2 territories (known as 'Part 2 cases');
Part 3 – Extradition to the United Kingdom;
Part 4 – Police powers;
Part 5 – Miscellaneous and general provisions.

Part 1 and Part 2 requests for extradition

1.11   The United Kingdom has extradition arrangements with over 100 territories. Part 1 warrants (referred to as 'EAW cases') are the most common types of request.

1.12   The following territories have been designated category 1 territories and all issue EAWs:

Austria, Belgium, Bulgaria, Cyprus, Croatia, Czech Republic, Denmark, Estonia, Finland, France, Germany, Gibraltar, Greece, Hungary, Ireland, Italy, Latvia, Lithuania, Luxembourg, Malta, the Netherlands, Poland, Portugal, Romania, Slovakia, Slovenia, Spain and Sweden.

1.13   Part 2 territories include the following:

Albania, Algeria, Andorra, Anguilla, Antigua and Barbuda, Argentina, Armenia, Aruba, Australia, Azerbaijan, The Bahamas, Bangladesh, Barbados, Belize, Bermuda, Bolivia, Bonaire, Bosnia and Herzegovina, Botswana, Brazil, British Antarctic Territory, British Indian Ocean Territory, Brunei, Canada, Cayman Islands, Chile, Colombia, Cook Islands, Cuba, Curaçao, Dominica, Ecuador, El Salvador, Falkland Islands, Faroe Islands, Fiji, The Gambia, Georgia, Ghana, Greenland, Grenada, Guatemala, Guyana, Hong Kong Special Administrative Region, Haiti, Iceland, India, Iraq, Israel, Jamaica, Kenya, Kiribati, Kosovo, Lesotho, Liberia, Libya, Liechtenstein, Macedonia (FYR), Malawi, Malaysia, Maldives, Mauritius, Mexico, Moldova, Monaco, Montenegro, Montserrat, Nauru, New Zealand, Nicaragua, Nigeria, Norway, Panama, Papua New Guinea, Paraguay, Peru, Philippines, Pitcairn, Henderson,

Ducie and Oeno Islands, Republic of Korea, Russian Federation, Saba, Saint Christopher and Nevis, Saint Helena, Ascension and Tristan da Cunha, Saint Lucia, Saint Vincent and the Grenadines, San Marino, Serbia, Seychelles, Sierra Leone, Singapore, Sint Eustatius, Sint Maarten, Solomon Islands, South Africa, South Georgia and the South Sandwich Islands, The Sovereign Base Areas of Akrotiri and Dhekalia, Sri Lanka, Swaziland, Switzerland, Tanzania, Thailand, Tonga, Trinidad and Tobago, Turkey, Turks and Caicos Islands, Tuvalu, Uganda, Ukraine, United Arab Emirates, United States, Uruguay, Vanuatu, Virgin Islands, Western Samoa, Zambia, Zimbabwe.

1.14   If a country does not appear above it does not mean that an extradition request cannot be made. Those countries that are not extradition treaty partners with the United Kingdom can still make extradition requests and be treated as if they were a category 2 territory. These arrangements are known as 'ad hoc arrangements' (see paragraph 8.4).

Framework Decision on the European Arrest Warrant

1.15   The EAW came into effect as a result of the Council Framework Decision 2002/584/JHA of 13 June 2002 (see appendix A). EAWs are valid throughout the European Union. They are intended to allow an issuing judicial authority to secure the return of a requested person quickly and easily. The aim of the Framework Decision was to replace the complex system of extradition with a system of *surrender* between member states.

Extradition proceedings – participants

1.16   Many organisations play a part in extradition proceedings in England and Wales. They are:
- CPS Extradition Unit;
- National Crime Agency (NCA);
- Home Office for Part 2 cases;
- Government Legal Department (GLD);
- Metropolitan Police Extradition and International Assistance Unit (Extradition Squad);
- Westminster Magistrates' Court (WMC);

- Administrative Court;
- Supreme Court; and
- extradition defence lawyers.

Crown Prosecution Service

1.17   The Director of Public Prosecutions (DPP) has a duty to conduct extradition proceedings.[4] The Crown Prosecution Service (CPS) acts as the representative of the requesting state. The Extradition Unit of the CPS is part of the Special Crime Division based at Rose Court, London. The Extradition Unit need not apply the Code for Crown Prosecutors in extradition proceedings. The role of the CPS can include providing advice to foreign states on the preparation of an extradition request; advising foreign states on the content and validity of an extradition request received from the NCA/Home Office; representing judicial authorities/requesting states in proceedings before WMC, the High Court and the Supreme Court; and advising foreign states on the merits of an appeal. Those representing the requesting state/judicial authority are referred to in the Criminal Procedure Rules as 'presenting officers.'[5]

1.18   It is possible for the requesting state to instruct a private firm of solicitors to act on its behalf under section 3(2A) of the Prosecution of Offences Act 1985. At the time of writing, this has only happened once since the EA 2003 came into force.

National Crime Agency

1.19   The NCA is the central authority designated to receive EAWs. The NCA certifies EAWs in accordance with EA 2003 s2 (including a proportionality exercise in accusation cases) and facilitates communication between the CPS and the issuing judicial authority. The NCA will also arrange for the surrender of those whose extradition has been ordered by the courts in EAW cases.

Home Office for Part 2 cases

1.20   The SSHD is responsible for certifying extradition requests from Part 2 territories and all extradition requests are received at the Home Office for processing. The Home Office is also responsible for

---

4   Prosecution of Offences Act 1985 s3(2)(ea).
5   Criminal Procedure Rules (Crim PR) 17.2.

arranging removal in Part 2 cases. The SSHD plays an important role in Part 2 cases.

Government Legal Department

1.21   The Government Legal Department (formerly Treasury Solicitor's Department)[6] is a non-ministerial government department that provides legal services to the majority of central government departments.[7] The GLD acts as private solicitor for the SSHD in extradition cases when the SSHD is a party to the proceedings in the High Court.

Metropolitan Police Extradition Squad

1.22   The extradition squad is responsible for all arrests of persons sought under Part 2 requests (whether carried out alone or with the assistance of a local force). It also carries out some arrests in EAW cases for those who are located within the Metropolitan Police area. Outside this area, the extradition squad offers support and provide assistance where required to local officers. The extradition squad is based at New Scotland Yard.

Westminster Magistrates' Court

1.23   Extradition proceedings can be conducted at any court where an 'appropriate judge' is sitting. However, the majority of cases are heard at Westminster Magistrates' Court. The International Jurisdiction Office (IJO) at WMC deals with the administration of extradition cases.

1.24   Extradition hearings will always be heard before specially trained district judges (known as 'appropriate judges'). A district judge is designated an appropriate judge by the Lord Chief Justice of England and Wales after consulting the Lord Chancellor.[8] The Senior District Judge (Chief Magistrate) is Howard Riddle and the Deputy Senior District Judge is Emma Arbuthnot.

---

6   On 1 April 2015 the Treasury Solicitor's Department became the Government Legal Department.

7   www.gov.uk/government/organisations/government-legal-department.

8   EA 2003 s139(1)(a).

Administrative Court

1.25 Appeals under the EA 2003 are heard in the Administrative Court, Royal Courts of Justice, London. Appeals are heard by a single judge or by a Divisional Court made up of two or three judges, one of whom will be a Lord/Lady Justice. The President of the Queen's Bench Division is Sir Brian Leveson. The Lord Justice with overall supervision of extradition appeals is Lord Justice Aikens.

1.26 Each appeal case is allocated to a lawyer at the Administrative Court who will be the initial contact for enquiries regarding the case. The Administrative Court also hears appeals against the refusal/grant of bail by WMC.

Supreme Court

1.27 In October 2009, the Supreme Court superseded the Appellate Committee of the House of Lords as the highest court in the United Kingdom. An appeal can only be brought to the Supreme Court if the High Court has certified that there is a point of law of general public importance and where the High Court or the Supreme Court has granted leave to appeal.

1.28 The Supreme Court has 12 justices and the President of the Supreme Court is Lord Neuberger.

Extradition defence lawyers

1.29 Those arrested under the EA 2003 are very often represented at the first court appearance by the duty solicitor. It is imperative that they receive competent advice and representation from a solicitor who is knowledgeable in extradition law.

1.30 The following chapters will go some way to providing practitioners with the foundations needed to adequately represent 'requested persons'[9] in extradition proceedings.

---

9 Crim PR 17.2 refers to 'requested persons' as the 'defendant'. This book will use the phrase 'requested person' to refer to those arrested under Part 1 or Part 2 of the EA 2003.

Practical considerations

Introduction

2.1   This chapter looks at practical matters for lawyers acting on behalf of those making their first appearance at the magistrates' court in extradition cases and, in particular, duty solicitors. It looks first at police powers and the arrest of a requested person, and goes on to describe a typical day of the duty solicitor in the extradition courts.

Arrest

2.2   A solicitor will often have minimal involvement when a requested person is first arrested. Police powers[1] allow for the arrest and search of a requested person for extradition and that person's treatment will be governed by the special code of practice that applies to extradition.[2] The police have the power to search both the person and the premises and to seize and retain material, but only if that material shows evidence of the requested person's identity, or relates to the extradition offence for which the person is sought.

2.3   The police will generally ask the requested person to identify themselves and seek to obtain evidence of their identity. Upon arrest, the police will caution the requested person. Anything that the requested person says (for example, 'Oh yes, I know all about this, it's the burglary that I committed in Krakow in 2007') will be noted and may be used in subsequent proceedings.

2.4   The right of access to legal advice at the police station under s58 Police and Criminal Evidence Act 1984 applies to those arrested in extradition cases.[3] However, for the vast majority of those requested persons who are unable to pay for legal advice, this will be limited to telephone advice. Given that the police do not interview requested persons, it is unlikely that physical attendance at the police station would pass the 'sufficient benefit' test as set out in the 2010 Standard Crime Contract provisions. The requested person will also have the right to have someone informed of their arrest, and, if necessary, will have access to an interpreter; very often by way of Language Line.

2.5   A person may not be granted bail by the police when arrested on an EAW. A person arrested under Part 2 of the Act may be granted

---

1   See EA 2003 Pt 4.
2   www.gov.uk/government/uploads/system/uploads/attachment_data/ file/117675/extradition-codes-of-practice.pdf.
3   EA 2003 s171(3)(d).

bail (EA 2003 ss72(4)(a) and 74(4)(a)). Where a person is held in custody following arrest, he or she must be brought before a court as soon as practicable.[4]

The duty solicitor's day

2.6 Unlike general criminal matters, it is unusual for those making their first appearance after an arrest under the EA 2003 to have their own solicitor. Many arrested will require the assistance of an interpreter.

2.7 The duty solicitor's day in the extradition courts can be a busy one. It is not unusual for the duty solicitor to be fully occupied throughout the day and until after 6 pm. There are five extradition court rooms at WMC and some have different functions. The court's work is generally separated as follows:

- Court 1 – full extradition hearings;
- Court 2 – full extradition hearings;
- Court 3 – video-link remand hearings, short hearings and initial hearings;
- Court 4 – full extradition hearings (fixed and 'floaters');
- Court 5 – remand hearings (custody and bail), short extradition hearings and applications.

2.8 The magistrates' court at Westminster sits at 10 am. Duty solicitors should arrive at 9 am and sign in at the first floor enquiries counter. Although the first hour or so may be quiet, requested persons arrive throughout the day, and any preparation that has been done before the court begins to sit will be useful later on in the day when it is likely to be very busy. It is important that duty solicitors make themselves known to the list caller in court 3 and to the CPS so that all the extradition work is handed to them. While those arrested on an EAW or extradition request will occasionally have their own solicitor, the majority will not. It is therefore advisable to obtain the EAWs/extradition requests from the CPS early on in the day to allow time to properly consider them (see chapter 3). The CPS should also provide a statement from the arresting officer and the requested person's record of previous convictions. The prosecution may be found in the extradition courts, or outside the courtrooms just before they open. They also have an unmarked office on the first floor of the

---

4 EA 2003 s4(3) for Part 1 cases and s72(3) for Part 2 cases (s74(3) for provisional arrest requests).

courthouse in the corridor opposite Courts 3 and 4, which is attended throughout the day by CPS caseworkers.

2.9   It is good practice for the duty solicitor to make him or herself known to the gaolers. By attending the cells, one can garner a considerable amount of information from the whiteboard that shows who is in custody and who is expected to be brought in to custody. The whiteboard displays information that can help in this regard. In particular, it will show the police station or prison that the person is coming from. If a person is coming from a police station or prison that is not in London, it is very likely that the person will be an extradition client. The gaolers should be able to give an indication of when the person is expected to arrive. Once the person has arrived, the gaolers will ask him or her whether an interpreter is required, and will note that information on the board. The cells are closed between 1.00 pm and 1.45 pm. This time can usefully be used either reading EAWs, speaking to family members about bail arrangements or completing legal aid forms.

2.10   Because requested persons are arrested all over the country, they will arrive throughout the day until the 'referral time',[5] which is 12.30 pm. Any persons arriving after that time will be referred to the judge, who will decide whether or not they will be accepted by the gaolers, or whether they will be detained in a local police station overnight to appear at court the following day. It is possible, therefore, to have a very quiet morning as duty solicitor but to have a number of clients in the afternoon. Generally, if there are more than four extradition clients per duty solicitor who require advice and representation, the court will ask another duty solicitor to assist. If it is apparent that there are a large number of cases to deal with, it is wise to seek assistance at an early stage. In every case, there is a significant amount of important information to convey to, and obtain from, the requested person and, particularly where an interpreter is required, this can take some time. In addition, it will often take time to obtain information from third parties required for a bail application, such as a bail surety or security, a suitable address, location of identity documents, or the nearest police station for a reporting condition. Duty solicitors should allow a minimum of 45 minutes for every client, allowing time for completion of legal aid and case management forms. Although there is sometimes pressure from the court, it is important that the necessary time is spent looking at the warrant and advising

---

5   While sometimes called the 'cut-off time', 'referral time' is a more accurate description – not all those arriving after 12.30 pm will be turned away.

the client. A failure to explain something at this stage, or to ask a particular question, could mean that a person is wrongly extradited.

2.11   If it is apparent that a client requires an interpreter for a language other than Polish, Lithuanian or Romanian, it is important that this is made known to the list caller as soon as possible. In theory, the court should be notified by the arresting police officers that an interpreter is needed, but this frequently fails to happen and, for more unusual languages, it can take hours for an interpreter to arrive. If no interpreter has been booked, the legal adviser should make arrangements to book one by notifying the IJO. At the time of writing, all interpreters are provided to the court by one company under contract. The quality of interpreters varies greatly, and solicitors should be alive to the possibility that the interpreter that has been provided may be inexperienced or unfamiliar with the terminology used in extradition cases.

2.12   New cases are likely to be heard in Court 3 after the video-link remand hearings have been concluded. Any overflow will go to any other available extradition court room.

2.13   Legal aid forms can be date stamped at the first floor enquiries counter on the day of the requested person's first appearance to ensure that any work done thereafter is covered. A requested person in custody should not have to provide evidence of income and, as long as the form is fully completed and he or she is financially eligible, legal aid will be granted in the interests of justice for all extradition cases.

2.14   Ideally, following the hearing the client should be seen and the outcome explained. This is often impracticable when dealing with several clients in succession in court. One may find at the end of the day that the client has been taken to prison before it has been possible to see him or her again. For this reason it is important to ensure that all matters, including appeal procedures, are covered before the court appearance.

Essential materials

2.15   Duty solicitors in the extradition court should take with them:

- a sufficient number of forms CRM14, CRM15 and the declaration for online submissions;
- an updated copy of the EA 2003, Criminal Procedure Rules 2015

and Criminal Practice Directions (an electronic copy can be stored, for example on a mobile phone or tablet device);

- this book;
- checklists.

Looking at a European Arrest Warrant

continued

Introduction

3.1 The purpose of the Framework Decision of 2002 (see appendix A), which created the EAW scheme, was to simplify and facilitate extradition procedures across EU countries. To this end, the extradition scheme became a form-filling exercise.[1] The model EAW form is annexed to the Framework Decision; its purpose is to ensure that all of the relevant information required by Article 8 of the Framework Decision is included by the judicial authority.[2] It should, however, be noted that if the form is incorrectly filled out, for example, if there are boxes that are not filled in, this does not in itself invalidate the warrant.[3] At the time of writing, a new 'Form A' is being distributed as an alternative to the translated EAW (under SIS II, see paragraph 7.7). A copy of this form is included in appendix D. It will be necessary to scrutinise these forms with great care to ensure compliance with EA 2003 s2. In addition it may be necessary to look at the warrant in the original language in order to determine whether there are any obvious omissions or discrepancies. This chapter will go on to look at the warrant and at each box of the form as set out in the appendix. It will look in some detail at challenges to the validity of the warrant, along with extradition offences.

The European Arrest Warrant

Certification by the National Crime Agency

3.2 EAWs in the United Kingdom must be certified by the NCA, the certificate being attached to the front of the warrant. To qualify for certification, the EAW must have been issued by a judicial authority (ie, an authority that the NCA believes has the function of issuing arrest warrants in the territory concerned: EA 2003 s2(7)).[4]

---

1 The transposition of the Framework Decision of 2002 into domestic law by the EA 2003 was not direct, and there are differences between the provisions set out in the Framework Decision and the implementing legislation.

2 The European Judicial Network website contains an 'EAW wizard', which provides an online form for judicial authorities to complete to create an EAW: www.ejn-crimjust.europa.eu.

3 See paragraph 3.23 and following below for the circumstances in which a warrant may be held to be invalid.

4 The case of *Assange v Swedish Prosecution Authority* [2012] UKSC 22 looked at whether a public prosecutor could be properly classified as a judicial authority or not, and concluded that, in that particular case, it could be. This issue was

3.3   The EAW must also contain a statement of purpose and specified information (EA 2003 s2(4) and (6)). The certificate will give the date that the requesting state issued the EAW and the date on which it was certified by the NCA. It should also be signed. If it is not signed[5] and dated, this may mean that the arrest and subsequent detention of the person named in the warrant are unlawful.[6] Once the warrant has been certified, it may be executed by a police officer or a customs officer in any part of the United Kingdom.

Proportionality check by the National Crime Agency

3.4   The Anti-social Behaviour, Crime and Policing Act 2014 s157 amended EA 2003 s2 to require the NCA to refuse to certify an EAW if it would be clear to them that a judge proceeding under section 21A would be required to order a person's discharge on the basis that extradition would be disproportionate (see paragraph 5.99 regarding EA 2003 s21A). In determining this question, the NCA must apply any general guidance issued by the Lord Chief Justice ('LCJ guidance').[7] This guidance sets out the type of offences for which a judge (absent exceptional circumstances) should generally determine that extradition would be disproportionate.[8] The table of offences can be found at Crim PD 17A.5 of the Criminal Practice Directions and is set out opposite:

revisited in relation to EAWs issued by ministries of justice in *Ministry of Justice, Lithuania v Bucnys* [2012] EWHC 2771 (Admin), which held that while the warrant had been issued by the Lithuanian Ministry of Justice, this could be classified as a judicial authority because the request for the EAW was based on an enforceable judgment of conviction and sentence. It also, however, looked at an EAW that had been issued by the Ministry of Justice in Estonia and found that it had not been issued by a judicial authority because the decision to issue that warrant could not be regarded as a 'judicial decision'. Any warrant issued by a body other than a court should be carefully checked against the case-law to determine whether it can be argued that the warrant was not issued by a judicial authority.

5   It is sufficient if the certificate contains an electronic signature or the initials of the person that certified it.

6   For a case in which this argument arose, see *Rimas v Lithuania* [2011] EWHC 2084 (Admin).

7   EA 2003 s2(7C) as inserted by Anti-social Behaviour, Crime and Policing Act 2014 s157(3).

8   Criminal Practice Directions (Amendment No 2) [2014] EWHC Crim 1569.

Table 3.1 Offences for which extradition will normally be disproportionate

Category of offence	Examples
Minor **theft** – (not robbery/burglary or theft from the person)	Where the theft is of a low monetary value and there is a low impact on the victim or indirect harm to others, for example: (a) Theft of an item of food from a supermarket (b) Theft of a small amount of scrap metal from company premises (c) Theft of a very small sum of money
Minor financial offences (**forgery, fraud** and **tax** offences)	Where the sums involved are small and there is a low impact on the victim and/or low indirect harm to others, for example: (a) Failure to file a tax return or invoices on time (b) Making a false statement in a tax return (c) Dishonestly applying for a tax refund (d) Obtaining a bank loan using a forged or falsified document (e) Non-payment of child maintenance
Minor **road traffic, driving** and related offences	Where no injury, loss or damage was incurred to any person or property, for example: (a) Driving whilst using a mobile phone (b) Use of a bicycle whilst intoxicated
Minor **public order** offences	Where there is no suggestion the person started the trouble, and the offending behaviour was for example: (a) Non-threatening verbal abuse of a law enforcement officer or government official (b) Shouting or causing a disturbance, without threats (c) Quarrelling in the street, without threats
Minor criminal damage, (other than by fire)	For example, breaking a window
Possession of controlled substance (other than one with a high capacity for harm such as heroin, cocaine, LSD or crystal meth)	Where it was possession of a very small quantity and intended for personal use

3.5   The exceptional circumstances (referred to in Crim PD 17A.3) are listed at Crim PD 17A.4 and include:

1) Vulnerable victim.
2) Crime committed against someone because of their disability, gender-identity, race, religion or belief, or sexual orientation.
3) Significant premeditation.
4) Multiple counts.
5) Extradition also sought for another offence.
6) Previous offending history.

3.6   Practitioners will be aware that while the first three factors above are relatively exceptional, at least one of the last three factors will very frequently be present. If any of these circumstances are present, the NCA is likely to certify the EAW despite the offence being one that falls within the LCJ's guidance.

Statement of purpose and box A

3.7   The first page of the EAW will usually contain the statement of purpose along with information required to identify the requested person, which is set out in box A.

(a) Information regarding the identity of the requested person:

Name:

Forename(s):

Maiden name, where applicable:

Aliases, where applicable:

Sex:

Nationality:

Date of birth:

Place of birth:

Residence and/or known address:

Language(s) which the requested person understands (if known):

Distinctive marks/description of the requested person:

Photo and fingerprints of the requested person, if they are available and can be transmitted, or contact details of the person to be contacted in order to obtain such information or a DNA profile (where this evidence can be supplied but has not been included).

3.8   In theory, the statement of purpose will be different for accused or convicted persons (see EA 2003 s2(3) and (5)), but in practice most warrants will contain the standard statement set out in the pro forma, which states:

> This warrant has been issued by a competent judicial authority. I request that the person mentioned below be arrested and surrendered for the purposes of conducting a criminal prosecution or executing a custodial sentence or detention order.

In order to determine whether the EAW has been issued for an accusation or following conviction, it will, therefore, be necessary to look at the warrant as a whole, but in particular boxes B and C of the EAW. Practitioners should note that a failure to delete the inapplicable part of the pro forma does not invalidate the EAW.

3.9   Box A sets out information that enables the authorities to identify the requested person. Frequently some fields in this box will be left blank. This will not invalidate the warrant, but the name of the requested person and the date of birth will clearly be essential in order to ensure that the correct person is arrested.

Box B

(b) Decision on which the warrant is based:
1. Arrest warrant or judicial decision having the same effect:
Type:
....
2. Enforceable judgment:
....
Reference:
....

3.10   Box B requires the judicial authority to state the decision on which the warrant is based, and will either be:

- an 'arrest warrant or judicial decision having the same effect' (in the case of an accusation warrant); or
- an 'enforceable judgment' (in the case of a conviction warrant).

3.11   It is from this box, therefore, that it will usually be possible to determine whether the requested person wanted by the judicial authority is being accused or has been convicted. In some cases, the requested person will be wanted for both accusation and conviction offences and the judicial authority will, therefore, have to provide both sets of information. These EAWs are known as 'hybrid warrants'. The judicial authority should state the type of decision along with its date and the case reference.

Box C

(c) Indications on the length of the sentence:

1. Maximum length of the custodial sentence or detention order which may be imposed for the offence(s):

....

2. Length of the custodial sentence or detention order imposed:

....

Remaining sentence to be served:

....

3.12 This section will contain information regarding either (in the case of (1) above) the maximum custodial sentence or, in the case of (2) above, the length of the sentence imposed and the remaining sentence to be served. As with box B, it is divided into two sections, which should correspond with those in the box above (ie if (1) is completed in box B, it should also be (1) that is filled in for box C).

3.13 The function of this box is to ensure that the offences for which the warrant has been issued meet the minimum requirements for the punishment threshold for which EAWs can be issued: that is, for those yet to be sentenced, an offence that carries imprisonment of 12 months or more, or, in the case of requested persons who have been sentenced, an offence for which the person has been sentenced to a term of four months' imprisonment or more. It is the sentence that will be imposed in the requesting state that is determinative, and not the sentence in the requested state. This means that, unlike in Part 2 cases, a person can be extradited for an offence that does not carry a sentence of imprisonment in this country, as long as the minimum sentence in the requesting state is 12 months (for those yet to be sentenced) and four months (for sentenced persons). Different minimum sentence periods apply to those offences in the Framework list (see paragraph 3.18 below).

3.14   Box C also allows the judicial authority to state the remaining sentence to be served. A failure to complete this part of box C or an error as to the amount of time left to serve will not invalidate the warrant.[9] The idea of an outstanding sentence to be served may be unfamiliar to many UK criminal practitioners who see their clients serving sentences immediately and then being released at the half-way point without returning to prison (apart from in very specific circumstances, such as breach of licence, or bail granted pending an appeal).

3.15   Many European countries, however, allow those sentenced for offences to be released part way through their sentence, with a requirement to return to prison at a date in the future. Some countries do not imprison people immediately following a sentence, but require them to surrender themselves to serve a sentence when notified. A very large proportion of Polish EAWs are issued in respect of those who have breached the Polish equivalent of a suspended sentence or licence, and are therefore required to serve a sentence of imprisonment. While the minimum period of imprisonment required for a warrant to be issued for sentenced prisoners is four months, there is no requirement for a minimum period to remain (of a sentence to be served) in order for an EAW to be issued. It is, therefore, theoretically possible for a person's extradition to be sought in order to serve a remaining sentence of, for example, one month as long as the original sentence was longer than four months. Such a case, however, may be open to challenge on the grounds that it would amount to a disproportionate interference with the requested person's rights under Article 8 of the European Convention on Human Rights. See paragraph 3.42 below regarding the requirement to state particulars of the sentence.

---

9 *Banasinski v District Court in Sanok, Poland* [2008] EWHC 3626 (Admin).

Box D (original)

> (d) Decision rendered in absentia and:
>
> The person concerned has been summoned in person or otherwise informed of the date and place of the hearing which led to the decision rendered in absentia.
>
> or
>
> The person concerned has not been summoned in person or otherwise informed of the date and place of the hearing which led to the decision rendered in absentia but has the following legal guarantees after surrender (such guarantees can be given in advance).
>
> Specify the legal guarantees:
>
> ....

3.16   Box D is used in conviction cases only to give details of the requested person's right to a retrial where he or she has been convicted in absentia (see paragraph 5.89). This box has been amended by Council Framework Decision 2009/299/JHA of 26 February 2009 to require more detail in the case of those convicted in absentia, although the provisions of EA 2003 s20 are such that the amendment makes no practical difference in the United Kingdom (see the amended box D below).[10] Whether or not the issuing state has used the old or the new pro forma for box D, it will still be necessary for the court to be satisfied to the criminal standard that a requested person who was not deliberately absent but convicted in absence will have a right to a retrial. Where a requesting state had filled in the original box D (above) with 'not applicable', this was taken by the court to be 'the clearest possible assertion on behalf of the judicial authority that the decision was not rendered in absentia but rather that he was present'.[11]

---

10   EA 2003 s20 is not to be read in light of Council Framework Decision 2009/299/JHA of 26 February 2009 (*Podlas v Koszalin District Court, Poland* [2015] EWHC 908 (Admin)).

11   *Kis (Emil) v District Court In Sokolov, Czech Republic* [2012] EWHC 938 (Admin).

Box D (as amended by Framework Decision of 2009)

(d) Indicate if the person appeared in person at the trial resulting in the decision:

1. ☐ Yes, the person appeared in person at the trial resulting in the decision.

2. ☐ No, the person did not appear in person at the trial resulting in the decision.

3. If you answered 'no' to question 2 above, please indicate if:

☐ 3.1a the person was summoned in person and thereby informed of the scheduled date and place of the trial which resulted in the decision and was informed that a decision may be handed down if he or she does not appear for the trial;

Date at which the person was summoned in person:

.... (day/month/year)

Place where the person was summoned in person:

....

OR

☐ 3.1b the person was not summoned in person but by other means actually received official information of the scheduled date and place of the trial which resulted in the decision, in such a manner that it was unequivocally established that he or she was aware of the scheduled trial, and was informed that a decision may be handed down if he or she does not appear for the trial;

Describe how it is established that the person concerned was aware of the trial:

....

OR

☐ 3.2 being aware of the scheduled trial the person had given a mandate to a legal counsellor, who was either appointed by the person concerned or by the State, to defend him or her at the trial, and was indeed defended by that counsellor at the trial;

Provide information on how this condition has been met:

....

OR

☐ 3.3 the person, after being served with the decision, expressly stated that he or she does not contest this decision.

Describe when and how the person expressly stated that he or she does not contest the decision:

....

OR

☐ 3.4 the person was entitled to a retrial or appeal under the following conditions:

☐ 3.4.1 the person was personally served with the decision on .... (day/month/year); and

– the person was expressly informed of the right to a retrial or appeal and to be present at that trial; and

– after being informed of this right, the person did not request a retrial or appeal within the applicable timeframe.

OR

☐ 3.4.2 the person was not personally served with the decision, but

– the person will be personally served with this decision without delay after the surrender; and

– when served with the decision, the person will be expressly informed of his/her right to a retrial or appeal and to be present at that trial; and

– after being served with the decision, the person will have the right to request a retrial or appeal within ..... days.

If you ticked this box 3.4.2, please confirm:

☐ that if the person sought, when being informed in the executing State about the content of the European arrest warrant, requests to receive a copy of the judgment before being surrendered, that person shall immediately after such request via the executing authority be provided with a copy of the judgment;

and

☐ that if the person has requested a retrial or appeal, the detention of the person awaiting such retrial or appeal shall, until the proceedings are finalised, be reviewed in accordance with the law of the issuing State, either on a regular basis or upon request of the person concerned; such a review shall in particular include the possibility of suspension or interruption of the detention;

and

☐ that if the person has requested a retrial or appeal, such retrial or appeal shall begin within due time after the surrender.

Box E

(e) Offences:

This warrant relates to in total: .... offences.

Description of the circumstances in which the offence(s) was (were) committed, including the time, place and degree of participation in the offence(s) by the requested person:

....

Nature and legal classification of the offence(s) and the applicable statutory provision/code:

....

I. If applicable, tick one or more of the following offences punishable in the issuing member state by a custodial sentence or detention order of a maximum of at least three years as defined by the laws of the issuing member state:

☐ participation in a criminal organisation;

☐ terrorism;

☐ trafficking in human beings;

☐ sexual exploitation of children and child pornography;

☐ illicit trafficking in narcotic drugs and psychotropic substances;

☐ illicit trafficking in weapons, munitions and explosives;

☐ corruption;

☐ fraud, including that affecting the financial interests of the European Communities within the meaning of the Convention of 26 July 1995 on the protection of European Communities' financial interests;

☐ laundering of the proceeds of crime;

☐ counterfeiting of currency, including the Euro;

☐ computer-related crime;

☐ environmental crime, including illicit trafficking in endangered animal species and in endangered plant species and varieties;

☐ facilitation of unauthorised entry and residence;

☐ murder, grievous bodily injury;

☐ illicit trade in human organs and tissue;

☐ kidnapping, illegal restraint and hostage-taking;

☐ racism and xenophobia;

☐ organised or armed robbery;

☐ illicit trafficking in cultural goods, including antiques and works of art;

☐ swindling;

☐ racketeering and extortion;

☐ counterfeiting and piracy of products;

☐ forgery of administrative documents and trafficking therein;

☐ forgery of means of payment;

☐ illicit trafficking in hormonal substances and other growth promoters;

☐ illicit trafficking in nuclear or radioactive materials;

☐ trafficking in stolen vehicles;

☐ rape;

☐ arson;

☐ crimes within the jurisdiction of the International Criminal Court;

☐ unlawful seizure of aircraft/ships;

☐ sabotage.

II. Full description of offence(s) not covered by section I above:

....

....

3.17　Box E is a particularly important part of the EAW. It is essential to examine it carefully to ensure that the warrant complies with both EA 2003 s2 and s10. As shown above, it requires the requesting state to provide information regarding the circumstances of the offence. Failure to provide sufficient detail here will invalidate the warrant (see paragraph 3.23 below).

3.18　　　The list set out in box E shows the 32 'Framework offences'. If the requesting state has ticked one of these boxes, and the offence is punishable in the member state by at least three years' imprisonment in the case of accusation warrants, or 12 months' imprisonment in the case of conviction warrants, it is not necessary to satisfy the dual criminality test (see paragraph 3.50 regarding dual criminality). The description of the offence must contain sufficient detail to establish that the conduct in question amounts to an offence in the United Kingdom (see paragraph 3.45 below for more information on extradition offences).

Box F

(f) Other circumstances relevant to the case (optional information):

....

3.19　Box F is used where the requesting state has identified potential problems with the execution of the warrant. It can be used, for example, where temporary surrender (see paragraph 7.38) is anticipated, or to give details of any limitation periods or extraterritoriality. It often also provides information on any attempts made to locate the requested person and statements about his or her knowledge of the proceedings.

Box G

(g) This warrant pertains also to the seizure and handing over of property which may be required as evidence:

This warrant pertains also to the seizure and handing over of property acquired by the requested person as a result of the offence:

Description of the property (and location) (if known):

....

3.20   This box allows for the seizure and return of evidence to the requesting state in pre-trial cases, or, post-conviction, for property which is the subject of a confiscation order. It is, at present, unusual for this box to be completed.

Box H

> (h) The offence(s) on the basis of which this warrant has been issued is(are) punishable by / has(have) led to a custodial life sentence or lifetime detention order:
>
> the legal system of the issuing member state allows for a review of the penalty or measure imposed – on request or at least after 20 years – aiming at a non-execution of such penalty or measure,
>
> and/or
>
> the legal system of the issuing member state allows for the application of measures of clemency to which the person is entitled under the law or practice of the issuing member state, aiming at non-execution of such penalty or measure.

3.21   Article 5(2) of the Framework Decision allows countries to refuse to execute an EAW if the warrant is issued for an offence punishable by a life sentence where there is no provision for a review. This provision was not transposed into UK law and this box is, therefore, irrelevant where the United Kingdom is the executing state.

Box I

> (i) The judicial authority which issued the warrant:
>
> Official name: ....
>
> Name of its representative: ....
>
> Post held (title/grade): ....
>
> File reference: ....
>
> Address: ....
>
> Tel. No.: (country code) (area/city code) (...) ....
>
> Fax No.: (country code) (area/city code) (...) ....
>
> E-mail: ....

Contact details of the person to contact to make necessary practical arrangements for the surrender:

....

Where a central authority has been made responsible for the transmission and administrative reception of European arrest warrants:

Name of the central authority: ....

Contact person, if applicable (title/grade and name): ....

Tel. No.: (country code) (area/city code) (...) ....

Fax No.: (country code) (area/city code) (...) ....

E-mail: ....

Signature of the issuing judicial authority and/or its representative:

....

Name: ....

Post held (title/grade): ....

Date: ....

Official stamp (if available):

3.22   The final boxes in the EAW, as set out above, are self-explanatory. It is necessary for this information to be provided so that practical arrangements can be made where extradition has been ordered. Box I should be referred to in order to determine whether the warrant has been issued by a 'judicial authority'.

Challenging the validity of a European Arrest Warrant

EA 2003 s2

3.23   When an EAW is received by the NCA, the latter must, according to EA 2003 s2, check that the warrant has been issued by a judicial authority of the requesting state and that it contains the following information:

- a statement that the person in respect of whom the warrant is issued is accused/convicted of an offence specified in the warrant and that it has been issued with a view to his arrest and extradition for the purpose of conducting a prosecution or executing a custodial sentence;

- particulars of the person's identity;
- (in the case of a conviction warrant) particulars of the conviction;
- particulars of any other warrant issued in the category 1 territory for the person's arrest in respect of the offence;
- (in the case of an accusation warrant) particulars of the circumstances in which the person is alleged to have committed the offence, including the conduct alleged to constitute the offence, the time and place at which he or she is alleged to have committed the offence and any provision of the law of the category 1 territory under which the conduct is alleged to constitute an offence;
- particulars of the sentence that may be imposed under the law of the category 1 territory in respect of the offence if the person is convicted of it/has not been sentenced; and
- (in the case of a sentenced person) particulars of the sentence that has been imposed.

3.24   If the warrant contains this information and the NCA believes that the authority which issued the Part 1 warrant has the function of issuing arrest warrants in the category 1 territory, the NCA may issue a certificate (see paragraph 3.2 above). In accusation cases, the NCA must not certify the warrant if it is clear that a judge would discharge the requested person on the basis that the warrant would be disproportionate. See paragraph 5.99.

3.25   While the NCA is initially responsible for checking that the information required by section 2 is included, EAWs that do not contain this information are frequently certified.[12] It is vital, therefore, that the warrant is carefully checked for compliance with section 2. Failure to comply with section 2 may mean that the warrant is invalid, and it may be possible for the requested person to be discharged.

3.26   In *Dabas v High Court of Justice, Madrid*[13] Lord Hope stated that a judge conducting an extradition hearing:

> ... must first be satisfied that the warrant with which he is dealing is a Part 1 warrant within the meaning of section 2(2). A warrant which does not contain the statements referred to in that subsection cannot be eked out by extraneous information. The requirements of section

---

12   Practitioners will clearly never come across an EAW that has not been certified, and it is, therefore, impossible to know how many warrants the NCA does not certify, but, given the number of warrants that are certified that do not comply with the requirements of section 2, it would appear that the process of checking the warrant is fairly rudimentary.

13   [2006] EWHC 971 (Admin).

2(2) are mandatory. If they are not met, the warrant is not a Part 1 warrant and the remaining provisions of that Part of the Act will not apply to it.

3.27   It would, however, appear from the case of *Zakrzewski v Regional Court in Lodz, Poland*[14] that if the statements made in a warrant cease to be true (for example, where a sentence is subsequently altered) or where the statement is wrong by way of omission, this can be cured by the provision of further information from the requesting state.[15] It should be noted that this does not apply to section 10; further information can be provided to show that an offence satisfies the dual criminality test (see paragraph 3.50 below).

Key principles for challenges under section 2

3.28   The main grounds of challenge under section 2 are as follows:

- lack of clarity as to the purpose of the warrant;
- deficient particulars of accusation or conviction;
- deficient particulars of other warrants; and
- deficient particulars of sentence.

3.29   This chapter will go on to look at each of these headings in turn. It is, however, important to bear in mind that the courts will generally take a 'cosmopolitan' approach and favour a purposive construction when looking at whether the requirements of section 2 are satisfied, in order to accommodate differences in legal systems across member states. The court will take the statements and information in the warrant at face value. Where the EAW contains information that is demonstrably incorrect, but is nevertheless valid at face value, it should be challenged as an abuse of process rather than under section 2, following the principles set out by Lord Sumption in *Zakrzewski v The Regional Court in Lodz, Poland.*[16] The court must, however, be satisfied that the abuse of process will cause prejudice to the requested person, either in the extradition process or in the requesting state if extradited.[17]

Lack of clarity as to the purpose of the warrant

3.30   By virtue of section 2(3), the warrant must contain a statement that it has been issued in respect of an accused or convicted person (see

---

14   [2013] UKSC 2.
15   At paragraph 10.
16   At paragraph 13.
17   *Belbin v The Regional Court in Lille, France* [2015] EWHC 149 (Admin).

paragraph 3.7 above regarding the statement of purpose). To seek a person's extradition in order to conduct an investigation with a view to possible prosecution is not a legitimate purpose. Where it is unclear from the warrant, when read as a whole, whether a person is wanted as an accused or a convicted person, or where it appears that the person is wanted as a suspect and not for prosecution, there may be grounds to challenge the validity of the warrant under section 2. It may, in some circumstances, be necessary to obtain expert evidence addressing the stage the proceedings have reached and the classification of the requested person under the law of the requesting state (although see point 7 in the list below). A helpful summary of the principles deriving from the case-law is set out by Aikens LJ in *Asztaslos v Szekszard City Court, Hungary:*[18]

(1) The court will look at the warrant as a whole to see whether it is an 'accusation case' warrant or a 'conviction case' warrant. It will not confine itself to the wording on the first page of the warrant, which may well be equivocal.

(2) In the case of an 'accusation case' warrant, issued under Part 1 of the Act, the court has to be satisfied, looking at the warrant as a whole, that the requested person is an 'accused' within *section 2(3)(a)* of the Act.

(3) Similarly, the court will look at the wording of the warrant as a whole to decide whether the warrant indicates, unequivocally, that the purpose of the warrant is for the purpose of the requested person being prosecuted for the offences identified.

(4) The court must construe the words in *section 2(3)(a)* and *(b)* in a 'cosmopolitan' sense and not just in terms of the stages of English criminal procedure.

(5) If the warrant uses the phrases that are used in the English language version of the EAW annexed to the Framework Decision, there should be no (or very little scope) for argument on the purpose of the warrant.

(6) Only if the wording of the warrant is equivocal should the court consider examining extrinsic evidence to decide on the purpose of the warrant. But it should not look at extrinsic material to introduce a possible doubt as to the purpose where it is clear on the face of the warrant itself.

(7) Consideration of extrinsic factual or expert evidence to ascertain the purpose of the warrant should be a last resort and it is to be discouraged. The introduction of such evidence is clean contrary to the aspiration of the Framework Decision, which is to introduce clarity and simplicity into the surrender procedure between member states

18   [2010] EWHC 237 (Admin) at para 38.

of the European Union. Therefore the introduction of extrinsic factual and expert evidence must be discouraged, except in exceptional cases.

3.31 In *Assange*,[19] the High Court examined the question of whether a person who had not been charged could properly be said to be an accused person. In such cases, it was said, the court must 'ask whether the case against him has moved from where he can be seen only as a suspect where proof may be lacking or whether there is an accusation against him supported by proof'[20] and found that, on the particular facts of that case (a detailed investigation and clear evidence of two complainants), he was plainly accused. Amendments made to the EA 2003 in 2014 included a new bar which prevents extradition in the absence of a prosecution decision. See paragraph 5.10.

Deficient particulars of accusation/conviction

3.32 The courts have recognised the differing requirements set out in the legislation for accusation and conviction warrants. While an accusation warrant must contain particulars of the circumstances of the offence (according to EA 2003 s2(4)(c)), a conviction warrant simply requires 'particulars of the conviction' (EA 2003 s2(6)(b)). Greater particularisation is therefore needed in accusation cases than in conviction cases.[21]

3.33 Each case will depend on its own particular facts. A useful guide to the necessary detail to be provided in a conviction warrant is set out in *Sandi v Craiova Court, Romania*:[22]

it will almost always be necessary for a conviction warrant to contain the number of offences for which the requested person has been convicted – and some information about when and where the offences were committed, and the requested person's participation in them, although not necessarily in the same level of detail as would be required in an accusation warrant. Furthermore, common sense dictates that it is likely that more particulars will be appropriate in more complex crimes such as fraud than in crimes such as simple theft. However, there is no formula for appropriate particularisation.[23]

3.34 In accusation cases, section 2(4)(c) requires that the circumstances of the alleged offence are set out, including the conduct, time, place and the relevant provision of law. The language of this section is 'not

---

19 *Assange v Swedish Prosecution Authority* [2011] EWHC 2849 (Admin).
20 At paragraph 152.
21 *Sandi v Craiova Court, Romania* [2009] EWHC 3079 (Admin) at para 32.
22 [2009] EWHC 3079 (Admin).
23 At paragraph 32.

obscure and [...] should be given its plain and ordinary meaning'.[24]
Successful challenges have been made to warrants that do not contain sufficient particulars of time or place. In general, however, the
courts do not require precision as to these particulars:[25]

> Providing that the description in a warrant of the facts relied upon
> as constituting an extradition offence identifies such an offence and
> when and where it is alleged to have been committed, it is not, in my
> view, necessary or appropriate to subject it to requirements of specifi-
> city accorded to particulars of, or sometimes required of, a count in an
> indictment or an allegation in a civil pleading in this country.

3.35   In one case, for example, offences were said to have been committed on unknown dates over four 12-month periods and one two-year
period. It was held that this was sufficiently particularised – the
use of the word 'time' does not mean that the exact date need be
specified.[26]

3.36   An obvious typographical error will not invalidate the warrant.[27]
While there is no requirement to cite the text of the provision of law
under which the alleged conduct constitutes an offence, the relevant
provision of law must be identified somewhere in the warrant – failure to do so will invalidate the warrant.[28]

3.37   By far the greatest number of challenges under EA 2003 s2(4)(c)
are made on the grounds that the conduct has not been sufficiently
particularised. As with section 2(6)(b), each case will depend on its
own facts. However, it is clear from the case-law that the particulars of
the offence must provide a person with 'a clear understanding of why
his extradition is being sought'.[29] Thus, 'a broad omnibus description
of the alleged criminal conduct, 'obtaining property by deception',
to take an English example, will not suffice'.[30] The conduct must be
fairly, accurately and properly set out in the warrant. Guidance was

---

24 *Von Der Pahlen v The Government of Austria* [2006] EWHC 1672 (Admin) at para
    21.
25 *Fofana and Another v Deputy Prosecutor Thubin Tribunal de Grande Instance de
    Meaux, France* [2006] EWHC 744 (Admin).
26 *Crean v Ireland* [2007] EWHC 814 (Admin) at para 17.
27 *Skrzypczak v The Circuit Court in Poznan* [2011] EWHC 1194 (Admin).
28 *Hunt v The Court at First Instance, Antwerp, Belgium* [2006] EWHC 165
    (Admin).
29 *Naczmanski v Regional Court in Wloclawek* [2010] EWHC 2023 (Admin) at
    para 17.
30 *Von der Pahlen v The Government of Austria* [2006] EWHC 1672 (Admin) at
    para 21.

given by Cranston J in *Ektor v National Public Prosecutor of Holland*,[31] who said:

> ... the person sought by the warrant needs to know what offence he is said to have committed and to have an idea of the nature and extent of the allegations against him in relation to that offence. The amount of detail may turn on the nature of the offence. Where dual criminality is involved the detail must also be sufficient to enable the transposition exercise to take place.[32]

3.38   In *Balint v Municipal Court in Prague, Czech Republic*[33] Jackson LJ stressed the importance of the cosmopolitan approach, saying:

> In examining the conduct alleged in the warrant and any further information the court must not be pedantic or overly technical. Instead, the court must make reasonable allowance for (a) the fact that methods of particularising criminal offences differ from one jurisdiction to another and (b) the fact (if it be the case) that the warrant has been translated from a foreign language into English.[34]

3.39   Where a conviction warrant sets out an aggregate sentence comprising a sentence for the index offence along with a suspended sentence that has been activated by the commission of the index offence, the EAW must contain the particulars of each conviction and particulars of both offences in order to be a valid EAW.[35]

3.40   In many cases where there is doubt as to the sufficiency of the particulars of conduct set out, there may be a parallel challenge as to whether the conduct amounts to an extradition offence (see paragraph 3.45 below).

Deficient particulars of other warrants

3.41   The requirement to provide particulars of 'any other warrant' does not amount to a requirement to include details of previous EAWs that have been withdrawn. Rather, it requires the requesting state to provide particulars of the domestic warrant on the basis of which the EAW was issued, for example a warrant of arrest or an order for surrender to custody.[36] The rationale for this is that it enables the court 'to ascertain that there are criminal proceedings in the requesting

---

31   [2007] EWHC 3106 (Admin).
32   [2007] EWHC 3106 (Admin) at para 7.
33   [2011] EWHC 498 (Admin).
34   At para 28.
35   See *Echimov v Court of Babadag, Romania* [2011] EWHC 864 (Admin) and *Presecan v Cluj-Napoca Court, Romania* [2013] EWHC 1609 (Admin).
36   *Louca v A German Judicial Authority* [2009] UKSC 4.

state'.[37] Practitioners should note that on 19 May 2015, the Supreme Court granted leave to appeal in two separate cases[38] where points of law of general public importance had been certified[39] and at the date of publication the Supreme Court has yet to rule on those questions. Until such a time that the Supreme Court has ruled, practitioners are advised to raise the issues that were before the Administrative Court in *Wojciechowski* and *Sas* so as to preserve the requested person's position.[40]

Deficient particulars of sentence

3.42   The EAW must set out either the sentence that may be imposed (where a person is yet to be sentenced), or the sentence that has been imposed (where a person has been sentenced). It is necessary to state the particulars of sentence to enable the court to determine whether the offence is an extradition offence under sections 64 and 65 of the Act.

3.43   Failure to state that a sentence has been suspended will not invalidate the warrant.[41] Indeed, practitioners will find that a large number

37 *Louca v Office of Public Prosecutor in Bielefeld, Germany* [2008] EWHC 2907 (Admin) at para 26.

38 *Poland v Wojciechowski* [2014] EWHC 4162 (Admin) and *Sas v Poland* [2015] EWHC 648 (Admin).

39 The certified questions were as follows: (1) When a European Arrest Warrant ('EAW') gives particulars of a judgment or order made by the court of a category 1 territory, requiring the requested person to serve an aggregated sentence of immediate imprisonment, is the EAW defective for the purposes of section 2(6)(c) of the Extradition Act 2003 if it does not also give particulars of domestic warrants issued in the category 1 territory to enforce that judgment or order within the issuing state? (2) Does the term 'any other warrant issued in the category 1 territory for the person's arrest in respect of the offence' in section 2(6)(c) of the Extradition Act 2003 only require the European arrest warrant to include the conviction of the requested person, or does it, following *Poland v Wojciechowski* [2014] EWHC 412 (Admin), require the particularisation of the decision that required the requested person to serve an immediate sentence of imprisonment and was the decision following which it could be said that the requested person was unlawfully at large? (3) When a European arrest warrant gives particulars of a judgment or order made by the court of a category 1 territory, convicting the requested person, is the European arrest warrant defective for the purposes of section 2(6)(c) of the Extradition Act 2003 if it does not also give particulars of domestic warrants issued in the category 1 territory to enforce that judgment or order within the issuing state?

40 The High Court has stayed all cases raising the s2(6)(c) issue on appeal until the final determination of the Supreme Court.

41 *Bulkowski (Kamil) v Regional Court of Elblag, Poland* [2012] EWHC 381 (Admin).

of Polish clients are subject to a suspended sentence that has been activated, although this will not be clear from the warrant.

3.44   Complications arise in relation to this requirement where a person's extradition is sought for multiple offences. In a conviction case, if there are several offences that are dealt with by way of an aggregate penalty, it is enough for the warrant to state the aggregate sentence.[42] Conversely, while it is necessary to state the sentence that has been imposed, if there is more than one offence, there is no requirement to state the aggregate penalty.[43] Indeed, a warrant will still be valid even if it can be shown that the sentence has been aggregated after the warrant has been issued (meaning that there is a different sentence to serve than that set out in the warrant). In an accusation case, the maximum sentence for each offence must be stated.[44]

Extradition offences

3.45   EA 2003 ss64 and 65 define extradition offences, drawing a distinction between sentenced persons and those who have not been sentenced (whether or not convicted), with different minimum periods of sentence applying in both cases. These sections are complicated and are by no means a direct transposition of the relevant provisions of the Framework Decision.[45] They were amended and, to a very limited extent, simplified by the Anti-social Behaviour, Crime and Policing Act 2014.

3.46   Where an appropriate authority within the issuing state has certified that the conduct falls within the Framework list contained within box E, it will not be necessary to look into whether the conduct alleged would amount to an offence had it taken place in this country, unless the classification is clearly erroneous.[46] It will, however, be necessary to check the sentence applicable to the offence against the minimum periods set out in the Act. If the offence does not appear in

---

42 *Pilecki v Circuit Court of Legnica, Poland* [2008] UKHL 7, [2008] 1 WLR 325.

43 *Bartkowiak v Judicial Authority of Poland* [2012] EWHC 333 (Admin).

44 *Taylor v Public Prosecutor's Office, Berlin* [2012] EWHC 475 (Admin).

45 See JR Spencer 'Implementing the European Arrest Warrant: A Tale of How Not to Do It' (2009) 30(3) *Statute Law Review* 184 at pp191–192.

46 See *Assange v Swedish Prosecution Authority* [2011] EWHC 2849 (Admin) at para 112: 'Thus it seems to us that although the court executing the EAW must scrutinise the EAW to ensure that it complies with the requirements of particularity, it should ordinarily accept the classification of the issuing member state, unless there is an obvious inconsistency which shows that the conduct alleged does not amount to the offence under the law of that state'.

the Framework list, the conduct alleged should be carefully analysed to determine whether it satisfies the dual criminality requirement. This is the primary area of challenge under these sections. This chapter will go on to look at the minimum periods of sentence, and will then cover dual criminality and the relevance of the location of the offence.

Minimum periods of sentence for extradition offences

3.47   If one of the boxes in the list of Framework offences set out in box E is ticked, it will be an extradition offence if it is punishable by at least three years' imprisonment (where a person has not been sentenced) or a sentence of 12 months' imprisonment was imposed (where a person has been sentenced) – see EA 2003 s64(5) and s65(5).[47]

3.48   If the offence is not on the Framework list, but would have constituted an offence had it taken place in the United Kingdom, it will be an extradition offence if it is punishable by at least 12 months' imprisonment (for persons not sentenced) or a sentence of four months' imprisonment was imposed (where a person has been sentenced). This can be contrasted with Part 2 cases, where the offence must be punishable in the United Kingdom by a minimum of 12 months' imprisonment.[48]

3.49   Note that these sections were amended in 2014, so that these minimum periods of sentence apply not only to imprisonment but also to other forms of detention.

Dual criminality

3.50   In order to determine whether an offence satisfies the dual criminality requirement, it is necessary to look at the conduct complained of in the warrant and, if the judicial authority has provided it, any further information. It would be wrong to look at whether the elements of the offence have a precise equivalent in this country.[49] If the mens

---

47   Although the legislation states that the conduct will constitute an extradition offence if (inter alia) 'a certificate issued by an appropriate authority of the category 1 territory shows that the conduct falls within the European Framework list', there is no need for a 'certificate' to be attached to the warrant: the warrant itself has been held to be the certificate: see *Dabas v High Court of Justice, Madrid* [2006] EWHC 971 (Admin) at para 26.

48   EA 2003 ss137 and 138.

49   *Norris v United States of America* [2008] UKHL 16 and *Zak v Regional Court of Bydgoszcz, Poland* [2008] EWHC 470 (Admin) at para 5.

rea is not specifically set out in the description of the conduct, it can be inferred, but only where the facts are such that the inference is the only reasonable one to draw.[50] If the conduct set out in the warrant would not amount to an offence in this country, the offence is not an extradition offence and the requested person should be discharged.

3.51   In looking at dual criminality, the courts will follow the same principles that apply to EA 2003 s2, that is, a cosmopolitan approach will be taken in order to give effect to the principle of mutual recognition.

Location of conduct

3.52   In most cases, the location of the conduct will not be an issue – the conduct will take place in the jurisdiction of the requesting state. There are, however, a number of offences that take place across borders and in such cases the location of the conduct may be crucial. In some cases, if the offence took place outside the requesting state, it may be possible to argue that it is not an extradition offence. The relevant provisions of the Act are sections 64 and 65.

3.53   Case-law has held that if conduct takes place outside the requesting state but has an intended effect within it, the court will consider that the conduct took place in that state.[51] Furthermore, while it may appear from reading EA 2003 ss64(5) and 65(5) that a Framework offence that occurs partially in the United Kingdom will not be an extradition offence, this is not the case: if the conduct set out in the warrant also satisfies the dual criminality test, it can be examined under sections 64(3) or 65(3).[52]

3.54   The flowcharts following at figure 3.1 and figure 3.2 illustrate the various ways in which conduct may be an extradition offence under sections 64 and 65 respectively. These flowcharts should be used in conjunction with the legislation, bearing in mind the provisions of sections 64(6) and 65(6) for tax or customs offences, and the rule in *Osunta v The Public Prosecutor's Office in Dusseldorf*,[53] which allows for excision from the warrant of conduct which would not amount to an extradition offence.

---

50 *Assange v Swedish Prosecution Authority* [2011] EWHC 2849 (Admin) at para 55.
51 *King's Prosecutor, Brussels v Cando Armas* [2005] UKHL 67 at para 35.
52 *At* para 17.
53 [2007] EWHC 1562 (Admin).

Figure 3.1 Part 1 extradition offence (persons not sentenced)

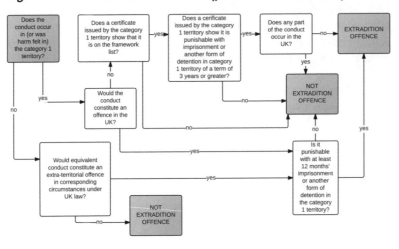

Figure 3.2 Part 1 extradition offence (sentenced persons)

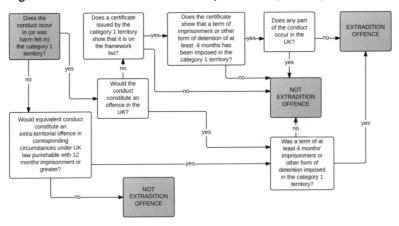

CHAPTER 4

Attending the client

Introduction

4.1   Often the first interaction a lawyer will have with the requested person will be in the cells at WMC. Time will often be limited, particularly for the duty solicitor, and it is therefore important to be able to give and to obtain the necessary information as quickly as possible. This chapter looks at what should be covered in the first meeting with the client, in particular how to explain the law and procedure. It also looks at the information that should be obtained at the first meeting in order to be in a position to properly represent the requested person at the initial hearing.

Seeing the client

4.2   Requested persons are unlikely to be familiar with the extradition process. When acting for those arrested on EAWs, it will be necessary briefly to explain the nature of the fast-track extradition procedure within Europe, specifically that the court's primary concern is to ensure that the procedural requirements have been met, and that the purpose of the hearing in this country is not to decide whether and by whom the offence was committed – guilt and innocence are for the courts in the requesting state to determine. Given the limited amount of time that will often be available, this should be explained at the outset. It is important for clients to be given a realistic assessment of their prospects of success: they should be informed of the difficulties inherent in contesting extradition, and that most requested persons are eventually extradited.

4.3   Using the procedure that the court will follow as a way of structuring the interview, the preliminary points regarding the question of production, service of the warrant (EA 2003 s4) and identity (EA 2003 s7) should be covered with the requested person. The law in relation to these areas is set out in detail in chapter 7. In brief, however, the requested person must be given a copy of the EAW (in both languages) as soon as practicable after arrest; failure to comply means a judge *may* grant his or her discharge. In addition, the requested person must be produced before WMC as soon as practicable; failure to comply means a judge *must* discharge the requested person. In relation to section 7, the judge must decide, on a balance of probabilities, whether the person before him or her is the person in respect of whom the warrant was issued.

Sections 4 and 7 of the Extradition Act 2003

4.4   While it will often be clear from the arrest statement whether or not the warrant has been served and whether the requested person has been produced as soon as practicable, it is always worth checking these points briefly with the client. If it is apparent from the arrest statement that the warrant has not been served, or that the person has not been produced as soon as practicable, these points will need to be covered in more detail. In particular, should there have been any obvious delay, a full chronology of events should be taken from the client, along with his or her understanding of any cause for the delay.

4.5   The question of identity (section 7) will often have been resolved by the arresting officer asking the person to confirm his or her name and date of birth, and seizing any identity documents in his or her possession. If the requested person disputes that he or she is the person who is the subject of the warrant, it will be necessary to take full instructions as to identity. Requested persons should, however, be warned that disputing identity could have an impact upon their credibility at the extradition hearing and therefore on their prospects of obtaining bail.

Persons facing charges in the United Kingdom

4.6   If the requested person has come from a prison, he or she is very likely to be a serving prisoner. The court will need confirmation of the early release date for any such requested persons, as the extradition hearing may be adjourned while that sentence is served. In the case of persons facing charges in England and Wales, the court must adjourn proceedings until the domestic case is disposed of.[1] Relevant dates should be established with the requested person. There is no equivalent provision for those on UK police bail. While requested persons in these circumstances may sometimes wish to return to the requesting state as quickly as possible, they will of course need to be warned about the consequences of failing to surrender in this jurisdiction (ie, that they may be committing a separate offence and that they may be circulated as wanted).

---

1   EA 2003 s214 states that a charge is disposed of when a person is either acquitted of it, or, if convicted, when there is no further possibility of an appeal against conviction.

Specialty and consent

4.7   The rule of specialty prevents a person being prosecuted in the requesting state for conduct not detailed in the warrant; it is therefore an important protection for those facing extradition.

4.8   A requested person may consent to extradition. The advantage of consenting to extradition is that it will result in an expedited process: a person who has consented cannot appeal, and he or she will not, therefore, have to wait to the end of the seven-day appeal period following the making of the extradition order.

4.9   Consent must be given in writing and is irrevocable.[2] The legal adviser will have a form that can be completed during the hearing for those who wish to consent. The requested person must have had the opportunity to receive legal advice before giving consent. As of 21 July 2014, consent to extradition is not to be taken as a waiver of specialty rights.[3]

4.10   It is worth noting that, if the requesting state does wish to prosecute an extradited person for offences for which they have not been extradited, it is possible for that state to seek consent from the United Kingdom to deal with the person for those offences.[4] Consent will be sought at a hearing where the person is unlikely to be represented. The grounds for refusing consent are limited.

Time on remand

4.11   In Part 1 cases, requested persons should be advised that any time spent on remand in the United Kingdom will count towards any sentence in the requesting state.[5] The requested state has the responsibility under the Framework Decision for transmitting information about the duration of detention to the requesting state at the time of surrender of the requested person. To fulfil this requirement, the NCA should provide the requesting state with a notice detailing the days spent in detention on the day that he or she is returned to the requesting state. Note that this does not apply to Part 2 countries: it is necessary to look at the specific arrangements with a Part 2 country to determine whether time spent on remand will count towards any

---

2 EA 2003 ss45/127.
3 Anti-social Behaviour, Crime and Policing Act 2014 s163.
4 EA 2003 ss54/129.
5 Framework Decision 2002 Article 26.

sentence.[6] In some cases, time spent on a curfew will count towards a sentence in the requesting state, but this will vary according to the specific circumstances of the requested person and the jurisdiction. It is therefore necessary, in those cases, to check with a lawyer in the requesting state whether time spent on a curfew will count towards a sentence.

Personal circumstances

4.12   Details of the client's personal circumstances should be taken. If it is clear that extradition will be contested, completion of the legal aid form will provide a good deal of necessary background information.[7] An interview with a client will inevitably be determined by the facts of the case; however the following questions should assist in providing a starting point both in advising as to any grounds on which the requested person may challenge the extradition proceedings and in preparing for a bail application:

General instructions

4.13   • When did he or she come to the United Kingdom?
- Why did he or she come to the United Kingdom?
- Has he or she been back to the requesting state?
- Is the requested person aware of the criminal proceedings (see paragraph 4.15 below)?
- Was he or she present at the trial (conviction cases). If not, why not?
- Does he or she have family in the United Kingdom/requesting state? Are they dependent? Full details should be taken;
- Is he or she employed? If so, what are the hours of work? Is it possible to contact the employer?
- What is his or her housing situation? How long has he or she been at the present address?
- Where was he or she arrested? At home/work?
- Has the requested person instructed lawyers in the requesting state?

---

6   The Privy Council in *Gomes v The State (Trinidad)* [2015] UKPC 8 held that the judge presiding over Mr Gomes' trial in Trinidad had been entitled not to credit him for the 45 months spent in custody in the UK while fighting his extradition.

7   Time should, however, not be wasted on completion of the legal aid form if it is clear that an extradition order will be made that day.

- What is his or her immigration status (see paragraph 4.16 below)?
- Does he or she have any health problems?
- Why does the requested person think that he or she should not be extradited?

Bail instructions

4.14
- Is any security or surety available? Contact numbers will need to be obtained.
- What is the nearest police station to the requested person's address? If possible, attempt to find out the opening hours prior to the hearing.
- Where are the identity documents of the requested person? Is it possible to obtain those that have not been seized by the police in order to surrender them?
- Does the requested person have any commitments that would make compliance with a curfew or a condition to report to the police station difficult?
- What are the circumstances of any offending whilst on bail/failure to surrender as listed with the list of previous convictions.

See chapter 7 for further information on making a bail application and refer to the checklists at appendices E and F.

Awareness of proceedings

4.15   The question of whether the requested person had been aware of the allegation or conviction prior to arrest will be relevant for any passage of time point: his or her knowledge of any outstanding proceedings will go to the question of the requested person's status as a fugitive. In the case of a conviction warrant, it will be crucial to ascertain for the purpose of EA 2003 s20 whether or not he or she was present upon conviction (see paragraph 5.32 in relation to EA 2003 s14).

Immigration status

4.16   The large majority of those facing EAWs will be exercising their right of residence in the United Kingdom as EU citizens. Sections 39 and 121 of the EA Act 2003,[8] however, prevent the extradition of a person who has claimed asylum (whether before or after the issue of the warrant), until the determination of that claim.

---

8   As amended by Anti-social Behaviour, Crime and Policing Act 2014 s162.

Issues to be taken

4.17 It is worth briefly explaining the most common bars and challenges to extradition to the client. Not only will this assist the requested person's understanding of the extradition process (and the limited grounds on which it is possible to contest extradition), it will also ensure that no possible grounds of challenge are overlooked. The list below sets out those most commonly relied on:

- rule against double jeopardy (s12);
- absence of a decision to charge or try (s12A) (accusation cases only);
- extraneous considerations (s13);
- passage of time (s14);
- forum (s19B) (accusation cases only);
- conviction in absence (s20);
- human rights considerations (s21):
  - Article 2 – right to life;
  - Article 3 – prohibition of torture and ill-treatment;
  - Article 5 – right to liberty and security;
  - Article 6 – right to a fair trial;
  - Article 8 – right to respect for private and family life;
- proportionality (s21A) (accusation cases only); and
- physical or mental health (s25).

4.18 In some jurisdictions, it will be possible to persuade the judicial authority to withdraw the warrant by negotiating a voluntary return to the issuing state. This is known as 'compromising the warrant' (see chapter 12). Given that a negotiated return will be on bail, this will be preferable to a return under a warrant. Indeed, it is far more likely that an extradition request will be defeated in this way than if surrender is contested in the United Kingdom and for this reason it is important that clients who wish to contest their extradition are made aware of this possibility. In order to pursue this route, it will be necessary for the requested person to instruct (and pay for) lawyers in the requesting state, who may be able to secure the withdrawal of the warrant on condition that the requested person will, for example, pay a security and return voluntarily or enter a guilty plea.[9] This will of course be more difficult for those in custody who will need assistance from a friend or relative should they wish to pursue this. In general, the courts are reluctant to adjourn extradition proceedings to allow the requested person to attempt to compromise the warrant.

9 This is sometimes referred to as an 'iron letter'. See para 12.6.

However, practitioners should familiarise themselves with the new provision in section 21B (see paragraph 12.6) as this allows for the requested person to request to speak to the prosecutor in the requesting state. See also paragraph 12.13 and following on transfer of sentenced prisoners.

Procedure if extradition is ordered

4.19   Requested persons should be advised of the timescales that apply if extradition is ordered. EA 2003 s35 provides that a requested person must be extradited before the end of a ten-day period, starting with either the day on which extradition is ordered (if the person has consented to be extradited) or on the eighth day after extradition has been ordered (ie after the period in which a person can lodge an application for leave to appeal has passed, for those who have not consented to be extradited). Section 35 does, however, allow the judge and the issuing authority to agree a later date. In practice, extensions of time are frequently sought and requested persons are rarely returned within the time limits set out in section 35. Where a person has not been removed within the required period, it is possible to apply for discharge: see paragraph 11.157.

Legal aid

4.20   Forms CRM14 and 15 should be completed as with any other legal aid case and can be date stamped by the enquiries counter at the court on the day of the first appearance for those cases where extradition is being contested. The majority of those arrested on EAWs will be in employment: if this is the case, they will need to provide supporting documentation unless they have been remanded in custody. Partners of applicants are also required to sign the form and if this is not possible, a full explanation should be provided on the forms stating why the partner of the requested person has not signed the form. Where a person has been remanded in custody, he or she can self-certify as to wages on form CRM15 and his or her partner need not sign the form (although note that the fact that the partner is unable to sign the form must be fully explained).[10] For those in custody, as long as the forms have been fully completed and they are eligible, the grant of legal aid

10   *Criminal Legal Aid Manual*, April 2013 paras 4.4.3 and 19.8 and para 4.4.7 (www.justice.gov.uk/downloads/legal-aid/eligibility/criminal-legal-aid-manual.pdf).

should not, in theory, be problematic. Unfortunately this is not the case in practice, and even those who have fully completed the form, self-certified and are apparently eligible will be likely to face delays and adjournments while awaiting the outcome of legal aid applications.[11] For those granted bail, they should be advised to prioritise obtaining supporting documentation for the legal aid application in order to ensure that it is dealt with expeditiously.

4.21   Applications for legal aid can be submitted online using the LAA Online Portal and will be processed more quickly than paper applications.

---

11 See the case of *Stopyra v District Court of Lublin, Poland* [2012] EWHC 1787 (Admin) 28 June 2012, in which there was an 11-week delay in the grant of legal aid: the Divisional Court pointed out the necessity of reform to prevent further breaches of the UK's obligations.

Bars to extradition

continued

Introduction

5.1 There are a limited number of grounds that can be relied upon to resist extradition. This chapter will look at the statutory bars to extradition, which are set out in EA 2003 ss11/79. It will then go on to look at the other grounds for resisting extradition, namely: conviction in absence; physical or mental condition; proportionality; death penalty; and finally, abuse of process. The judge will follow these in the order set out in the statute in looking at each ground during the extradition hearing (if raised). The structure of the Act envisages a 'step-by-step' approach by the judge (see figure 5.1).[1]

Statutory bars to extradition

5.2 Under section 11 (Part 1 cases) and section 79 (Part 2 cases) the judge must decide whether a person's extradition is barred by reason of:

- sections 12/80[2] – the rule against double jeopardy;
- section 12A – absence of prosecution decision (Part 1 cases only);
- sections 13/81 – extraneous considerations;
- sections 14/82 – passage of time;
- section 15 – the person's age (Part 1 cases only);
- sections 83 – hostage-taking considerations (Part 2 cases only);
- section 94 – death penalty (Part 2 cases only);
- sections 17/95 – specialty;
- sections 18, 19 and 19A/96 and 96A – earlier extradition from territory or by the ICC; and
- sections 19B/83A – forum.

5.3 Having considered these, the judge will go on to look at conviction in absence (ss20/85); human rights (and, in Part 1 cases only, proportionality) (ss21A/87) and whether a person's mental or physical condition should prevent extradition (ss25/91). This chapter will follow the statutory numbering in looking at each of these in turn, and end by looking at abuse of process, which, although not a statutory bar, is within the court's jurisdiction and has on occasion prevented a person's extradition. Human rights considerations are explored in chapter 6.

1 *Mihai Sonea v Mehedinti District Court* [2009] EWHC 89 (Admin) at para 16.
2 Where EA 2003 Parts 1 and 2 set out the same bar to extradition, this is indicated using a slash, for example sections 12/80.

5.4   In addition to these bars, there is also the possibility of making a request for either temporary transfer to the requesting territory or for arrangements to be made for discussions with investigators/prosecutors from the requesting territory under EA 2003 s21B. See paragraph 12.6 for further detail.

Double jeopardy – sections 12/80

5.5   Section 12 provides that:

> A person's extradition to a category 1 territory is barred by reason of the rule against double jeopardy if (and only if) it appears that he would be entitled to be discharged under any rule of law relating to previous acquittal or conviction.

5.6   In order for the bar to apply the requested person must previously have been put in 'peril of conviction' for the offence for which he or she now faces extradition.[3] The court must therefore assess whether the requested person has been previously acquitted or convicted of the same offence, or an offence arising out of the same or substantially the same facts as those set out in the warrant.[4] Any conviction or acquittal must be final, and finality 'is to be judged by the process in the requesting state'.[5] In Part 1 cases, the judge is then required to proceed on the basis of two statutory assumptions, that:

- the English courts had jurisdiction to try him or her for those offences; and
- he or she was facing trial for them in England.[6]

The court has then to ask itself whether English rules of law on double jeopardy would apply.[7]

5.7   It is important to bear in mind that the doctrine of autrefois convict can only be relied upon once sentence has been passed,[8] although there is no requirement for the sentence to have been completed, or indeed commenced.

---

3   *Connelly v DPP* [1964] AC 1254 (HL), *Mitchell v High Court of Boulogne sur mer* [2007] EWHC 2006 (Admin), *Zdinjak v Croatia* [2012] EWHC 1554 (Admin).

4   *Fofana v Deputy Prosecutor Thubin Tribunal de Grande Instance de Meaux, France* [2006] EWHC 744 (Admin).

5   *R (Oncel) v Governor of Brixton Prison, Government of the Republic of Turkey* [2001] EWHC 1142 (Admin) at para 32.

6   In relation to Part 2 cases, the judge is not required to make these assumptions (EA 2003 s80).

7   *Hamburg Public Prosecutor's Office v Altun* [2011] EWHC 397 (Admin) at para 19.

8   *Richards v The Queen* [1993] AC 217, PC.

5.8   This is a bar to extradition that is likely to become of increasing relevance, and can arise in cases where there is an element of cross-border activity, such that one country has already taken action against the requested person. A person, for example, committing a customs fraud may commit an offence in two jurisdictions. It may be that a prosecution in jurisdiction A deals with one part of the conduct and that jurisdiction B then seeks to prosecute for another part of the conduct or indeed a larger conspiracy that subsumes the element that has already been prosecuted. Depending on the particular facts of the case, this may give rise to an argument that the requested person's extradition falls within the double jeopardy bar. For an example of unusual facts giving rise to extradition being barred by reason of double jeopardy, see *Ninedeys v District Prosecutor's Office of Varna, Bulgaria.*[9]

5.9   To establish this bar, evidence from both lay and expert witnesses will almost certainly be required.

Absence of prosecution decision – section 12A

5.10   This bar, inserted by the Anti-social Behaviour, Crime and Policing Act 2014, prevents the extradition of a person where the requesting state has not made a decision to charge or try the requested person. It applies only to Part 1 requests.

5.11   It will be apparent that there is some overlap between this bar and the provisions of EA 2003 s2(3) which require the EAW to contain a statement that the person in respect of whom the warrant is issued is accused of the commission of an offence and that the warrant has been issued with a view to his arrest and extradition for the purpose of being prosecuted for the offence (see paragraph 3.30). Familiar principles apply to the judge's task under section 12A. The judge must take 'a cosmopolitan approach' and avoid '[approaching] the construction of the phrases "decision to charge" and "decision to try" in section 12A by reference solely to the domestic law and practice of criminal procedures in England and Wales [...]'.[10]

5.12   There are two stages to the application of this section.

---

9   [2014] EWHC 4416 (Admin).
10 *Kandola and Others v Generalstaatwaltschaft Frankfurt, Germany and Others* [2015] EWHC 619 (Admin) at para 27.

First stage

5.13   Under section 12A, the first stage is that the judge must have reasonable grounds for believing that –

> (i) the competent authorities in the category 1 territory have not made a decision to charge or have not made a decision to try (or have made neither of those decisions), and
> (ii) the person's absence from the category 1 territory is not the sole reason for that failure.[11]

5.14   In *Kandola and Others v Generalstaatwaltschaft Frankfurt, Germany and Others,*[12] the Divisional Court said that the default position will be that the requesting state has made the decision to charge or try and that the burden at this stage will therefore be on the requested person to raise the challenge before the judge.[13] In that case, Aikens LJ went on to say that 'Reasonable grounds for believing' involves something less than proof on a balance of probabilities, but more than simple assertion, or a fanciful view or "feeling"'.

5.15   In considering the first stage of section 12A, the judge must begin by looking at the EAW itself. If it is clear from the EAW that decisions have been taken, the judge should look no further. If there is a lack of clarity, the judge will be entitled to consider extraneous evidence.[14] The court in Kandola disapproved however of the deployment of 'elaborate "expert" evidence' and indicated that it would not, at this stage, be necessary or appropriate for enquiry to be made of the requesting state.[15]

5.16   In relation to the question as to whether the sole reason for the failure to make a decision to try or charge is the person's absence, this again will be for the requested person to provide sufficient evidence to raise a case that her absence is not the sole reason for the lack of a decision to charge or to try that person.[16] In practice, this is likely to require expert evidence from a lawyer in the requesting state.

---

11   EA 2003 s12A(1)(a).
12   [2015] EWHC 619 (Admin).
13   At para 30.
14   At para 31.
15   At para 32.
16   At para 33.

Second stage

5.17 If the requested person is able to satisfy the judge as to both (i) and (ii) above, the judge must then move on to consider the second stage. Under section 12A(1)(b) the requested person's extradition will be barred unless the prosecution is able to prove to the criminal standard that –

(i) the competent authorities in the category 1 territory have made a decision to charge and a decision to try, or

(ii) in a case where one of those decisions has not been made (or neither of them has been made), the person's absence from the category 1 territory is the sole reason for that failure.

5.18 It is at this stage that it will be necessary for the prosecution to make enquiry of the requesting state. Aikens LJ states that a short, clear, statement from the judicial authority answering the following questions should be determinative:

(i) has a decision been taken in this case (a) to charge the requested person and (b) to try him, if not,

(ii) is the sole reason for the lack of each of the decisions that have not been taken the fact that the requested person is absent from the category 1 territory of which you are a/[sic]the judicial authority?[17]

5.19 Whilst this may appear on the face of it to be a straightforward requirement, in reality (as practitioners will be aware) obtaining a short, clear, statement from a judicial authority may not be easy. Should the requesting state be unable to prove either matter under section 12A(1)(b), the requested person will be discharged.

Extraneous considerations – sections 13/81

5.20 Section 13 states:

A person's extradition to a category 1 territory is barred by reason of extraneous considerations if (and only if) it appears that –

(a) the Part 1 warrant issued in respect of him (though purporting to be issued on account of the extradition offence) is in fact issued for the purpose of prosecuting or punishing him on account of his race, religion, nationality, gender, sexual orientation or political opinions; or

(b) if extradited he might be prejudiced at his trial or punished, detained or restricted in his personal liberty by reason of his

---

17 *Kandola and Others v Generalstaatwaltschaft Frankfurt, Germany and Others* [2015] EWHC 619 (Admin) at para 34.

race, religion, nationality, gender, sexual orientation or political opinions.

5.21   Section 81 uses precisely the same formulation in relation to Part 2 requests.

5.22   The 'extraneous considerations' are:

- race;
- religion;
- nationality;
- gender;
- sexual orientation; or
- political opinions.

5.23   There are two categories within the extraneous considerations bar that are set out as alternatives: it is enough to show one or the other. The bar prevents the extradition of a person if, broadly, the 'extraneous considerations' have resulted in the issue of the warrant or request, or will prejudice the person upon his return. The first category (subsection (a)) looks at the reasons behind the issue of the warrant or request: it prevents extradition where a country has ostensibly sought the return of a person for a particular offence, but where the real motive for seeking his or her return is to prosecute or punish that person because of the 'extraneous considerations.' The second category (subsection (b)) is directed at what might happen to the person if he or she is extradited. If he or she will suffer prejudice, punishment or detention by reason of the 'extraneous considerations' then extradition will be barred.

5.24   There is an obvious overlap between this bar and human rights considerations, in particular Articles 3, 5 and 6, and in practice they are often argued in parallel (see chapter 6).[18]

Test

5.25   The test is set out in the pre-2003 Act case of *Fernandez v Government of Singapore*,[19] which was summarised by Scott-Baker LJ as follows:

The burden is on the appellant to show a causal link between the issue of the warrant, his detention, prosecution, punishment or the prejudice which he asserts he will suffer and the fact of his race or his religion. He does not have to prove on the balance of probabilities that the events described in s13(b) will take place, but he must show that

18 Different tests do, however, apply. See *Nikolics v The City Court of Szekszard (A Judicial Authority in Hungary)* [2013] EWHC 2377 (Admin) para 14.
19 [1971] 1 WLR 987.

there is a 'reasonable chance' or 'reasonable grounds for thinking' or a 'serious possibility' that such events will occur. [20]

5.26 As such, while it may appear that the test is easily satisfied (less than the balance of probabilities), in reality it is difficult to succeed on this bar because of the problems one may face in adducing evidence to show the causal link between the issue of the warrant, the person's detention, prosecution, punishment or the prejudice the person asserts he or she will suffer and any extraneous considerations.

5.27 By way of example, it may be helpful to consider a case in which reliance was unsuccessfully placed on this bar alongside a case in which extraneous considerations did bar a person's extradition.

5.28 In *Tamarevichute v Russian Federation*[21] the defence sought to argue that there was a 'reasonable chance' or a 'serious possibility' that, as a person of Roma origin, the appellant might be prejudiced at her trial in Kaliningrad on account of her race. The Administrative Court found that the appellant had 'adduced powerful evidence of widespread discrimination against the Roma within the Russian Federation ... [which included] attacks on Roma people and their property, the voicing of anti-Roma sentiments in the media and in political speeches, and human rights abuses by the law enforcement authorities'.[22]

5.29 This, however, was not enough to bar her extradition. The judge said:

> The fact that, if returned to the Russian Federation, the appellant would be at risk of suffering general prejudice as a result of her Roma origin is not, however, sufficient to constitute a bar to her extradition under the provisions of section 81(b) of the Act. She must demonstrate that there exists a 'reasonable chance' or a 'serious possibility' of her being prejudiced at her trial, or 'punished, detained or restricted in her personal liberty' by reason of her race.

In deciding that the causal link had not been demonstrated, the judge looked at whether the appellant had actually suffered prejudice when in Russia on account of her Roma origin, and found that she had not.

5.30 This can be contrasted with the case of *Government of the Republic of Serbia v Ejup Ganic*[23] in which the district judge found that

---

20 *Hilali v The National Court in Madrid and Another* [2006] EWHC 1239 (Admin) at para 62.

21 [2008] EWHC 534 (Admin) (DC).

22 At para 98.

23 [2010] EW Misc 11 (MC).

extradition was barred under both subsection (a) and (b) of EA 2003 section 81. In that case, the return of the former acting President of Bosnia was sought for war crimes. The requested person had been subject to two international investigations, both of which had found that there was no case to answer. The defence called a number of witnesses who gave evidence to say that the prosecution was politically motivated, resulting in the discharge of the requested person under both section 81(a) and (as a result of evidence called to show that he would be prejudiced at trial on account of his race) section 81(b).

5.31   Again, as can be seen from the above examples, a requested person will need to obtain a significant body of evidence from experts and others to persuade a judge that extraneous considerations should bar his or her extradition.

Passage of time – sections 14/82

5.32   Passage of time is frequently raised by requested persons seeking to resist their extradition. Under section 14 of EA 2003 Part 1, or section 82 of Part 2, a person's extradition is barred if it appears that it would be *unjust or oppressive* to extradite him or her by reason of the passage of time since he or she is alleged to have committed the offence or since he or she is alleged to have become unlawfully at large.

5.33   To rely on this bar, it is not enough to show a long delay. It is also necessary to show either injustice or oppression occasioned by the time that has passed. This bar replicates provisions in earlier Acts, and a significant body of pre-2003 case-law on passage of time still applies.

Fugitives and passage of time

5.34   Perhaps the most important point that can be derived from the case-law is that delay brought about by the accused fleeing the country will prevent that person from relying on the passage of time in all but the most exceptional circumstances. In *Kakis v Government of the Republic of Cyprus*[24] Lord Diplock said:

> Delay in the commencement or conduct of extradition proceedings which is brought about by the accused himself by fleeing the country, concealing his whereabouts or evading arrest cannot, in my view, be relied upon as a ground for holding it to be either unjust or oppressive to return him.

24 [1978] 1 WLR 779.

5.35   This principle was refined in the more recent case of *Gomes and Goodyer v Trinidad and Tobago*[25] in two important ways. First, the court decided that if a defendant deliberately flees, he or she cannot then rely on passage of time, even if the requesting state has significantly contributed to the delay.[26] Second, the burden is on the requesting state to prove beyond all reasonable doubt that the requested person has deliberately fled the jurisdiction.

When does the passage of time start to run where a person has been convicted in absence?

5.36   It was established in *Rahman v County Court of Boulogne sur Mer, France*[27] that a person remains 'accused' of a crime for the purposes of s14/82 unless or until there has been a conviction in a trial in which he was required to participate but failed to attend and is therefore a fugitive from justice. This approach was developed from paragraph 38 of the House of Lords decision in *Gomes and Goodyer* where Lord Brown said:

> The final question discussed before the House was the period of time for consideration under s82. It starts of course with the date of the alleged offence (s82(a)) or when the fugitive became unlawfully at large (s82(b)) – (a fugitive tried in his absence without having deliberately absented himself from his trial falling for this purpose under s82(a)).

5.37   In a conviction in absence case where the requested person has not deliberately absented herself therefore, practitioners will be able to rely on the length of time that has passed since the date of the commission of the offence (ss14(a)/82(a)).

Necessary questions

5.38   In all cases which raise a potential passage of time bar, it will be important to establish with requested persons the circumstances in which they came to leave the country. In accusation cases, lawyers will need to ask questions such as:

- whether they knew of the offence;
- whether they were arrested;
- what they had understood to have happened following arrest;
- whether any assertions were made by the authorities.

25   [2009] UKHL 21.
26   In *Gomes*, the requesting state had lost the file.
27   [2014] EWHC 4143 (Admin).

5.39   Similarly, in conviction cases, it will be necessary to carefully establish:

- whether they were present when convicted;
- if so, why they then left the country;
- what contact they had with the authorities; and so on.

Injustice or oppression

5.40   The burden of proof is on the requested person to establish on the balance of probabilities that it would be unjust or oppressive to extradite him or her.

5.41   In *Kakis*, Lord Diplock set out a definition of injustice or oppression. He stated that:

> 'Unjust' I regard as directed primarily to the risk of prejudice to the accused in the conduct of the trial itself, oppressive as directed to the hardship to the accused resulting from changes in his circumstances that have occurred during the period to be taken into consideration.[28]

5.42   The case of *Gomes and Goodyer* also looked again at injustice, approving a definition of injustice endorsed in a 2006 Privy Council case,[29] as follows:[30]

> First, the question is not whether it would be unjust or oppressive to try the accused but whether ... it would be unjust or oppressive to extradite him ... [Second], if the court of the requesting state is bound to conclude that a fair trial is impossible, it would be unjust or oppressive for the requested state to return him ... But, [third], the court of the requested state must have regard to the safeguards which exist under the domestic law of the requesting state to protect a defendant against a trial rendered unjust or oppressive by the passage of time ... [Fourth], no rule of thumb can be applied to determine whether the passage of time has rendered a fair trial no longer possible: much will turn on the particular case ... [Fifth], there can be no cut-off point beyond which extradition must inevitably be regarded as unjust or oppressive.

5.43   The judgment emphasises the strong public interest in honouring extradition arrangements. Following the principles set out, it will be difficult for a requested person to establish that it would be unjust to extradite him or her by reason of passage of time.

---

28   *Kakis v Government of the Republic of Cyprus* [1978] 1 WLR 779 at para 782.
29   *Knowles Jr v United States of America (The Bahamas)* [2006] UKPC 38.
30   [2009] UKHL 21 at para 32.

5.44   The judgment did not, however, give significant further guidance on the meaning of oppression, save to approve of what was said by Lord Diplock in *Kakis*:[31]

> ... the gravity of the offence is relevant to whether changes in the circumstances of the accused which have occurred during the relevant period are such as would render his return to stand his trial oppressive.

5.45   If a person therefore is sought for a minor offence and a lengthy period of time has passed, he or she will be more likely to be able to establish that their extradition will be oppressive than if the offence for which he or she is requested is grave.[32]

5.46   The gravity of the offence will be clear from the warrant. To show oppression, a detailed proof of evidence from the requested person will be required, alongside evidence from family members and, in some cases, expert witnesses such as social workers or psychologists who can comment on the impact that extradition will have on family members. There will often be an overlap between passage of time and Article 8 and they are often relied on by requested persons in tandem.

Cases where passage of time has barred extradition

5.47   The passage of time bar will always be fact-specific, but practitioners may find it helpful to consider examples of cases where passage of time has been successfully raised by requested persons.

La Torre v Italy[33]

5.48   The requested person in this case was the subject of five extradition requests from Italy, both accusation and conviction covering serious offences. There had been delays of between 6 and 16 years. Mr La Torre had been in custody since 1999, and the Italian authorities had been aware of this. He was only partially successful, but the case is useful in that it emphasises an important point: specifically, that in a marginal case, culpable delay on the part of the state could tip the balance in the requested person's favour. The judgment says:[34]

> All the circumstances must be considered in order to judge whether the unjust/oppressive test is met. Culpable delay on the part of the State may certainly colour that judgment and may sometimes be

---

31 *Gomes and Goodyer v Trinidad and Tobago* [2009] UKHL 21 at para 31.
32 *Sapstead v Governor of HMP Belmarsh* [2004] EWHC 2352 (Admin) at para 34.
33 [2007] EWHC 1370 (Admin).
34 At para 37.

decisive, not least in what is otherwise a marginal case ... And such delay will often be associated with other factors, such as the possibility of a false sense of security on the extraditee's part.

Wenting v High Court of Valenciennes[35]

5.49   Mr Wenting had been sentenced to five years' imprisonment imposed 20 years earlier for importation of 585 grams of cocaine. He had left France with the express permission of the French authorities, having been granted bail to live in the Netherlands. He had been living a law-abiding life; he had built up two successful businesses over the years and he had a partner who was seriously ill. Although he had been aware that he had been convicted after a trial had taken place in his absence, he had been informed by the Dutch probation service that he should wait for a summons. He was not ever notified that he was required to return to France to serve the sentence. The court found that it would be oppressive to extradite him.

Kovac v Regional Court in Prague[36]

5.50   In this case, the requested person had been convicted on six occasions for 18 offences of coercion of a young girl into prostitution and had been sentenced to nine years' imprisonment. There was, however, a 16-year unexplained delay between the conviction and the issue of the warrant, and the court found that this inactivity on the part of the authorities had lulled Mr Kovac into a false sense of security. In the intervening period, he had married and was the father of three children and two adopted children. He had also been working until his remand in custody as a night shift cleaner. The judge concluded that this was a borderline case and that the Czech authorities' failure to offer any explanation meant that it was a case of oppression.

Italy v Merico[37]

5.51   This case illustrates the principle that the court must take all factors into account cumulatively, in considering the passage of time bar. Ms Merico had been convicted of drug-trafficking offences in 1997 and sentenced to six years' imprisonment. She was released from prison having served two years of that sentence.

5.52   In 2005 the Italian authorities were notified that she was living in the United Kingdom. Since she had left, however, her circumstances

35 [2009] EWHC 3528 (Admin).
36 [2010] EWHC 1959 (Admin).
37 [2011] EWHC 1857 (Admin).

had altered drastically. The court took into account the following factors in deciding that it would be oppressive to extradite her by reason of the passage of time:

- the offences were committed a very long time ago;
- she had been released from prison 12 years before, after she had served nearly two years' imprisonment;
- she had travelled on a valid passport to the United Kingdom, where she had lived openly;
- she had not been convicted of any further offences;
- she had been bringing up her children and looking after her mother who was suffering from a terminal illness.

5.53 Those were factors which, taken together, were relevant to the decision that it would be oppressive to order her extradition. The court stated that each reason individually would not suffice but, taken together, they were capable of amounting to oppression.

R (Cepkauskas) v District Court of Marijampole, Lithuania[38]

5.54 The requested person was wanted on an accusation warrant for four offences of theft of cars, and one offence of theft, from 1997 to 1998. He had numerous convictions in the United Kingdom, including one that had resulted in an 18-month period of imprisonment. This sentence had led to a deportation order being made, although it was subsequently appealed successfully. The court found that it would be oppressive to extradite him for the following reasons: he had lived in the United Kingdom since 2003 and had no remaining family ties in Lithuania; it was an accusation rather than a conviction warrant; there had been no explanation for the delay in issuing the warrant and he had had no knowledge that there were matters outstanding against him in Lithuania; he had one child and four stepchildren who were dependent on him.

Summary of the case-law

5.55 In summary, some of the factors considered relevant to a finding of oppression in the cases above were:

- culpable delay on the part of the requesting state (in a marginal case);
- length of delay;
- whether a false sense of security has been engendered;
- whether the person's circumstances have changed significantly;

- the circumstances in which the person left the requesting state;
- the effect on those reliant on the requested person.

Person's age – section 15

5.56   Section 15 provides that a person's extradition is barred by reason of his age if it would be conclusively presumed because of his age that he or she could not be guilty of the extradition offence. The judge will be required to assess whether extradition is barred on the assumptions that the conduct would amount to an offence in the United Kingdom, had it taken place in the United Kingdom and that the person had carried out the conduct.

5.57   In short, given that the age of criminal responsibility in this country is ten, if a person is said to have committed an offence when he or she was younger than ten, extradition will be barred. This bar only applies in Part 1 cases. Practitioners may have difficulty imagining circumstances in which a warrant for a child younger than ten would be issued, particularly given that there is now no EU country with a lower age of criminal responsibility than England and Wales.

Hostage taking considerations – section 83

5.58   Section 83 sets out another highly unusual bar to extradition which does not apply to Part 1 cases. It only applies where:

- the conduct set out in the warrant would constitute an offence under section 1 of the Taking of Hostages Act 1982 or an attempt to commit such an offence;[39] and
- the requesting country is a party to the Hostage Taking Convention.

5.59   If both of these conditions apply, the court will have to examine whether the requested person might be prejudiced at trial because

---

39   Section 1 of the Taking of Hostages Act 1982 states that:
A person, whatever his nationality, who, in the United Kingdom or elsewhere –
(a) detains any other person ('the hostage'), and
(b) in order to compel a State, international governmental organisation or person to do or abstain from doing any act, threatens to kill, injure or continue to detain the hostage, commits an offence.
     The Taking of Hostages Act 1982 was enacted to implement the International Convention against the Taking of Hostages.

communications between him or her and the appropriate authorities (ie consular authorities) would not be possible.[40]

Specialty – sections 17/95

5.60   The principle of specialty[41] provides that, where a person is extradited, he or she will be prosecuted or proceeded against only for the offences in respect of which he or she is extradited, that is, those set out in the warrant or request.

5.61   In respect of Part 1 cases, section 17 is a bar to extradition to be considered by the appropriate judge at the extradition hearing. For Part 2 cases, it falls to be considered by the Secretary of State after the extradition hearing.

5.62   To rely on the specialty bar, a requested person must show that there are no specialty arrangements with the requesting state. This will be difficult to show in Part 1 cases, given that all EU countries are signatories to the 1957 European Convention on Extradition, which includes a provision preventing an extraditee from being dealt with for offences other than those for which he or she has been extradited.[42] The specialty rule also features in the Framework Decision.

Earlier extradition – sections 18, 19, 19A/96, 96A

5.63   Sections 18, 19 and 96 offer some (limited) protection to a person who has been extradited *to* the United Kingdom and subsequently faces a new warrant or request to be extradited from the United Kingdom.[43]

5.64   If the country that originally extradited the requested person to the United Kingdom is required to give consent to onward extradition and does not do so, that will act as a bar to extradition. As with

---

40   The Convention carries a clause which modifies extradition arrangements between state signatories and indeed allows extensive extradition which goes beyond that provided for in EA 2003.

41   Specialty is also sometimes referred to as 'speciality'.

42   For an example of a case where the requested person sought to rely on this bar in respect of a Part 1 state, see the case of *Hilali v National Court of Madrid* [2006] EWHC 1239 (Admin). Although the court did not rule out reliance on this bar in Part 1 cases, it gave the argument short shrift, saying (at para 52): 'It seems to us a surprising submission that Spain is likely to act in breach of the international obligations to which it has signed up. There is no evidence before us that it has done so in the past and in these circumstances we would need compelling evidence that it is likely to do so in the future'.

43   There is a similar provision in s19A which applies when a person has been transferred to a country by the International Criminal Court.

the specialty bar, this is considered by the judge at the extradition hearing for Part 1 cases and by the Secretary of State where the requesting state is a Part 2 territory.

Forum – sections 19B–F/83A–E[44]

5.65   Criminal conduct is increasingly cross-jurisdictional, meaning that there will often be more than one country in which a prosecution may take place. *Forum non conveniens* is a civil law doctrine that gives courts power to refuse to hear a case where there is a more appropriate jurisdiction. In an extradition context, the forum bar operates by way of EA 2003 ss19B–F and 83A–E. These sections prevent extradition 'by reason of forum' if the extradition would not be in the interests of justice. They only apply in accusation cases.[45] These provisions are complex and allow the judge to take into consideration a circumscribed set of factors.

Gateway

5.66   Section 19B/83A states that extradition will not be in the interests of justice if the judge –

(a) decides that a substantial measure of D's relevant activity was performed in the United Kingdom; and

(b) decides, having regard to the specified matters relating to the interests of justice (and only those matters), that the extradition should not take place.

5.67   The first condition, described as a 'gateway' in the case-law[46] is that a substantial measure of the activity must have been performed in the UK. Relevant activity is defined as activity 'material to the commission of the extradition offence' and which is alleged to have been performed by the requested person. It is described as a gateway as, if the judge is not satisfied as to this, it will not be necessary to go on to consider the specified matters relating to the interests of justice.

---

44   As inserted by Schedule 20 to the Crime and Courts Act 2013.

45   The fact that a person is requested under a conviction warrant means that they cannot rely on the forum bar, even if that person is entitled to a re-trial having been convicted *in absentia* – see *Bagri (Paramjit) v Public Prosecutor Bordeaux Court of First Instance* [2014] EWHC 4066 (Admin) and *Douglas Belbin v Regional Court of Lille, France* [2015] EWHC 149 (Admin).

46   *Pham v United States of America* [2014] EWHC 4167 (Admin) at para 85; *Atraskevic v Prosecutor General's Office, Republic of Lithuania* [2015] EWHC 131 (Admin) at para 16.

Specified matters

5.68 The second condition imposes limits on the judge's discretion in looking at the interests of justice and allows the judge to 'have regard' only to the seven matters which are specified in the provisions, and to no other matters. The specified matters are as follows:

a) the place where most of the loss or harm resulting from the extradition offence occurred or was intended to occur;

b) the interests of any victims of the extradition offence;

c) any belief of a prosecutor that the United Kingdom, or a particular part of the United Kingdom, is not the most appropriate jurisdiction in which to prosecute D in respect of the conduct constituting the extradition offence;

d) were D to be prosecuted in a part of the United Kingdom for an offence that corresponds to the extradition offence, whether evidence necessary to prove the offence is or could be made available in the United Kingdom;

e) any delay that might result from proceeding in one jurisdiction rather than another;

f) the desirability and practicability of all prosecutions relating to the extradition offence taking place in one jurisdiction, having regard (in particular) to –
   (i) the jurisdictions in which witnesses, co-defendants and other suspects are located, and
   (ii) the practicability of the evidence of such persons being given in the United Kingdom or in jurisdictions outside the United Kingdom;

g) D's connections with the United Kingdom.

5.69 The court has observed that these sections contain no indication as to the weight to be given to each of these matters, and that the relative importance and weight to be accorded to each of them may vary.[47] Case-law states that 'having regard' means bearing in mind each of the specified matters, although in the particular case being considered one factor may be irrelevant, or not present, or of little weight, or of great importance.[48] Nonetheless, the judge must have regard to each of the specified matters individually.[49]

---

47   *Dibden v Tribunal de Grande Instance de Lille, France* [2014] EWHC 3074 (Admin) at para 18.

48   *Shaw v Government of the United States of America* [2014] EWHC 4654 (Admin) at para 40.

49   *Shaw* at para 40.

Prosecutor's belief – sections 19B(3)(c)/83A(3)(c)

5.70   EA 2003 defines 'A prosecutor' in these sections as a person who has responsibility for prosecuting offences in any part of the United Kingdom, whether or not the person also has other responsibilities.[50] This will exclude a prosecutor from the CPS Extradition Unit.[51]

5.71   Whilst a prosecutor's belief is just one of the specified matters to which the judge must have regard, it will be an important one, particularly given that, if the judge does find that extradition is barred by reason of forum, she cannot order a prosecution to take place. The court has provided some guidance as to the exercise it must carry out in looking at sections 19B(3)(c)/83A(3)(c) under which the judge must take into account any belief of a prosecutor that the United Kingdom is not the most appropriate jurisdiction. In *Dibden v Tribunal de Grande Instance de Lille, France*, Simon J set out the limited basis upon which the court should review a prosecutor's belief saying: 'In my judgment, section 19B(3)(c) was not intended to invite a review of the prosecutor's belief as to the more appropriate jurisdiction on grounds short of irrationality. It was certainly not intended to invite a debate with demands for documents justifying the belief.'[52] He went on to say that the prosecutor's belief can be set out in a letter or statement but should be in writing, akin to a decision letter in immigration proceedings, and setting out the reasons for the prosecutor's belief.

5.72   Further principles regarding the 'prosecutor's belief' are set out in *Shaw v United States of America*:

> 48. In my view, the correct construction of section 83A(3)(c) is, for present purposes, as follows: first, it is important to note the word 'any' at the start of the paragraph. There may or may not be a belief that is stated to the court in some form or another. It is only if there is one that this factor is going to be relevant. The judge has to ask whether there is a belief; but if there is not, then he cannot have any further 'regard' to this factor. [Second], the key-word is 'belief'. It is not 'decision' or some similar word. A 'belief' in this context is more akin to a point of view or a conclusion based upon certain facts and other considerations. [Third], for these purposes, 'a prosecutor' must mean a domestic prosecutor within the United Kingdom: see the definition in section 83E(2). In England and Wales this means someone within the domestic branch of the CPS, rather than the separate

---

50 EA 2003 s19F.
51 *Shaw* at para 48.
52 *Dibden* at para 35.

and independent branch of the CPS, called the CPS Extradition Unit, which deals with extradition matters.

49. [Fourth], the 'belief' has to be a firm one in the sense that the prosecutor has to have concluded that the United Kingdom is 'not the most appropriate jurisdiction in which to prosecute' the person whose extradition is sought. Note the words 'the most appropriate'; therefore, it might be an appropriate jurisdiction but not necessarily 'the most appropriate'. [Fifth], it is important to note what precisely is the subject of the prosecution 'belief'. It is that the prosecution of the requested person for an offence (or offences) 'in respect of the conduct constituting the extradition offence' is not the most appropriate in the United Kingdom. In other words, the prosecutor has to consider the conduct that founds the alleged extradition offence itself, not other offences or other conduct that might be involved.

5.73 Further guidance relating to the prosecutors belief was provided in *Atraskevic v Prosecutor General's Office, Lithuania*[53] at para 37:

The third general point concerns the construction of the statutory wording of factor *(c)*: viz. 'any belief' of a prosecutor that the United Kingdom or a particular part of it, is not the most appropriate jurisdiction in which to prosecute the requested person for the extradition offence. In our view, the use of the words 'any belief of a prosecutor' is important. The 'prosecutor' in question here is a domestic prosecutor, that is someone in the domestic CPS. Such a prosecutor may or may not have formed any such belief at the time of the extradition hearing. If none has been formed or expressed, the statutory wording does not require that any party or the court should demand that a prosecutor must then take steps to create a 'belief' on the part of the prosecutor. The initiative to declare 'a belief' or not lies with the domestic CPS. There is no statutory mechanism that enables the court to compel further investigation by the CPS so as to put it in a position to have a 'belief'. That view of the construction of this factor is consistent with the rule, applicable in extradition cases, that a decision by domestic authorities not to investigate whether there should be a criminal prosecution in the United Kingdom is not susceptible to judicial review except in wholly exceptional circumstances such as bad faith: *R (Bermingham) v DPP* [2007] QB 207 at [64]; *R (McKinnon) v Secretary of State for Home Affairs* [2009] EWHC 2021 at [53].

5.74 Practitioners should also note that under sections 19B(5)/83A(5) a prosecutor can apply to be made a party to the proceedings. If it appears to the judge that the prosecutor has considered the offences for which the requested person could be prosecuted in the United Kingdom in respect of the conduct constituting the extradition

53 [2015] EWHC 131 (Admin).

offence, the judge must make the prosecutor a party to the proceedings if an application is made by the prosecutor.

Other specified matters

5.75   Under sections 19B(3)/83A(3) the judge will have regard to the place where most of the loss or harm occurred or was intended to occur. This would cover offences such as those where a person in the United Kingdom uses the internet to commit an offence in another jurisdiction, without leaving this one. The judge will also look at the interests of the victims. In looking at this specified matter, the judge will consider the views of the victims as to where the trial should take place but is also required to have regard to where the interests of the victim would best be served by having a trial.[54] The judge must also consider whether evidence could be made available in the United Kingdom for an offence which corresponds to the extradition offence.

5.76   Another consideration for the judge under sections 19B(3)/83A(3) will be the delay that might result in proceeding in one jurisdiction. Under subsection (f), the legislation envisages a multi-handed case that engages the forum bar and requires the judge to look at where witnesses and other co-defendants are located and how practicable it would be for their evidence to be given in the United Kingdom. Judges are entitled to consider cost under the heading of practicability.[55] The judge is also required to have regard to the defendant's connections with the United Kingdom.

5.77   Under a separate subsection (ss19B(4)/83A(4)) that follows, the judge must also have regard to the desirability of not requiring the disclosure of material which is subject to restrictions on disclosure in the requesting state. It is not clear on what information a decision can be taken that there are concerns about the disclosure of sensitive material.

Prosecutor's certificate

5.78   Further complexity is added to the forum provisions by sections 19C/83B which allows the prosecutor to prevent an argument on forum by issuing a certificate. If the prosecutor does so, the only mechanism for challenge will be on appeal on judicial review

---

54   *Shaw* at para 61.
55   *Piotrowicz v Regional Court in Gdansk, Poland* [2014] EWHC 3884 (Admin) at para 30.

principles. The certificate must certify particular matters, which are set out in sections 19D/83C (see below).

5.79　It will be evident that the legislation allows prosecutors a great deal of latitude. Sections 19C/83B also enable prosecutors to obtain adjournments to consider whether to issue a certificate. If an application is made, the judge must grant the adjournment application and continue to adjourn for as long as appears reasonable. In addition, a prosecutor cannot be required to give a prosecutor's certificate.

5.80　Under sections 19D/83C, the certificate must certify both matter A and Matter B and either Matter C or Matter D – as follows.

Matter A

The responsible prosecutor has considered the offences for which D could be prosecuted in the UK

AND

Matter B

The responsible prosecutor has decided that there are one or more such offences that correspond to the extradition offence.

5.81　It is mandatory for the prosecutor to certify that they have considered the offences and that they are extradition offences. In practice, this is unlikely to be contentious.

5.82　The prosecutor must also certify either Matter C or Matter D.

Matter C

The responsible prosecutor has made a formal decision that D should not be prosecuted for the corresponding offences, and the reason for that decision is a belief that –
(i) there would be insufficient admissible evidence for the prosecution; or
(ii) the prosecution would not be in the public interest.

OR

Matter D

The responsible prosecutor believes that D should not be prosecuted because there are concerns about the disclosure of sensitive material in –
(a) the prosecution of D for the corresponding offences, or
(b) any other proceedings.

5.83   With regard to Matter C, the prosecutor must have taken a formal decision not to charge. The test here is effectively the same as the test for a charging decision under the Code for Crown Prosecutors. The formal decision is defined as referring to a decision made after complying with any relevant code of practice that the requested person should or should not be prosecuted. In most cases this will be the Full Code test.[56]

5.84   With regard to Matter D the prosecutor will need to certify that there are concerns about the disclosure of sensitive material. As with section 19B(4) the information which the prosecutor will have which will enable her to make the decision about the disclosure of sensitive material is unclear.

5.85   Although the prosecutor's certificate may appear to be a powerful tool, in reality, it is unlikely to be frequently deployed. This is because, once a certificate is issued, it allows decisions taken by the prosecutor to be subjected to scrutiny by the court, albeit only on appeal on judicial review principles.

5.86   Given the way that the earlier provisions of the forum bar operate, a successful challenge to extradition where the prosecuting authorities have already come to a firm decision as to jurisdiction appears unlikely. In such circumstances, a prosecutor will be unlikely to need to resort to the issue of a certificate to ensure an extradition goes ahead, particularly in light of the specified matter of the 'prosecutor's belief' under sections 19B(3)(c)/83A(3)(c).

CPS guidance

5.87   Any lawyer dealing with a case engaging the forum bar should have regard to both the CPS Internal Process for dealing with Forum Bar cases (see appendix H) along with the guidance issued by the DPP on the handling of cases where the jurisdiction to prosecute is shared with prosecuting authorities overseas.[57]

---

56 www.cps.gov.uk/publications/docs/code_2013_accessible_english.pdf.

57 See: Director's Guidance on the handling of cases where the jurisdiction to prosecute is shared with prosecuting authorities overseas available at www.cps. gov.uk/publications/directors_guidance/director_s_guidance_on_concurrent_ jurisdiction.html . See also the Attorney-General's Domestic Guidance for handling criminal cases affecting both England, Wales or Northern Ireland and the United States at www.publications.parliament.uk/pa/ld200607/ldlwa/ 70125ws1.pdf.

Death penalty – section 94

5.88 The death penalty bar prevents the Secretary of State from ordering a person's extradition to a Part 2 country if he or she could be, will be or has been sentenced to death. If, however, the Secretary of State receives a written assurance that the death penalty will not apply to the requested person or will not be carried out (and he considers that assurance adequate), the requested person will not be able to rely on this bar. In a case where an assurance has been provided that the death penalty will not be carried out if imposed, consideration should be given as to whether remaining on death row in 'limbo' amounts to a violation of Article 3 ECHR.[58]

Conviction in absence – sections 20/85

5.89 This bar prevents the extradition of persons convicted in absence where they will not have a right to a retrial. There is, however, an important caveat: if the requested person deliberately absented themselves from their trial, he or she will not be able to rely on sections 20/85 to prevent extradition.

5.90 The steps that the judge must follow in deciding this question are prescribed by EA 2003 ss20/85. In the extradition hearing, the judge must decide whether the person was convicted in absence, and if so, whether he or she deliberately absented himself. It is the judicial authority that bears the burden of proving, to the criminal standard, that a person was deliberately absent.[59] In any conviction case, it is imperative for the duty solicitor to ascertain whether the person was present when convicted, and if not, whether that person was deliberately absent from the trial.[60]

Deliberate absence?

5.91 In many civil law jurisdictions the 'trial' will not be a single hearing but rather a 'continuing process'.[61] Requested persons who were present at trial, but absent from appeal (albeit duly summoned), are therefore likely to be deemed to have been convicted in their presence as they were present for 'part of the trial process'.

---

58 *Ghana v Gambrah* [2014] EWHC 1569 (Admin).
59 *Murtati v Albania* [2008] EWHC 2856 (Admin); *Benko v Hungary* [2009] EWHC 3530 (Admin); *Mitoi v Romania* [2006] EWHC 1977 (Admin).
60 *Emil Kis v District Court In Sokolov, Czech Republic* [2012] EWHC 938 (Admin).
61 *Caldarelli v Court of Naples Italy* [2008] 1 WLR 1724.

5.92   There have been numerous authorities that have looked at the construction of 'deliberate absence' under EA 2003 s20(3). In *Bicioc v Baia Mare Local Court, Romania*,[62] Mitting J stated that the issue of whether a requested person was 'deliberately absent from his trial' was a 'vexed question' to which 'a clear answer has not been given by our courts.'

5.93   In *Podlas v Koszalin District Court, Poland*[63] the Divisional Court sought to give a clear answer and provided guidance on 'deliberate absence' as follows:

> 1.   Section 20(3) (and its Part 2 equivalent) cannot be construed in the light of Framework Decision 2009/299/JHA of 26 February 2009.
> 2.   What constitutes 'the trial' for the purposes of s20(3) is a question of fact and in many member states, 'the trial' is a process and not a single hearing.
> 3.   Section 20(3) is only relevant where a 'trial process' has been initiated against the requested person. Whether the 'trial process' has been initiated will be a question of fact in each case depending on the requesting states procedures.
> 4.   It is for the judicial authority to establish to the criminal standard that the requested person has absented himself from the 'trial process' and that it was done deliberately. How the requested person knows of the process is irrelevant, it is the fact of his knowledge of the process that is relevant.
> 5.   Deliberate absence requires a consideration of what is in the mind of the requested person. A requested person cannot have deliberately absented himself from the 'trial process' if he or she did not know the process is taking place or is about to be commenced.
> 6.   The fact that the requested person has taken steps to make it difficult or impossible to serve a summons on him or her that notifies him or her of the fact, date and place of the trial is not of itself proof that the requested person has 'deliberately absented himself from his trial'.

'Entitled' to a re-trial

5.94   If the judge finds that the person was convicted in absence without having deliberately absented herself, the judge must then go on to look at whether the person would be entitled to a retrial, or (on appeal) a review amounting to a retrial. Section 20(8) provides that the judge must not decide that a person would be entitled to a retrial unless:

---

62   [2014] EWHC 628 (Admin).
63   [2015] EWHC 908 (Admin).

... in any proceedings that it is alleged would constitute a retrial or a review amounting to a retrial, the person would have these rights –

(a) the right to defend himself in person or through legal assistance of his own choosing or, if he had not sufficient means to pay for legal assistance, to be given it free when the interests of justice so required;

(b) the right to examine or have examined witnesses against him and to obtain the attendance and examination of witnesses on his behalf under the same conditions as witnesses against him.

5.95   A warrant or request may sometimes contain information on the right to a retrial, or it may be addressed by the requesting authority in further information provided to the court. Nevertheless, in cases where there is doubt it may be necessary to instruct a defence expert (such as a legal academic or an experienced lawyer practising in the requesting state) to address this point. EAWs from Italy and Romania in particular should be carefully scrutinised to check whether the requested person will be entitled to a retrial, and that any retrial will conform to Article 6 ECHR standards.

5.96   A number of cases have examined the meaning of 'entitled', looking at whether a person can be said to be entitled where the entitlement to a retrial is subject to a court's discretion. In the single judge decision of *Bohm v Romania*,[64] it was said that 'the right has to be automatic, and cannot be automatic if it is subject to the exercise of discretion, since the discretion might be exercised against retrial'. Contrast this however with the judgment of Rafferty LJ in *Nastase v Office of the State Prosecutor, Italy*:[65]

> The existence of procedural steps does not remove the entitlement to a retrial. Rather, the Italian authorities must be [permitted] to regulate their own proceedings by imposition of their own rules. Section 20 may create entitlements, but procedural rules set parameters within which such rights are exercisable.

5.97   When considering the differing views of the courts in numerous cases raising the section 20(5) issue of a right to a retrial, Rafferty LJ stated:

> These decisions in my view show a difference between on the one hand an exercise of what one might term pure discretion when considering

---

64 [2011] EWHC 2671 (Admin).

65 [2012] EWHC 3671 (Admin) at para 45. See also *Rexha v Officer of the Prosecutor, Court of Rome* [2012] EWHC 3397 (Admin) in which extradition was ordered where the judicial authority stated that whilst an absolute assurance of that the requested person would be entitled to a retrial, it was 'highly probable' (para 43).

an application for a retrial (Bohm) and the application of the law to the facts in accordance with a criminal code on the other.

5.98   While *Nastase* is a Divisional Court judgment, this is an unsettled area in extradition law and it will be necessary to check the developing case-law if relying on sections 20/85.

Proportionality – section 21A

5.99   On 21 July 2014, EA 2003 s21 was amended to include a new section 21A entitled 'Persons not convicted: human rights and proportionality.' The amendment added a new statutory consideration for judges, to be dealt with after having looked at whether extradition would be compatible with a person's Convention rights. In effect, it brought into force a new proportionality bar to extradition that had long been called for. Controversially, it only applies to Part 1 cases (EAWs) and those that are accused. The logic behind these exclusions is not apparent.[66]

5.100   EA 2003 s21A states:

(1) If the judge is required to proceed under this section (by virtue of section 11) he must decide both of the following questions in respect of the person ('D') –
  (i) Whether the extradition would be compatible with the Convention rights within the meaning of the Human Rights Act 1998;
  (ii) Whether the extradition would be disproportionate.
(2) In deciding whether the extradition would be disproportionate, the judge must take into account the specified matters relating to proportionality (so far as the judge thinks it appropriate to do so); but the judge must not take any other matters into account.
(3) These are the specified matters relating to proportionality –
  (a) the seriousness of the conduct alleged to constitute the extradition offence;
  (b) the likely penalty that would be imposed if D was found guilty of the extradition offence;
  (c) the possibility of the relevant foreign authorities taking measures that would be less coercive than the extradition of D.
(4) The judge must order D's discharge if the judge makes one or both of these decisions –

---

66   The House of Lords Select Committee on Extradition recommended that the legislation be amended so that the bar would also apply to conviction cases. See www.publications.parliament.uk/pa/ld201415/ldselect/ldextradition/126/12602.htm.

(a) that the extradition would not be compatible with the Convention rights;

(b) that the extradition would be disproportionate.

(5) The judge must order D to be extradited to the category 1 territory in which the warrant was issued if the judge makes both of these decisions –

(a) that the extradition would be compatible with the Convention rights;

(b) that the extradition would not be disproportionate.

5.101   In determining whether extradition is disproportionate the judge must have regard to only those specified matters set out in section 21A(3). The proportionality bar does however come as a secondary review of proportionality, given that the NCA should already have carried out a proportionality check at the certification stage and in doing so, should have applied the LCJ's guidance (see paragraph 3.4 above). The Divisional Court has provided guidance as to how the appropriate judge should determine the issues in EA 2003 s21A(3). In *Miraszewski and Others v District Court in Torun, Poland and Others*,[67] Pitchford LJ set out the following principles:

5.102   **Seriousness of the offence (s21A(3)(a))**

a. The LCJ's guidance contained within the Criminal Practice Directions Amendment No 2 [2014] EWHC Crim 1569 provides a measure of assistance to the assessment of seriousness.[68]

b. The LCJ's guidance is appropriate for identifying a 'floor' rather than a ceiling for the assessment of seriousness.[69]

c. The LCJ's guidance is aimed at offences at the very bottom end of the scale of seriousness about which it is unlikely there could be any dispute.[70]

d. The guidance states that in the identified cases the triviality of the conduct alleged would alone require the judge to discharge the requested person.[71]

e. A judge making the proportionality decision is not limited by the categories identified within the guidance provided for by the Lord Chief Justice. A judge may conclude that an offence is not serious

---

67 [2014] EWHC 4261 (Admin).

68 At para 27.

69 At para 28.

70 At para 28.

71 At para 28.

even though it does not fall within the categories listed in the guidance.[72]

f.   Other offences may be assessed by the judge as being non-serious or trivial offences.[73]

g. The seriousness of conduct alleged to constitute the offences is to be judged, in the first instance, against domestic standards although, as in all cases of extradition, the court will respect the views of the requesting state if they are offered.[74]

h. The main components of the seriousness of the conduct are the nature and quality of the acts and the harm caused to the victim. The appropriate judge should not adjourn to seek the requesting state's views on the subject.[75]

5.103   **Likely penalty that would be imposed if D was found guilty of the extradition offence (EA 2003 s21A(3)(b))**

i.   The principal focus is on the question of whether it would be proportionate to order the extradition of a person who is not likely to receive a custodial sentence in the requesting state.[76]

j.   Appropriate respect for the sentencing regime of a member state is required, however, in the extremely rare case when a particular penalty would be offensive to a domestic court in the circumstances of the particular criminal conduct the judge may adjust the weight to be given to 'the likely penalty'.[77]

k. The broad terms of subsection (3)(b) permit the judge to make the assessment on the information provided and, when specific information from the requesting state is absent, the judge is entitled to draw inferences from the contents of the EAW and to apply domestic sentencing practice as a measure of likelihood.[78]

l.   It does not follow that the likelihood of a non-custodial penalty precludes the judge from deciding that extradition would be proportionate.[79]

---

72   At para 28.
73   At para 28.
74   At para 36.
75   At para 36.
76   At para 37.
77   At para 38.
78   At para 38.
79   At para 39.

5.104 **Possibility of the relevant foreign authorities taking measures that would be less coercive than the extradition of D (EA 2003 s21A(3)(c))**

    m. There is an evidential burden on the requested person to identify less coercive measures that would be appropriate in the circumstances.[80]

    n. Where the requested person has left the requesting state with knowledge of his obligations to the requesting state's authorities, but in breach of them, it is unlikely that the appropriate judge will find less coercive methods appropriate. However, there may be occasions when the less coercive procedure is appropriate. If the requested person fails to respond to those alternative measures the issue of a further warrant and extradition could hardly be resisted.[81]

5.105 The specified matters in section 21A(3) are not listed in order of importance[82] and the appropriate judge will need to specifically address each of the subsection (3) issues and should give reasons for the weight he attaches to each factor.[83]

Effectiveness?

5.106 It is understood that in the period between the proportionality bar coming into force and 5 September 2014, the NCA refused to certify 14 EAWs on the basis that they believed the EAW would be discharged by an appropriate judge under the proportionality bar. If the NCA continue to refuse to certify disproportionate warrants, it may be that the courts will not deal with large numbers of cases under EA 2003 s21A. Those that slip through the net will still be dealt with by the court and, at the time of writing, the authors are aware of at least half a dozen cases that have been discharged under the new bar. Practitioners should keep the words of Pitchford LJ at the forefront of their minds: extradition for an offence which falls outside the category of offences set out in the LCJ's guidance can still be disproportionate. It is likely that the new proportionality bar will be an important weapon in the armoury of the defence advocate.

---

80 At para 41.
81 At para 41.
82 At para 32.
83 At para 33.

Physical or mental health – sections 25/91

5.107   If, during the extradition hearing, it appears to the judge that it would be unjust or oppressive to extradite the person by virtue of his physical or mental condition, the judge must either order his discharge,[84] or adjourn the hearing[85] until it appears to the judge that the person's physical or mental condition is such that it would no longer be unjust or oppressive to extradite him.[86] It is important to note that the mere fact that a person suffers from an illness is not enough to prevent extradition. It must be shown that, because of the illness or complaint, it will be unjust or oppressive to extradite the requested person.

5.108   In order to satisfy a finding of 'oppression' a high threshold must be reached. The Administrative Court has said that: 'The term "unjust or oppressive" requires regard to be had to all the relevant circumstances, including the fact that extradition is ordinarily likely to cause stress and hardship; neither of those is sufficient.'[87] The court may consider that the standard of care will be less satisfactory for a requesting person in the requesting state. That said, the High Court has emphasised that the test is whether or not the extradition would be oppressive.[88]

5.109   There is a significant body of case-law that looks, in particular, at those requested persons who are at risk of suicide.[89] In *Richen Turner v Government of the United States of America*,[90] Aikens LJ summarised the following propositions from the case-law:

84   EA 2003 s25(3)(a).

85   EA 2003 s25(3)(b).

86   See paragraphs 5.40–5.46 for more detail on injustice or oppression: the Administrative Court in *Government of the Republic of South Africa v Shrien Dewani* [2012] EWHC 842 (Admin) confirmed that the words are 'to be read in the sense used in cases such as *Kakis*'.

87   *Government of the Republic of South Africa v Shrien Dewani* [2012] EWHC 842 (Admin) at para 73.

88   See *R (Mikolajczyk) v Wroclaw District Court* [2010] EWHC 3503 (Admin) at para 17: 'It is of course possible that treatment will be less satisfactory in Poland than in the United Kingdom, but the question is whether the difference in treatment would mean that extradition was oppressive. It is for the appellant to demonstrate that that is so.'

89   See, for example: *Jansons v Latvian Judicial Authority* [2009] EWHC 1845 (Admin), *R (Rot) v District Court of Lublin, Poland* [2010] EWHC 1820 (Admin), *R (Prosser) v Secretary of State for the Home Department* [2010] EWHC 845 (Admin), *Wrobel v Poland* [2011] EWHC 374 (Admin), *R (Griffin) v City of London Magistrates' Court* [2011] EWHC 943 (Admin).

90   [2012] EWHC 2426 (Admin) at para 28.

(1) The court has to form an overall judgment on the facts of the particular case.

(2) A high threshold has to be reached in order to satisfy the court that a requested person's physical or mental condition is such that it would be unjust or oppressive to extradite him.

(3) The court must assess the mental condition of the person threatened with extradition and determine if it is linked to a risk of a suicide attempt if the extradition order were to be made. There has to be a 'substantial risk that [the appellant] will commit suicide'. The question is whether, on the evidence[,] the risk of the appellant succeeding in committing suicide, whatever steps are taken[,] is sufficiently great to result in a finding of oppression.

(4) The mental condition of the person must be such that it removes his capacity to resist the impulse to commit suicide, otherwise it will not be his mental condition but his own voluntary act which puts him at risk of dying and if that is the case there is no oppression in ordering extradition.

(5) On the evidence, is the risk that the person will succeed in committing suicide, whatever steps are taken, sufficiently great to result in a finding of oppression?

(6) Are there appropriate arrangements in place in the prison system of the country to which extradition is sought [such] that those authorities can cope properly with the person's mental condition and the risk of suicide?

(7) There is a public interest in giving effect to treaty obligations and this is an important factor to have in mind.

5.110 Approving the above propositions in *Wolkowicz v Polish Judicial Authority*[91] the President of the Queen's Bench Division stated that the key issue in almost every case will 'be the measures that are in place to prevent any attempt at suicide by a requested person with a mental illness being successful'. These should be examined in three stages:

1) The position while the requested person is being held in custody in the United Kingdom.

2) Arrangements that will be in place when the person is being transferred to ensure there are proper arrangements in place to prevent suicide. Medical records should be sent to those who will have custody during transfer.

3) It is to be presumed (in the absence of strong evidence to the contrary) that the receiving state within the EU will discharge its responsibilities to prevent the person committing suicide. It

---

91 [2013] EWHC 102 (Admin) at para 10.

should not be necessary to require any assurances from requesting states within the EU.

5.111   In *Wolkowicz* the court emphasised that, following these principles, it is 'only in a very rare case that a requested person will be likely to establish that measures to prevent a substantial risk of suicide will not be effective'.

5.112   The solicitor representing any requested persons with physical or mental health problems will need to obtain medical evidence which will show the court why their complaint will lead to injustice or oppression. The solicitor should also carefully consider whether there are any other facts that lend support to a finding of oppression, for example: family circumstances; delay or a significant change in circumstance. It may be helpful to consider the examples given above of cases where oppression caused by the passage of time has led to discharge.

Abuse of process

5.113   Although EA 2003 does not state that an abuse of the court's process will bar extradition, the courts have found that in certain circumstances it will. Abuse of process arguments can only be deployed if all other bars to extradition have failed, ie it is a residual jurisdiction.[92]

5.114   The implied jurisdiction of the court to consider abuse of process in the context of extradition proceedings was decided in relation to the 2003 Act in *R (Bermingham) v Director of the Serious Fraud Office.*[93] The court will start from the assumption that a requesting state is acting in good faith, which may be displaced by evidence.[94] A person requested by a Part 1 territory will also face the difficulty of overcoming the principle of mutual trust and recognition inherent in the operation of the system of EAWs.

5.115   Procedural guidance from the case of *United States of America v Tollman*[95] is succinctly set out in *Haynes v Malta:*[96]

---

92   *Loncar v County Court in Vukovar (Croatia)* [2015] EWHC 548 (Admin) at para 22.

93   *R (Bermingham) v Director of the Serious Fraud Office* [2006] EWHC 200 (Admin).

94   *Ahmad and Aswat v The Government of the United States of America* [2006] EWHC 2927 (Admin), [2007] UKHRR 525 at para 101.

95   *United States of America v Tollman* [2008] EWHC 184 (Admin).

96   *Haynes v Malta* [2009] EWHC 880 (Admin) at para 6.

To sustain an allegation of abuse of process in relation to proceedings under the Act, it is necessary, first to identify with specificity what is alleged to constitute the abuse; [second] to satisfy the court that the matter complained of is capable of amounting to an abuse; and [third] to satisfy the court that there are reasonable grounds for believing that such conduct has occurred. If the matter gets that far, then the court should require the judicial authority to provide an explanation. The court should not order extradition unless satisfied that no such abuse has taken place.

5.116 As stated above, the requested person bears the burden of satisfying the judge that, not only is the issue raised capable of amounting to an abuse, but also that there are reasonable grounds for believing that the abuse has occurred. It will be essential therefore for the requested person to bring cogent evidence of the abuse in order to satisfy the court that the conduct has occurred.

5.117 While the Administrative Court has stated that 'abuse of process in the extradition context is not confined to bad faith on the part of the requesting state'[97] the circumstances in which abuse of process can be argued will be limited. In relation to Part 1 cases, the court has drawn a distinction between an abuse of the extradition process by the prosecuting authority and an abuse resulting from the misconduct or bad faith of the police of the requesting state in the investigation of the case or the preparation of evidence for trial. Abuse arising from misconduct or bad faith by the police is a matter to be resolved by the requesting state and will not be capable of preventing a person's extradition.[98] Where the requesting state seeks the 'extradition of someone for a collateral purpose, or when they know that the trial cannot succeed',[99] this will fall into the former category and will be capable of amounting to an abuse of the court's process.

5.118 Various categories of abuse of process that the courts have examined in the context of extradition proceedings include: re-issue of an

---

97 *Janovic v Prosecutor General's Office, Lithuania* [2011] EWHC 710 (Admin) at para 18.

98 *Symeou v Public Prosecutor's Officer, Patras, Greece* [2009] EWHC 897 (Admin) at para 34.

99 At para 33.

extradition request;[100] collateral motive;[101] disclosure;[102] incorrect particulars;[103] and forum issues.[104]

Immigration status

5.119   If a requested person has made a claim for asylum she cannot be extradited while the asylum claim is pending.[105] The question of whether extradition proceedings should be adjourned pending the outcome of the asylum claim is currently moot: in *R (Chichvarkin) v Secretary of State for the Home Department*[106] the Divisional Court stated that, in circumstances where an asylum claim is being actively considered by the SSHD and the extradition court is considering whether extradition would lead to a breach of a person's human rights, this would 'weigh heavily in favour of an adjournment of the extradition proceedings'.[107] See also, however, in *Kozlowski v District Court of Torun Poland*,[108] Ouseley J (in the face of a growing number of Polish appellants seeking to adjourn proceedings to await the outcome of asylum claims) warned against drawing a general point of principle from *Chichvarkin* and said that 'in cases involving Council of Europe and EU countries there ought to be a very firm approach not to grant adjournments'.[109] Nonetheless, where a requested person has made a realistic claim for asylum and the country of origin is within the Council of Europe but not an EU member state, careful consideration should be given to whether evidence given in the extradition hearings could adversely impact on her or any family members that remain in the requesting state. If there is such a risk, an adjournment could well be in her best interests.

100 *Office of the Prosecutor-General of Turin v Franco Barone* [2010] EWHC 3004 (Admin); *Sofia City Court, Bulgaria v Atanasova-Kalaidzhieva* [2011] EWHC 2335 (Admin).

101 *Republic of Serbia v Ejup Ganic* [2011] EWHC 878 (Admin); *R (Lotfi Raissi) v Secretary of State for the Home Department* [2008] EWCA Civ 72.

102 *Government of Ukraine v Kononko* [2014] EWHC 1420 (Admin).

103 *Zakrzewski v Regional Court in Lodz, Poland* [2013] UKSC 2.

104 Albeit prior to the implementation of the forum provisions under the Crime and Courts Act 2013. See for example *Kulibaba and Konovalenko v Government of the United States of America* [2014] EWHC 176 (Admin).

105 EA 2003 ss39 and 121.

106 *R (Chichvarkin) v Secretary of State for the Home Department* [2010] EWHC 1858 (QB).

107 At para 61.

108 *Kozlowski v District Court of Torun, Poland* [2012] EWHC 1706 (Admin).

109 At para 20.

5.120   The Refugee Convention prohibits the return of refugees to their home country.[110] While this is not explicitly covered in the EA 2003, it has been resolved by the Divisional Court in *District Court in Ostroleka v Dytlow*.[111] Similarly, recent amendments to the EA 2003 provide that if a person is granted leave to remain or enter on the grounds that it would be a breach of the Human Rights Convention to remove the person to the territory to which extradition would be requested, the Secretary of State may order the person's discharge.[112]

5.121   If the requested person is a refugee whose extradition is sought by the country of origin, or where a requested person sought by her country of origin has been granted leave to remain in the United Kingdom as a person with humanitarian protection she should be discharged.[113] It will be important to obtain the decision letter from the Home Office to satisfy the court that she is indeed a refugee or has been granted humanitarian protection.

5.122   Requested persons who have been granted asylum and then obtain British citizenship will not be afforded the protection afforded by the EA 2003 as they will no longer be a refugee and as a British citizen will have other protections.[114]

5.123   The following chapter looks at human rights considerations as grounds for resisting extradition.

---

110   This is known as the principle of *'non-refoulement'*.

111   *District Court in Ostroleka, Second Criminal Division (A Polish Judicial Authority) v Dytlow* [2009] EWHC 1009 (Admin).

112   EA 2003 s93(6A) as amended by Anti-social Behaviour, Crime and Policing Act 2014 s162(3).

113   *Government of Ukraine v Polishchuk*, Westminster Magistrates' Court, 5 September 2014

114   *Turkey v Ozbek* [2014] EWHC 3469 (Admin).

Human rights

Introduction

6.1   In dealing with both Part 1 (EA 2003 s21) and Part 2 (s87) cases, the judge will be required to consider whether extradition would be compatible with a person's rights under the European Convention on Human Rights ('the Convention') within the meaning of the Human Rights Act 1998. If the judge decides the question in the negative, he or she must order the person's discharge.

6.2   Although in law the same considerations apply, the treatment of human rights by the courts differs in practice as between Part 1 and Part 2 cases. This chapter will begin by looking at how human rights considerations are applied in Part 1 and Part 2 cases. It will then go on to look at the specific human rights that are protected by the Convention.

Human rights in Part 1 cases

6.3   All EU countries have signed and ratified the Convention. The Framework Decision states that the EAW 'is the first concrete measure in the field of criminal law implementing the principle of mutual recognition, which the European Council referred to as the "cornerstone" of judicial cooperation.' It goes on to say that the mechanism of the EAW is 'based on a high level of confidence between member states'.[1]

6.4   It is important to have this context in mind when considering human rights in Part 1 extradition cases. There is a presumption that EU countries will comply with their human rights obligations. As stated in *Dabas*: 'The important underlying assumption of the Framework Decision is that member states, sharing common values and recognising common rights, can and should trust the integrity and fairness of each other's judicial institutions.'[2]

6.5   Nevertheless, the way in which human rights are considered in Part 1 cases has not always been consistent. A line of case-law developed in 2010 suggesting that the presumption of compliance with human rights in EU countries was tantamount to being irrebuttable.[3]

---

1   Framework Decision 2002 paras 6 and 10 of the Preamble.
2   *Dabas v High Court of Justice in Madrid, Spain* [2007] UKHL 6.
3   See, for example, *Dabkowski v Poland* [2010] EWHC 1712 (Admin); *R (Rot) v District Court of Lublin, Poland* [2010] EWHC 1820 (Admin) and *Klimas v Prosecutor General's Office of Lithuania* [2010] EWHC 2076 (Admin). In the latter

6.6   There was, however, a shift following the case of *MSS v Belgium*,[4] in which the European Court of Human Rights dealt with the case of an Afghan asylum-seeker who had been deported from Belgium to Greece, where he had been held in 'appalling' conditions. In that case, the court observed that:

> ... the existence of ... international treaties guaranteeing respect for fundamental rights in principle are not in themselves sufficient to ensure adequate protection against the risk of ill-treatment where, as in the present case, reliable sources have reported practices ... which are manifestly contrary to the principles of the Convention.

6.7   The Administrative Court followed this approach in *Agius v Malta*,[5] emphasising that section 21 imposed an obligation on the district judge to 'reach a decision as to whether extradition would be compatible with the appellant's Convention rights'. While maintaining that the starting point is the presumption (which is not easily displaced) that the requesting state will comply with its Convention obligations, the court stated it is 'capable of being rebutted by clear and cogent evidence, which establishes that ... extradition would not be compatible with the defendant's Convention rights'. The court went on to say that:

> In practical terms [...] the burden of displacing the assumption will be a heavy one, and it may well be the case that as a matter of fact successful reliance on section 21(1) will be the exception rather than the rule, but that does not mean that there is a legal obligation on an appellant relying on section 21(1) to demonstrate 'exceptional circumstances'.[6]

6.8   In spite of this presumption, in very recent years, the courts have on occasion found that the extradition of persons to particular European countries would be incompatible with their Convention rights: see paragraph 6.19 below.

---

case, Mitting J said: 'Accordingly, and as a matter of principle, I would hold as I did in *Jan Rot* that when prison conditions in a Convention category 1 state are raised as an obstacle to extradition, the district judge need not, save in wholly extraordinary circumstances in which the constitutional order of the requesting state has been upset for example by a military coup or violent revolution examine the question at all ...'.

4   *MSS v Belgium*, Application No 30696/09, 21 January 2011.
5   *Agius v Court of Magistrates, Malta* [2011] EWHC 759 (Admin).
6   At para 19.

Human rights in Part 2 cases

6.9   All Council of Europe countries are signatories to the Convention.[7] There is therefore a presumption that non-EU Council of Europe countries will also be capable of offering adequate protection of a requested person's human rights,[8] although at the time of writing the Russian Federation does not benefit from this presumption.[9]

6.10   Indeed, even for countries that have not signed the Convention, there will often be a presumption of compliance with international human rights norms. For many years, the courts have asserted that there are 'fundamental assumptions that the requesting state is acting in good faith and that the fugitive will receive a fair trial in the courts of the requesting state'.[10] Although this presumption can be rebutted by evidence, it will be all the more difficult to displace 'where the requesting state is one in which the United Kingdom has for many years reposed the confidence not only of general good relations, but also of successive bilateral treaties consistently honoured'.[11]

---

7 Council of Europe countries who are not EU member states are as follows: Norway, Albania, Turkey, Iceland, Switzerland, Liechtenstein, San Marino, Moldova, Macedonia, Ukraine, Russia, Georgia, Armenia, Azerbaijan, Bosnia and Herzegovina, Serbia, Monaco, Montenegro and Andorra.

8 See *Gomes and Goodyer v Trinidad and Tobago* [2009] UKHL 21 at para 35: 'Council of Europe countries in our view present no problem. All are subject to Article 6 of the Convention and should readily be assumed capable of protecting an accused against an unjust trial – whether by an abuse of process jurisdiction like ours or in some other way.'

9 No requested persons have been extradited to Russia in recent years save for one exceptional case: Mr Maxim Vintskevich was extradited to Russia in March 2013. It is understood that he was advised of the possibility of resisting his extradition on the grounds that it would lead to a violation of his Article 3 Convention rights but chose not to contest his extradition on this ground. See the judgments of the Chief Magistrate in *Russian Federation v Fotinova* in the Westminster Magistrates' Court, 21 March 2013 and of District Judge Nicolas Evans in *Russian Federation v Trefilov* in the Westminster Magistrates' Court, 16 November 2012.

10 *Serbeh v Governor of HMP Brixton* [2002] EWHC 2356 (Admin) at para 31.

11 *Ahmad v USA* [2006] EWHC 2927 (Admin). See also the comments of Sir Brian Leveson in *Ravi Shankaran v The Government of the State of India* [2014] EWHC 957 (Admin) at para 66: 'It is true that India is not party to the ECHR or other international treaties that accord specific human rights to those within its jurisdiction. Nevertheless, it is a democracy governed by the rule of law with a developed and effective system of law. It has a constitution requiring respect for fundamental rights including the protection of life, liberty and access to a court. There have been long and extensive bi-lateral relations between the governments of the United Kingdom and India. India is a leading member of the Commonwealth and there have been friendly exchanges between the judiciary of the United Kingdom and India.'

An example of such a state is the United States. In practice, a court's willingness to find that a country will not comply with its human rights obligations will differ by country, according to its record of compliance. When seeking to persuade a court that a person should be discharged under section 87, it is therefore of the utmost importance to put before the court persuasive evidence of a lack of compliance with human rights obligations.

European Court of Human Rights

6.11 There have been several recent refusals to extradite persons on human rights grounds (and in particular Article 3 in relation to prison conditions) notwithstanding the difficulties set out above. This can be seen in the light of the codification of the 'pilot judgment' procedure by the ECtHR in 2011.[12] This procedure aims to deal with systemic or structural human rights violations in Council of Europe states. In relation to prisons in several countries, the ECtHR has handed down pilot judgments that point to structural problems in the countries concerned which cause a violation of the Article 3 rights of prisoners (see paragraph 6.19 below). Under section 2(1) of the Human Rights Act 1998, the UK courts are bound to take into account the decisions of the ECtHR so far as they are relevant to the proceedings.[13] Where the Strasbourg court has found a systemic violation of human rights in the requested state, the court in this country will be likely to find that this rebuts the presumption of compliance with the Convention. In such cases, it will be for the requesting state to 'dispel the doubts' raised by the Strasbourg court.[14] The principal means by which requesting states have sought to meet this challenge is examined in paragraph 6.21 below.

6.12 The unsettled approach of the courts to this question goes to the very heart of the (essentially political) reckoning that must be carried out by judges in extradition cases. Whilst they must have regard to the human rights of requested persons, they are also acutely aware of the two things: first, that extradition arrangements are reciprocal, ie

12 See ECtHR press release issued by the Registrar of the Court, No 256, 24 March 2011.
13 Although this does not necessarily mean that the judgment is binding. See the comments of McCombe LJ in *Badre v Court of Florence, Italy* [2014] EWHC 614 (Admin) at para 44: 'As is well known, and recently much debated, the requirement to take the judgment into account does not necessarily mean that the judgment has to be followed.'
14 See *Saadi v Italy* (2009) 49 EHRR 30 at para 129.

a refusal to extradite to a country may lead to an extradition request from this country being refused; and second, that blanket refusals to extradite to a particular country carry the possibility of creating a safe haven for fugitives in England and Wales.

Article 2 (right to life) and Article 3 (prohibition of torture and inhuman and degrading treatment)

6.13   Article 2 states that everyone's right to life shall be protected by law. Article 3 provides that no one shall be subjected to torture or to inhuman or degrading treatment or punishment.[15] Challenges under Article 2 have been brought where it is alleged that a person will be killed by other prison inmates (*Dewani*);[16] by gang members (*McLean*);[17] by the State (*Bah*);[18] or where a person's extradition is sought by a country that applies the death penalty. In relation to Article 3, requested persons have argued that their Convention rights will be violated by, for example, inter-prisoner violence arising from being targeted as a result of ethnicity (*Konuksever*);[19] the prison conditions in a particular country (*Krolik*);[20] or life imprisonment without parole (*Harkins and Edwards*).[21] As these examples show, the risk may be from the state, or may arise from threats by non-state actors or could relate to grossly disproportionate sentences or medical treatment.

6.14   In seeking to persuade a court that a requested person should not be extradited under these Articles, the burden will be on the requested person to bring clear and cogent evidence showing that there are substantial grounds for believing that the person, if extradited, faces a real risk of either being killed[22] or being subjected to

---

15   Where Article 2 is argued, Article 3 will frequently be argued alongside it, given that inhuman or degrading treatment will often be a corollary of a threat to life.

16   *Government of South Africa v Dewani* [2010] EWHC 3398 (Admin).

17   *McLean v High Court of Dublin, Ireland* [2008] EWHC 547 (Admin).

18   *The Government of the Republic of Gambia v Bah* (3 February 2012) Westminster MC.

19   *Konuksever v Government of Turkey* [2012] EWHC 2166 (Admin).

20   *Krolik v Several Judicial Authorities of Poland* [2012] EWHC 2357 (Admin).

21   *Harkins and Edwards v UK* Application No 9146/07, 17 January 2012.

22   Although, as Lord Bingham points out in *R (Ullah) v Special Adjudicator* [2004] UKHL 26, the test that the court applied in *Dehwari v Netherlands* (2000) 29 EHRR CD 74 was 'near certainty' rather than real risk: at para 24.

torture or to inhuman or degrading treatment.[23] Where the risk is from a non-state actor, it will be necessary to show that protection from the requesting state will be inadequate.[24]

6.15 Given the heavy burden on the requested person, it will not be enough to rely simply on the requested person's own evidence.[25] Witnesses of fact who can support the requested person's account may be appropriate, along with expert witnesses who can speak to the specific risk faced by the requested person. Case-law from the European Court of Human Rights can be used along with reports from governmental and non-governmental organisations, such as the US State Department and the Council of Europe Committee for the Prevention of Torture, to bolster the evidence of expert witnesses.

Prison conditions – presumption of compliance

6.16 The High Court, having encountered numerous appeals premised on poor prison conditions in Poland, provided guidance in *Krolik v Several Judicial Authorities of Poland*[26] for these cases as follows:

- Any appeal raising the issue must:
  - clearly identify any new factual issues not considered in this appeal or earlier cases which are said to give rise to a breach of Article 3 by reason of the conditions in Polish prisons;
  - set out a summary of the evidence relied on in support; and
  - explain how it meets the criteria for evidence of the type to which we have referred at paragraphs 6.6 and 6.7.
- Any such appeal will be listed within days of it being lodged at the court. If there are no new factual issues and the evidence is not of the type identified, the court will consider whether it should be heard then and there and, if appropriate, dismissed.
- As it is highly unlikely that new factual issues will arise or that the type of evidence required will be provided, it is anticipated that there will be few, if any, further appeals that raise the issue.
- District judges should require a requested person or the advocate representing the requested person who seeks to raise an Article 3 issue relying on Polish prison conditions to identify any new factual issues not considered in this appeal or earlier cases and

---

23 *Soering v UK* (1989) 11 EHRR 439 at para 91.
24 *R (Bagdanavicius) v Secretary of State for the Home Department* [2005] UKHL 38 at para 24.
25 *G v District Court of Czestochowa, Poland* [2011] EWHC 1597 (Admin).
26 [2012] EWHC 2357 (Admin).

whether the evidence in support is of the type to which we have referred. If the requested person or his advocate fails to do so, then the district judge should ordinarily be entitled to deal with the claim briefly by relying on the decisions of this court.

6.17   The Administrative Court has considered a wide range of factual issues in relation to prison conditions. The most common issue raised is overcrowding. In order to satisfy the first condition set out in the High Court guidance above, it will be necessary for the requested person to raise a novel issue relating to prisons in Poland. A Polish client should be advised of the difficulties that he or she will face in raising any argument on Polish prison conditions.

6.18   Evidence of a risk of a breach of Article 3 has been examined in the Administrative Court in relation to requests from other EU member states, such as Lithuania and Greece which have not yet been the subject of any pilot judgments. In *Aleksynas and Others v Minister of Justice, Republic of Lithuania and Another*[27] and *Ilia v Appeal Court in Athens, Greece*[28] assurances were examined. The Administrative Court has also looked at prison conditions in Latvia[29] and Romania.[30] Whilst none of the appeals in these cases were allowed, some requested persons have succeeded in persuading the magistrates' court that they face a real risk that their Article 3 rights will be breached. In such cases, a successful argument has been put forward on the basis of very specific facts. Practitioners seeking to bring such challenges should be aware of the indication of the Chief Magistrate (which has been expressly approved by the Divisional Court in *Brazuks and Others v Prosecutor's General Office, Latvia*)[31] 'that in all EAW cases, bearing in mind that the requesting state will be a member of the Council of Europe and a signatory to the ECHR, the court will not hear evidence challenging general prison conditions unless the defendant identifies from an internationally recognised source new factual issues that could amount to clear, cogent and compelling evidence to show that there is a real risk of treatment contrary to Article 3.'

---

27 [2014] EWHC 437 (Admin).
28 *Ilia v Appeal Court in Athens, Greece* [2015] EWHC 547 (Admin).
29 *Brazuks and Others v Prosecutor General's Office, Latvia* [2014] EWHC 1021 (Admin).
30 *Florea v Judicial Authority Carei Courthouse, Satu Mare County, Romania* [2014] EWHC 2528 (Admin); *Blaj and Others v Court of Alesd, Romania and Others* [2015] EWHC 1710 (Admin).
31 See footnote 29 above.

Prison conditions where presumption has been displaced

6.19   At the time of writing, the ECtHR has handed down pilot judgments (see paragraph 6.11 above) relating to prison conditions in the following countries: Russia,[32] Italy,[33] Bulgaria[34] and Hungary.[35] The Strasbourg court has also been critical, to a greater or lesser extent, of conditions in a number of EU member states, as well as the majority of non-EU Council of Europe countries.

6.20   If the presumption of compliance has been displaced by a pilot judgment, it will be open to the requesting state to attempt to persuade the court that there has been a general improvement since the pilot judgment such that all prisons are now Article 3 compliant. If the court is persuaded of this, it will be unnecessary to consider assurances, as the court can rely on the compliance of the requesting state with the Convention. Requesting states have also, however, attempted to deal with the displacement of the presumption of compliance with the Convention by offering an assurance that, in respect of the requested person alone, the requesting state will comply with their obligations under the Convention.[36] The way in which the court has dealt with these assurances will be examined below.

---

32   *Ananyev and Others v Russia*, Application Nos 42525/07 and 60800/08 (10 January 2012).

33   *Torreggiani and Others v Italy*, Application No 43517/09 (8 January 2013).

34   *Neshkov and Others v Bulgaria*, Application Nos 36925/10, 21487/12, 72893/12, 73196/12, 77718/12 and 9717/13 (27 January 2015).

35   *Varga and Others v Hungary*, Application Nos 14097/12, 45135/12, 73712/12, 34001/13, 44055/13, and 64586/13 (10 March 2015).

36   See Hickinbottom J in *Badre v Court of Florence, Italy* [2014] EWHC 614 (Admin) at para 65: '[...] where the European Court of Human Rights has made a finding in a pilot judgment that the prison regime of a state is in systemic breach of Article 3, absent other specific evidence, there is a risk that, if detained in that prison system, a returned individual will be subjected to prison conditions that breach his human rights. Of course, it is open to that state to adduce evidence that there is no such risk. For example, it could produce evidence that, since the pilot judgment, prison conditions have improved, so that there is no longer a systemic problem with them; or give an assurance that, if the individual is returned and then detained, he will be kept in a particular prison (or in one of a number of identified prisons) which does not suffer from the general problem identified by the European Court.'

Assurances

6.21   In *Othman (Abu Qatada) v United Kingdom*,[37] the ECtHR looked at whether assurances received from Jordan were sufficient to remove any real risk of ill-treatment. It set out the following principles in relation to Article 3 expulsion cases:

> 187. In any examination of whether an applicant faces a real risk of ill-treatment in the country to which he is to be removed, the Court will consider both the general human rights situation in that country and the particular characteristics of the applicant. In a case where assurances have been provided by the receiving State, those assurances constitute a further relevant factor which the Court will consider. However, assurances are not in themselves sufficient to ensure adequate protection against the risk of ill-treatment. There is an obligation to examine whether assurances provide, in their practical application, a sufficient guarantee that the applicant will be protected against the risk of ill-treatment. The weight to be given to assurances from the receiving State depends, in each case, on the circumstances prevailing at the material time [...].

> 188. In assessing the practical application of assurances and determining what weight is to be given to them, the preliminary question is whether the general human rights situation in the receiving State excludes accepting any assurances whatsoever. However, it will only be in rare cases that the general situation in a country will mean that no weight at all can be given to assurances [...].

> 189. More usually, the Court will assess first, the quality of assurances given and, second, whether, in light of the receiving State's practices they can be relied upon. In doing so, the Court will have regard, inter alia, to the following factors:
> (i) whether the terms of the assurances have been disclosed to the Court [...];
> (ii) whether the assurances are specific or are general and vague [...];
> (iii) who has given the assurances and whether that person can bind the receiving State [...];
> (iv) if the assurances have been issued by the central government of the receiving State, whether local authorities can be expected to abide by them [...];
> (v) whether the assurances concern treatment which is legal or illegal in the receiving State [...];
> (vi) whether they have been given by a Contracting State [...];
> (vii) the length and strength of bilateral relations between the sending and receiving States, including the receiving State's record in abiding by similar assurances [...];

---

37   Application No 8139/09 [2012] ECtHR 56 (17 January 2012).

(viii) whether compliance with the assurances can be objectively verified through diplomatic or other monitoring mechanisms, including
providing unfettered access to the applicant's lawyers [...];
(ix) whether there is an effective system of protection against torture
in the receiving State, including whether it is willing to cooperate
with international monitoring mechanisms (including international
human rights NGOs), and whether it is willing to investigate allega-
tions of torture and to punish those responsible [...];
(x) whether the applicant has previously been ill-treated in the receiving State [...]; and
(xi) whether the reliability of the assurances has been examined by the
domestic courts of the sending/Contracting State [...].

6.22   The use of this list in the context of extradition proceedings has been
approved by the Administrative Court, which has warned, however,
that the factors should not be treated as a 'tick-box' list and that the
circumstances of each person's case should be examined carefully.[38]

6.23   In *Badre v Court of Florence, Italy*[39] the court considered whether
a general assurance would be sufficient following a pilot judgment
(*Torreggiani*)[40] which was critical of prison conditions in Italy, and in
particular overcrowding. The prosecution sought to rely on the following assurance:

> Our Ministry assures you that should the Somali national ABDI
> BADRE Hayle be surrendered by the Authorities of the United King-
> dom of Great Britain and Northern Ireland under the European Arrest
> Warrant, he will be kept in conditions complying with the provisions
> of Article 3 of the European Convention for the protection of human
> rights and fundamental freedoms signed in Rome on 4 November
> 1950 as modified on 11 May 1994.
>
> Following his surrender ABDI BADRE Hayle shall not be necessarily
> incarcerated in the Detention Institution of Busto Arsizio or Piacenza
> in that he can be imprisoned in other correctional institutions

6.24   In the light of the *Othman* criteria above (and in particular (i), (ii),
(iv), (vi), (vii) and (viii)), the court was of the view that the assurance
was insufficient to dispel the belief that there was a real risk of ill-
treatment on extradition. The Divisional Court remarked on the non-
specific nature of the assurance, and the fact that it failed to address,
inter alia, whether the requested person would be granted bail and
where the requested person would be confined. Hickinbottom J

---

38   *Ilia v Appeal Court in Athens, Greece* [2015] EWHC 547 (Admin) at para 39.
39   [2014] EWHC 614 (Admin).
40   Application No 43517/09 (8 January 2013).

(who concurred with McCombe LJ) commented on the assurance as follows:

> Whilst of course every case will be fact specific, in my view, in the face of a pilot judgment identifying a systemic failure of a state's prison system, a simple assurance from that state that the Article 3 rights of an individual (who if returned is at risk of being detained) will not be breached, will, without more, rarely if ever be sufficient to persuade a court that there is not a risk of such a breach.

6.25   It will not be necessary to examine the sufficiency of an assurance if the requesting state is able to satisfy the court that there is no longer a systemic problem with prison conditions in a requesting state. In *Elashmawy v Court of Brescia, Italy and Others*[41] (which came a year after *Badre*) the court looked at remedial measures that had been taken by Italy since the pilot judgment of *Torreggiani*[42] 'which have then been implemented and upon which the Committee of Ministers or the ECtHR have then indicated views.' It held that events had moved on in Italian prisons such that '[e]ither the presumption is restored that Italy, as an EU state, will fulfil its Article 3 obligations; or Italy has proved, by cogent evidence, to relieve the doubts.'

Article 4 (prohibition of slavery and forced labour)

6.26   Article 4, which prohibits slavery, servitude and forced labour, imposes a positive obligation on state authorities to take operational measures to protect victims, or potential victims, of trafficking where they are aware, or ought to have been aware, of circumstances giving rise to a credible suspicion that an identified individual had been, or was at real and immediate risk of being, trafficked or exploited.[43] In the United Kingdom, the National Referral Mechanism ('NRM') provides a framework for the authorities to identify victims of human trafficking.

6.27   In *Igbinovia v President of the Criminal Division (Seccion Segunda de la Audencia Provincial De Santa Cruz de Santa Cruz de Tenerife)*,[44] the possibility of a challenge under Article 4 of the ECHR was raised. In the context of that particular case, and specifically given that the

---

41   [2015] EWHC 28 (Admin).
42   Application No 43517/09 (8 January 2013).
43   *Rantsev v Cyprus and Russia*, Application No 25965/04 (7 January 2010) at para 286.
44   [2014] EWHC 4512 (Admin).

NRM's eventual finding was that the requested person was not a victim of human trafficking, the challenge was unsuccessful. Nevertheless the Court of Appeal has made it clear that defence lawyers must make enquiries if there is credible material that they have a client who might have been the victim of trafficking in relation to criminal proceedings.[45] It is the authors' view that this should apply equally in extradition cases.

6.28 In *Polish Judicial Authorities v Celinski and Others*[46] the Divisional Court considered the position of an appellant who had referred herself to the UK Human Trafficking Centre (UKHTC). Aikens LJ provided guidance as to how the appropriate judge is to approach such a referral:

> A District Judge, having heard the evidence, must therefore himself determine the issue as to whether the requested person has been trafficked, having been assisted by the CPS and the UKHTC by provision of the relevant evidence in their possession, subject to principles of public interest immunity from disclosure. Judges should not normally adjourn hearings for a referral to the UK Competent Authority, nor defer the effect of their extradition decisions pending a decision on a referral by the UK Competent Authority.[47]

Article 5 (right to liberty and security) and Article 6 (right to a fair trial)

6.29 Under Article 5, everyone has the right to liberty and security of person. This is not an absolute right, and the provision specifies the circumstances in which a person may be deprived of their liberty and the procedural protections.

6.30 Article 6 safeguards the right to a fair trial, and sets out the basic rights of those charged with a criminal offence. There is often an overlap between this Article and the abuse of process jurisdiction.

6.31 Article 5 challenges will frequently arise in tandem with those under Article 6, where, for example, it is suggested that, if a person is

---

45 See for example *R v O* [2008] EWCA Crim 2835. See also the Law Society's practice note on Criminal Prosecutions of Victims of Trafficking, 6 October 2011.

46 [2015] EWHC 1274 (Admin).

47 At para 52.

returned to the requesting state, they will be held in pre-trial detention for lengthy periods.[48]

6.32   In relation to both Articles, the burden of proof will be on the
requested person to show substantial grounds for believing that
there is a real risk of a flagrant denial of the rights. In *R (Ullah) v
Special Adjudicator*,[49] the House of Lords stated that 'where reliance
is placed on Article 6 it must be shown that a person has suffered or
risks suffering a flagrant denial of a fair trial in the receiving state ...
Successful reliance on Article 5 would have to meet no less exacting
a test.'[50]

6.33   Further guidance on this test can be found in the case-law. First,
'real risk' is less than the balance of probabilities. Real risk 'means a
risk that is substantial and not merely fanciful; and it may be established by something less than proof of a 51 per cent probability'.[51]
The meaning of 'flagrant' was elaborated on by Lord Bingham in
EM (Lebanon) v Secretary of State for the Home Department,[52] quoting
from a European Court of Human Rights case that stated that 'the
use of the adjective is clearly intended to impose a stringent test of
unfairness going beyond mere irregularities or lack of safeguards in
the trial procedures such as might result in a breach of Article 6 if
occurring within a contracting state itself'.[53]

6.34   Where the requested person has been able to show a real risk of
a breach of Articles 5 or 6, the requesting state may seek to respond
by offering assurances (as with Article 3). In such cases, the *Othman*

---

48   The application of Article 5 to those held in detention pending extradition,
ie in the requested state, was examined in *Lukaszewski v The District Court in
Torun, Poland* [2012] UKSC 20, where it was argued that the Article 5 rights
of requested persons should operate to extend the period in which an appeal
against an order for extradition could be served on the prosecution beyond that
set out in the Civil Procedure Rules. The court held, following the decision
in *MT (Algeria) v Secretary of State for Home Department* [2009] UKHL 10,
that Article 5 did not apply to the proceedings as they were not challenging
detention per se, but challenging the underlying decision to extradite the
appellants. Nevertheless, as that case also points out, Article 5 rights were
relied on in *R (Kashamu) v Governor of Brixton Prison* [2002] QB 887 to hold
that the district judge should consider whether there had been an abuse of
process rendering the detention unlawful under Article 5(4).

49   [2004] UKHL 26.

50   At para 24. Although that was an asylum case, the test nevertheless also
applies in extradition cases. See para 24 of *Janovic v Prosecutor General's Office,
Lithuania* [2011] EWHC 710 (Admin).

51   *Brown v Government of Rwanda* [2009] EWHC 770 at para 34.

52   *EM (Lebanon) v Secretary of State for the Home Department* [2008] UKHL 64.

53   *Mamatkulov and Askarov v Turkey* (2005) 41 EHRR 25, 537 at para OIII 14.

principles regarding assurances set out above (at paragraph 6.21) will apply.[54]

6.35   For the reasons set out at the beginning of this chapter, there have been relatively few successful challenges to extradition under these Articles. A notable recent exception can be found in *Shawn Sullivan v USA*,[55] a successful challenge under Article 5 where it was held that a man who risked being detained under a 'civil commitment order' faced a real risk of a flagrant denial of his rights because such an order fell outside the provisions of Article 5.1(e) (lawful detention of persons of unsound mind). In relation to Article 6, the Divisional Court held in *Office of the Prosecutor General of Turin v Barone*[56] that in circumstances where no steps had been taken to contradict the expert evidence of the defence (which sought to demonstrate that the trial was not compliant with Article 6), a decision refusing to order extradition under section 21 would be inevitable. In *Abu Qatada*,[57] a ECtHR decision on deportation, the court held[58] the admission of torture evidence:

> ... is manifestly contrary, not just to the provisions of Article 6, but to the most basic international standards of a fair trial. It would make the whole trial not only immoral and illegal, but also entirely unreliable in its outcome. It would, therefore, be a flagrant denial of justice if such evidence were admitted in a criminal trial.

6.36   Expert evidence, such as a report or witness statement from an appropriately qualified lawyer, academic or NGO with knowledge of the justice system in the requesting state will almost always be required. Any other evidence of, for example, ways in which the requesting

---

54 See *Ravi Shankaran v The Government of the State of India and Another* [2014] EWHC 957 (Admin) which applied the *Othman* principles in respect of an Article 5 challenge.

55 *Sullivan (Shawn) v Government of the United States of America* [2012] EWHC 1680 (Admin).

56 *Office of the Prosecutor General of Turin v Barone* [2010] EWHC 3004 (Admin). See also *Konuksever v Turkey* [2012] EWHC 2166 (Admin). In this case, the court found that there was a risk of a breach of the appellant's Article 3 rights. They also, however, expressed concern over the procedural history and stated that the way the requesting state had proceeded 'is capable of being viewed as an abuse of process and as a breach of Article 6', although failed to fully apply the test as set out in *Ullah*.

57 *Othman (Abu Qatada) v United Kingdom*, Application No 8139/09, [2012] ECHR 56 (17 January 2012).

58 At para 267. See also para 259 of that judgment for examples of cases where it has been accepted that certain forms of unfairness could amount to a flagrant denial of justice.

state has breached the requested person's Article 5 or 6 rights in the past, will of course also be of assistance.

Article 8 (right to respect for private and family life)

6.37   Article 8 provides that everyone has a right to respect for his private and family life, his home and his correspondence. It goes on, however, to qualify that right, saying that:

> There shall be no interference by a public authority with the exercise of this right except as is in accordance with the law and is necessary in a democratic society in the interests of national security, public safety or the economic well-being of the country, for the prevention of disorder or crime, for the protection of health or morals, or for the protection of the rights and freedoms of others.

6.38   It is, therefore a heavily qualified right and a number of cases have emphasised that there is a strong public interest in honouring extradition treaties.

6.39   At the time of publication, Article 8 is raised as a challenge to extradition on behalf of the requested persons in the majority of Part 1 cases. Out of 461 extradition hearings to take place in the three months preceding 17 March 2015 at WMC, 280 raised Article 8 arguments.[59] Prior to the decision of the Supreme Court in *HH*[60] it was only in rare cases that Article 8 was successfully raised as a challenge that defeated an extradition request.

6.40   In deciding whether a person's extradition would be compatible with his or her Article 8 rights, the question is always 'whether the interference with the private and family lives of the extraditee and other members of his family is outweighed by the public interest in extradition'.[61] In assessing the proportionality of the interference, the court will take into account a number of considerations, among which are the gravity of the offence; time to be served (and how much time has been served in this country);[62] delay; and the effect of extradition on innocent members of an extraditee's family. The Supreme Court judgment in *HH*[63] cautioned against the assumption

---

59 *Polish Judicial Authorities and Others v Celinski and Others* [2015] EWHC 1274 (Admin).

60 *HH v Deputy Prosecutor of the Italian Republic, Genoa* [2012] UKSC 25.

61 As stated by Baroness Hale giving the leading judgment in *HH v Deputy Prosecutor of the Italian Republic, Genoa* [2012] UKSC 25.

62 *Wysocki v Polish Judicial Authority* [2010] EWHC 3430 (Admin).

63 *HH v Deputy Prosecutor of the Italian Republic, Genoa* [2012] UKSC 25.

that there is an 'exceptionality test', while stating, however, that given the constant and weighty public interest in extradition, the cases in which extradition is held to be a disproportionate interference with a person's Article 8 rights are likely to be exceptional.

6.41 In this judgment, Lady Hale discussed the information that the court requires in assessing a child's interests in the light of Article 8. She stated:

> If the children's interests are to be properly taken into account by the extraditing court, it will need to have some information about them. There is a good analogy with domestic sentencing practice, although in the first instance the information is likely to come from the parties, as there will be no pre-sentence report. The court will need to know whether there are dependent children, whether the parent's removal will be harmful to their interests and what steps can be taken to mitigate this. This should alert the court to whether any further information is needed. In the more usual case, where the person whose extradition is sought is not the sole or primary carer for the children, the court will have to consider whether there are any special features requiring further investigation of the children's interests, but in most cases it should be able to proceed with what it has.[64]

6.42 Lady Hale went on to say that:

> The important thing is that everyone, the parties and their representatives, but also the courts, is alive to the need to obtain the information necessary in order to have regard to the best interests of the children as a primary consideration, and to take steps accordingly.[65]

6.43 In cases where the requested person is the sole carer of a child or where the extradition of both parents is sought, it is imperative that evidence be put before the court as to the consequences for the child of a separation from his or her parents and evidence from a child psychologist and/or social worker should be obtained. Guidance on the areas which such experts should cover can be found at paras 82–86 of the judgment.

A re-evaluation of *Norris* and *HH*?

6.44 In May 2015, the Lord Chief Justice gave a judgment in the Divisional Court in *Celinski*[66] that looked at the way in which Article 8 had been applied by the appropriate judges at the extradition hearing

---

64 *HH v Deputy Prosecutor of the Italian Republic, Genoa* [2012] UKSC 25 at para 82.

65 At para 86.

66 *Polish Judicial Authorities v Celinski and Others* [2015] EWHC 1274 (Admin).

following the decision of *HH*. The LCJ reiterated the principles laid down in *Norris* and *HH* and stated that it should rarely be necessary to cite any other decisions made in Article 8 cases.[67] The LCJ also highlighted the following factors:

i)   The public interest in ensuring that extradition arrangements are honoured is high as is the public interest in not creating a safe haven for fugitives in the United Kingdom.[68]

ii) Decisions of the judicial authority of a member state making a request for extradition should be afforded a proper degree of mutual confidence and respect.[69]

iii) Factors that mitigate the gravity of the offence or culpability in an accusation case are matters that will be considered by the court in the requesting state in the event of a conviction.[70]

iv) In a conviction case, it will rarely be appropriate for the appropriate judge to consider whether the sentence imposed significantly differs from what a UK court may impose because a) the appropriate judge will not have details of the person's previous offending behaviour, b) each member state is entitled to set its own sentencing regime and levels of sentence provided they are in accordance with the Convention.[71]

6.45   The LCJ stated that it was important that appropriate judges clearly set out an analysis of the facts as found at the extradition hearing and give 'sufficient and clear, adequate reasons' for the conclusion arrived at by balancing the relevant considerations. The LCJ proposed incorporating a 'balance sheet' into the decisions of the appropriate judge that sets out the 'pros' and 'cons' of extradition. Practitioners may therefore wish to incorporate the 'balance sheet approach' into their skeleton arguments.

6.46   Article 8 is still the most common objection to extradition raised by requested persons when first appearing at WMC. Solicitors must therefore ensure that clients are given realistic advice about their likelihood of success if they do seek to raise it.

---

67 At para 14(iii).
68 At para 9.
69 At para 10.
70 At para 12.
71 At para 13.

The initial hearing in EAW cases

Introduction

7.1   This chapter covers the initial hearing that takes place following a requested person's arrest under Part 1 of EA 2003. Part 1 of the Act governs EAWs. This chapter will consider:

- procedural requirements;
- challenging production and service;
- identification issues;
- requested persons facing domestic proceedings/sentence;
- issues to be raised to challenge extradition;
- bail;
- proceeding to an uncontested extradition hearing;
- competing EAW requests;
- removal where no appeal.

Provisional or certified EAW request?

7.2   The most common way for a person to be arrested under EA 2003 is by way of a certified[1] EAW. In such cases, the procedure as set out in paragraph 7.8 below will be followed.

7.3   However, arrest under EA 2003 Part 1 can also be provisional. A provisional arrest takes place where a constable, customs officer or a service policeman has reasonable grounds for believing that a Part 1 warrant (EAW) has been or will be issued by a category 1 territory.[2]

7.4   A person arrested under a provisional EAW must be brought before the appropriate judge within 48 hours of arrest and must be given a copy of the warrant as soon as practicable after arrest. An EAW and NCA certificate must also be produced to the judge within 48 hours of arrest.

7.5   If the person is brought before the court within 48 hours but the EAW and NCA certificate have not been so produced, the judge may extend the period by a further 48 hours if the judge decides (on the balance of probabilities) that production of the documents could not reasonably be complied with within the initial 48-hour period. If this time limit is not complied with, it is possible to apply for the requested person to be discharged.[3]

---

1   The NCA is responsible for certifying EAWs.
2   EA 2003 s5.
3   See Crim PR 17.16(2) for the procedure to be followed where the failure to comply with this time limit gives rise to an application to discharge

7.6 Provisional arrest is used where the NCA has yet to certify an issued EAW.

SIS II Forms

7.7 Since 13 April 2015, the United Kingdom became part of the Schengen Information System (second generation – SIS II). SIS II is a pan-European database that passes real-time information from one participating member state to another, in the form of alerts relating to people and property. A person can be arrested on the basis of a SIS II alert (known as Form A) and this will usually be under the 'provisional arrest' scheme under the EA 2003 unless the SIS II form has been certified by the NCA. Throughout this chapter, reference to an EAW will include the SIS II Form unless stated otherwise. As stated in paragraph 3.1, this will need to be checked very carefully to ensure compliance with EA 2003 s2.

The initial hearing

7.8 The initial hearing starts when the requested person is brought before the appropriate judge.

7.9 In almost all cases the requested person will appear in custody. As in all court proceedings, persons brought before the court will be asked to give their name and date of birth. The requested person will have an interpreter present with them to assist in translation if required.

7.10 Once the requested person has been identified, the CPS representative acting on behalf of the judicial authority will introduce him or herself and the person acting on behalf of the requested person.

7.11 The judicial authority (ie the CPS representative) will confirm that the court has a copy of the EAW, Part 1 certificate and the arrest statement. The judicial authority will then summarise the EAW and provide the court with the circumstances of arrest. The court will be asked to find that the requested person has been served with a copy

the requested person. Whilst this rule requires the defendant to make an application for discharge in writing unless the court directs otherwise, in practice such applications should be made orally at the first opportunity for requested persons who are remanded in custody, given that continued detention in such circumstances may be unlawful.

of the EAW as soon as practicable after arrest[4] and produced before the appropriate judge as soon as practicable.[5]

Service of the EAW

7.12   Section 4(2) states that a copy of the warrant must be given to the person as soon as practicable after his or her arrest. If this section is not complied with and the person applies to the judge to be discharged, the judge *may* order his or her discharge.[6]

7.13   The arrest statement will usually say when the EAW was served upon the requested person. It may be the case that the arresting officer merely gives the EAW to the person upon arrest and then immediately takes it from that person and places it in his or her property bag while the requested person is in custody. It appears from practice that this would be sufficient for the purpose of the EA 2003. The warrant must be in the language of the state requesting the person's extradition. Furthermore, the NCA certificate should be attached. There is no requirement that the warrant be in the native language of the requested person.

7.14   If the requested person has not been served with the EAW then an application should be made to the judge for discharge. It should be noted, however, that although EA 2003 s4(4) gives the judge discretion as to whether to discharge, this is not normally exercised in favour of the requested person. Judges will look at what prejudice has actually been suffered by the EAW not being served upon the requested person and will often seek to remedy the problem by ensuring that a copy of the EAW is given to the requested person in the dock. The duty solicitor will also have had an opportunity to provide advice to the requested person on the content of the EAW before going into court.

---

4 EA 2003 s4(2).
5 EA 2003 s4(3).
6 EA 2003 s4(4). See Crim PR 17.16(2) for the procedure to be followed where the failure to comply with this time limit gives rise to an application to discharge the requested person. Whilst this rule requires the defendant to make an application for discharge in writing unless the court directs otherwise, in practice such applications should be made orally at the first opportunity for requested persons who are remanded in custody, given that continued detention in such circumstances may be unlawful.

Production before the appropriate judge

7.15 Section 4(3) states that the person must be brought as soon as practicable before the appropriate judge. If this requirement is not complied with and the person applies to the judge to be discharged, the judge *must* order his or her discharge.[7] Unlike section 4(4) the judge has no discretion and must discharge if they find that the person has not been produced before the judge as soon as practicable.

7.16 What is deemed to be 'as soon as practicable' is a factual determination that will differ from case to case and from judge to judge. The leading authority on production is *Nikonovs v Governor of Brixton Prison*.[8] The facts of that case were set out in paragraph 4 of the judgment:

> At 5.45 on the morning of Saturday 17 September GSL Court Services, who were responsible for conveying Mr Nikonovs to court, telephoned the Boston Custody Suite to say that Mr Nikonovs would not be collected until Monday as Bow Street Magistrates' Court was not open over the weekend. In fact this was an error, the court was open on Saturday. In the event Mr Nikonovs was not brought before a judge at Bow Street until 14:00 hours on Monday 19 September, which was nearly 66 hours after his arrest at Boston police station and some 74 hours after his arrest at his home.

7.17 The judge at the magistrates' court refused to discharge Nikonovs who subsequently sought a writ of *habeas corpus ad subjiciendum*. The High Court granted the writ of *habeas corpus* and discharged Nikonovs. As part of their reasoning the court stated that: 'the criterion is practicable rather than the more elastic reasonably practicable' and:[9]

> No one suggests it was not practicable to bring him to London that day. He could have been brought to Bow Street and the district judge was very unhappy that he was not. He was not, in the event, brought before District Judge Wickham at Bow Street until 14:00 hours on the Monday afternoon. In these circumstances I have no hesitation in concluding that the applicant was not brought before an appropriate judge as soon as practicable.

7.18 This approach appears to have been tempered by the High Court in *Huczko v Governor of HMP Wandsworth*.[10] This was also a case where a writ of *habeas corpus ad subjiciendum* was sought following

---

7   EA 2003 s4(5).
8   [2005] EWHC 2405 (Admin).
9   At para 21.
10 [2012] All ER (D) 47 (Jun).

the refusal of the judge to order the requested person's discharge. In this case, Huczko was arrested and taken the following day to Hammersmith Magistrates' Court in West London. This was an error, as he should have been taken to WMC in order to be produced before an appropriate judge. Huczko was detained for four hours at Hammersmith Magistrates' Court until it was appreciated that he should have been taken to WMC. He was transferred to the correct court where he arrived at about 1 pm. He was then brought before a judge just after 4 pm. The judge found that, despite the human error, he had been produced within 18 hours of his arrest and therefore as soon as practicable. The Divisional Court agreed.

7.19 The 'referral' time at WMC for receiving new cases is 12.30 pm. After that time a case can only be accepted if it is referred to an appropriate judge and the judge agrees to accept the late arrival. If the judge refuses then the person will be lodged overnight in a London police station to be produced the following day.

7.20 When deciding whether to argue that a person has not been brought before an appropriate judge as soon as practicable, it is important to consider the following:

- What time was the person arrested?
- Was the arrest a planned arrest or unexpected?
- What time did the person arrive at the police station and when was his detention authorised?
- When were arrangements made for the collection of the requested person to be taken to court?
- What time was the person transported from the police station to the court?
- How far was the distance between the police station and the court?
- Was the case referred to an appropriate judge the previous day after the referral time?
- If so, what information was conveyed to the court about the estimated time of arrival and what was the response of the judge?
- Did anything occur during the transportation to the court that unexpectedly delayed the arrival?

7.21 Only after considering these questions will a duty solicitor be able realistically to determine whether or not to challenge the person's production.

7.22 As general guidance, if it has taken two working days to get to court, production should be challenged. If the person was produced before the appropriate judge on the day of arrest or even the following day, unless the distance to be travelled was short, an argument that the person was not produced as soon as practicable will usually be untenable.

7.23 After the CPS representative acting on behalf of the judicial authority has made the introductions the judge will ask the defence representative if there are any challenges to service and production. If there are, submissions should be made there and then.[11] Once the case has moved beyond the initial hearing these issues cannot be revisited.[12] If there are no challenges, then the judicial authority will ask the judge to move on to the issue of identity.

7.24 If the defence submissions on either service of the EAW or production at court are successful then the person is discharged from the extradition request. This does not mean that the EAW is automatically withdrawn and that the person is immune from extradition. A new EAW can be issued and certified by the NCA and proceedings would then start again. It does, however, provide the requested person with an opportunity to try and compromise the EAW (see chapter 12).

Identity

7.25 The appropriate judge must decide whether the person brought before him is the person who is referred to in the EAW. Very often identity will not be in dispute – the requested person will have already given details of their identity on arrest and when asked by the court – but it may be challenged by the defence.

7.26 The appropriate judge must determine identity on the balance of probabilities.[13]

7.27 There are many sources from which the court can determine identity. As already mentioned above, the requested person will have given their details when asked by the court. The appropriate judge will also have recourse to the arrest statement and the details that were given to the police upon arrest. Furthermore, identity documents may have been seized. Finally the PNC may determine

---

11 See Crim PR 17.16(2) for the procedure to be followed where the failure to comply with this time limit gives rise to an application to discharge the requested person. Whilst this rule requires the defendant to make an application for discharge in writing unless the court directs otherwise, in practice such applications should be made orally at the first opportunity for requested persons who are remanded in custody, given that continued detention in such circumstances may be unlawful.

12 *Hilali v The National Court of Madrid* [2006] EWHC 1239 (Admin).

13 EA 2003 s7(3).

their true identity if the requested person has been the subject of a livescan check.[14]

7.28   If identity is still in doubt, the judicial authority may seek a set of fingerprints from the requesting state in order to compare them with those taken upon arrest.

7.29   EAWs also contain a section in box A that allows for the judicial authority to enter details about the requested person's 'distinctive marks' or to provide a description. Many judicial authorities take advantage of this and provide a full description including known tattoos and scars.

7.30   EAWs may be accompanied by a photograph of the person sought that could help the appropriate judge determine identity.

7.31   If the judge decides that the person before him or her is not the person in respect of whom the warrant was issued, he or she must order discharge. If the judge concludes that it is the correct person then the case must proceed to EA 2003 s8 and the issue of consent.

7.32   The requested person must be warned that if identity is unsuccessfully challenged, this may affect the weight to be attached to his or her evidence at the extradition hearing.[15]

Appealing service, production and identity

7.33   Appeals under the EA 2003 in EAW cases are brought under section 26 (for the defence) and section 28 (for the issuing judicial authority). Sections 26 and 28 relate to appeals regarding decisions made at the extradition hearing. Sections 4 to 8 are considered to involve issues dealt with at the 'initial hearing' and are therefore not subject to the statutory appeal provisions of sections 26 or 28. Furthermore, such decisions cannot be re-opened under the Magistrates' Courts Act 1980 s142, as would be the case in criminal proceedings.[16]

7.34   The only way of challenging an adverse decision under sections 4 to 8 is by way of a judicial review or, if the person is in custody, applying for a writ of *habeas corpus ad subjiciendum*. This approach was approved by the High Court in *Nikonovs*.

---

14   See *Prendi v Government of the Republic of Albania* [2015] EWHC 1809 (Admin) in which information from an Interpol Red Notice was held to be inadmissible.

15   *Adedeji v Public Prosecutor's Office, Germany* [2012] EWHC 3237 (Admin).

16   *Klimeto v Westminster Magistrates' Court* [2013] 1 WLR 420.

Other issues before consent

7.35   If the person before the court is subject to a charge in the United Kingdom then the extradition hearing *must* be adjourned prior to dealing with consent[17] until the charge is disposed of. Consent will not be taken and the court will proceed to deal with bail.[18]

7.36   If the person before the court is subject to a sentence of imprisonment in the United Kingdom then the judge *may* adjourn the extradition hearing until the sentence of imprisonment has been served. A judge can adjourn the hearing for up to six months before the matter has to be brought back before the court. Again, under section 8B consent will not be taken if the appropriate judge exercises his decision to adjourn.

7.37   Sections 8A and 8B were introduced into the legislation in order to prevent a requested person escaping prosecution in the United Kingdom or escaping a sentence by consenting to extradition and being removed from the jurisdiction before being prosecuted or completing their sentence.[19] The Criminal Procedure Rules also require a court to adjourn if informed that a requested person has been charged with an offence in the United Kingdom.[20]

7.38   If a requested person is subject to a lengthy sentence of imprisonment, the CPS will obtain instructions from the judicial authority as to whether it wishes to seek the requested person's temporary extradition known as 'temporary surrender'. The requesting state will be required to provide an undertaking stating that the requested person will be kept in custody pending their trial and returned to the United Kingdom after proceedings have concluded in that state. If the court agrees to temporary surrender, the requested person will be returned to the United Kingdom to serve the remainder of the sentence.

Consent

7.39   Once the court has progressed through sections 4 to 7 of the Act the next issue to be dealt with is that of consent. The consent procedure was discussed in chapter 4. The clerk of the court will put the consent procedure to the requested person, who will be asked to indicate whether he or she wishes to consent to their extradition. If the

---

17 EA 2003 s8A.
18 The required information about consent must be given: *Morozovs v Latvian Judicial Authority* [2013] EWHC 367 (Admin).
19 *R (Governor of Wandsworth Prison) v Kinderis* [2008] QB 347.
20 Criminal Procedure Rules 17.3(4).

requested person consents to their extradition they will be asked to sign the consent form. The interpreter will translate this. It is advisable to ask the court for a copy of the signed consent order to keep on the requested person's file.

7.40   The effect of consent is that a person consenting to extradition will waive appeal rights, and will be extradited within ten days of having consented to be extradited. This ten-day period can be extended upon an application from the judicial authority if it is not possible to effect removal within that time.

7.41   Where requested persons do not consent to their extradition they will be informed that they can change their mind at any time.

Opening proceedings

7.42   The permitted period within which the extradition hearing is to begin is within 21 days of the date of arrest.[21] In the vast majority of cases this is not possible due to difficulties with listings. The judge will therefore 'formally open' proceedings but make no decisions. This satisfies the requirement that the hearing is to begin within 21 days of the date of arrest.

7.43   If proceedings have been adjourned under s8A or s8B then the permitted period within which the extradition hearing is to begin is extended by the number of days for which the proceedings have been adjourned.[22]

Issues to be raised at extradition hearing to resist extradition

7.44   The court will next ask the advocate to indicate whether any issues will be raised or whether the matter can proceed to an uncontested hearing. If there are any issues to raise these should be outlined by the advocate at the initial hearing. These issues may come under intense scrutiny from the judge and the advocate must be prepared to fully justify why the issue to be raised is tenable, why time is required to prepare the case and why it is in the interests of justice to adjourn.

7.45   The issues raised to challenge extradition may be one or more of the following:

21 EA 2003 s8(4).
22 EA 2003 s8(4A) as inserted by Anti-social Behaviour, Crime and Policing Act 2014 s155.

- validity of the EAW (s2);
- the offence(s) contained in the EAW is/are not extradition offences (s10);
- one (or more) of the bars to extradition (ss11–19B);
- conviction in absence (s20);
- extradition would be disproportionate and/or incompatible with Convention rights (ss21, 21A);
- physical/mental health of requested person (s25).

Case management forms and directions

7.46 The defence advocate should complete a case management form at the initial hearing for all cases where extradition is contested. The case management form can be found at appendix G. The form warns the advocate that 'the information you provide must be accurate as it may be checked, and it may be referred to at a later hearing'. The form must therefore be completed accurately.

7.47 Should issues arise later in the proceedings that were not included in the form it is important to notify both the court and the CPS as soon as they arise so that all parties are on notice in advance of the extradition hearing.

7.48 Having identified the issues to be contested, the court will then proceed to fix a date for the extradition hearing to take place. If the requested person is based in or around London and on bail, then the court may list the extradition hearing as a 'floater'. This means that it may not proceed on that day if there is insufficient court time to hear the case as it will often be in a list of several 'floating' cases. The court will also fix a date for a case management hearing to take place, usually one month before the extradition hearing. A judge will often be allocated to the case to ensure judicial continuity in case management, although this may not happen until close to the extradition hearing date unless the case is particularly complex.

7.49 The advocate will need to provide a realistic time estimate in order to assist the court in finding a date for the hearing. By way of example, a section 10 extradition offence argument could take as little as 30 minutes, whereas a substantial issue where expert evidence is to be called could last a day or two. The court will build judgment writing into the hearing time and cases may be given a half-day time estimate that will include 90 minutes for the hearing and 90 minutes for judgment writing.

7.50 Once a date is fixed the court will make directions. A signed directions form will be provided to the parties setting out the agreed directions to be complied with. These will include directions for the service of a skeleton argument, defence evidence (if any), and a proof of evidence. In extradition proceedings, where the requested person is to be called to give evidence, a signed proof of evidence has to be served in advance (see paragraph 9.27). This allows the CPS acting on behalf of the judicial authority to seek instructions on issues raised within the statement. It can also then be adopted in evidence by the requested person, drastically reducing the amount of time required for examination in chief.

7.51   A skeleton argument will also be required in most, if not all, contested cases. The preparation of the skeleton argument and other documents for the extradition hearing will be explored in chapter 9.

7.52   When agreeing to directions, it is important to remember that it may take at least a week for the requested person's legal aid application to be determined. Work is unlikely to start straight away on a case unless the requested person is paying privately and has put the representative in funds.

7.53   On occasions the duty solicitor may have too many cases to deal with to allow time for the completion of the case management form for each case. The court makes allowance for this and the last question on the form asks: 'have you had sufficient time to advise your client on potential challenges? If not why not?' It is acceptable to indicate 'no' and in these cases the court will direct that the case management form be completed and submitted within seven days of the initial hearing or by the second hearing, whichever is sooner.

Bail

7.54   The final issue for the court to determine at the initial hearing is that of bail. Bail applications in all proceedings, but especially in extradition proceedings, need to be structured. As discussed in chapter 4, there are enquiries specific to extradition proceedings that the court will make of the advocate if bail is to be granted. It is important to have a good bail package in place and for that reason telephone calls will very often need to be made to family members in order to obtain a security or locate travel documents.

7.55   There is no presumption in favour of bail in conviction cases and, in reality in both accusation and conviction cases, a requested person is unlikely to be granted bail without a security.

7.56   The conditions usually imposed in extradition cases include:

- security/surety or both (pre-release condition);
- surrender/retention of travel documents (pre-release condition);
- residence;
- not to apply for international travel documents;
- reporting to a police station;
- curfew;
- geographical restriction.

7.57   All securities need to be paid at WMC and sureties are taken at the same court. Assistance is provided at the first floor helpdesk. Those offering securities do not need to attend court if they can deposit the funds via an electronic transfer. In this situation the proposed security contacts the WMC bail department, which will provide them with the court's bank details and court reference number. If a security is to be paid in cash, the person offering the security will need to bring proof of identity (passport/ID card/driver's licence) to court together with proof of address (bank statement/utility bill) to comply with Anti-Money Laundering Regulations. Where the depositor is able to provide a photocard driving licence (UK or EEA) or a full government issued passport it is not necessary to provide proof of address. The requested person cannot usually be released from custody until the court has received cleared funds into their central bail account. It is therefore imperative that the court reference number is recorded accurately as a mistake could lead to a delay on the payment being identified. A surety will need to attend court with proof of identity and proof of the availability and liquidity of funds being offered.

7.58   If a male requested person is remanded into custody he will be taken to HMP Wandsworth unless he is assessed on arrival at the prison to be a category A prisoner, in which case he will be transferred to HMP Belmarsh. Female requested persons remanded into custody will go to HMP Holloway.

7.59   If the requested person is remanded into custody it is important to inform family, friends or partners (if instructed to do so) that HMP Wandsworth operates induction visits on Mondays to Thursdays between 8 am and 9 am. These visits do not have to be booked in advance and are only for prisoners who have been in custody for seven days at the most.

7.60   If the requested person subsequently breaches any bail condition, EA 2003 s198 allows the local court to deal with the breach.

Bail appeals

7.61   An appeal of a bail decision is made to the High Court by submitting Form EX244 to the Administrative Court Office together with the fee of £155. An appeal can only be made after two refusals of the grant of bail by WMC. An appeal can also be made against the imposition of certain bail conditions.[23] The CPS will need to be put on notice of such an application and the Administrative Court will usually list the hearing within 48 hours (excluding weekends and bank holidays). A fully completed CRM 14 to cover the High Court bail application will need to be submitted at the time the Form EX244 is lodged to ensure a representation order is granted without delay.

7.62   If the requested person is granted bail, the CPS can appeal the decision. If they do so, they must give written notice within two hours of giving their notice of an intention to appeal the bail decision. The bail appeal will be heard at the High Court within 48 hours.

Uncontested extradition hearings

7.63   If there are no issues to be raised on behalf of the requested person – or the person wishes to return to the requesting state but does not consent to his or her extradition – the matter will very often proceed to an uncontested extradition hearing there and then and it is therefore important for the advocate to be prepared for this as a possibility.

7.64   The court has to be satisfied of the following before ordering extradition:

- the extradition request is a valid request within the meaning of EA 2003 s2;
- the offences contained in the EAW are extradition offences;
- there are no bars to extradition;
- there is no conviction in absence, or the requested person accepts deliberately absenting themselves (conviction cases only);
- extradition would be compatible with the requested person's Convention rights within the meaning of the Human Rights Act 1998 (and in accusation cases, that extradition would not be disproportionate).

7.65   At an uncontested extradition hearing the prosecutor acting on behalf of the judicial authority will conduct most of the hearing, taking the

23 *Sarao v United States of America* [2015] EWHC 1570 (Admin).

judge through the warrant. The prosecutor will refer to sections 64 or 65 in establishing extradition offences and will submit that no bars to extradition are raised and that extradition would be compatible with the requested person's Convention rights.

7.66 The judge will ask the advocate on behalf of the requested person if there are any representations to be made. Having received confirmation that there are none, the judge will make the extradition order pursuant to section 21(3) of the Act if it is a conviction warrant or section 21A(5) if it is an accusation warrant.

7.67 The judge should then inform the requested person that he or she has seven days to apply for permission to appeal the decision to order extradition (see chapter 11). If no application for permission to appeal is lodged, then arrangements are made for extradition within the ten days that follow the end of the seven-day period. The requested person will also be informed that due to the numbers awaiting extradition, this period can be – and very often is – extended on application to the court. If the requested person is not removed in the relevant period and there has been no extension of time application granted, then the court must order their discharge unless reasonable cause can be shown for the delay.[24]

7.68 The requested person – if remanded in custody – will be informed that every day spent in custody awaiting extradition will be deducted from any sentence outstanding in the requesting state, or if convicted the time will count against any sentence of imprisonment imposed. This information is transmitted to the requesting judicial authority by the NCA on surrender of the requested person.

Competing EAW requests

7.69 On rare occasions an EAW will be issued by two different category 1 territories. If during the relevant period[25] the judge is informed that there are competing EAW requests he or she may:

- order further proceedings on the warrant under consideration to be deferred until the other warrant has been disposed of, if the warrant under consideration has not been disposed of;
- order the person's extradition on the warrant under consideration to be deferred until the other warrant has been disposed of,

24 EA 2003 s35(5).
25 The relevant period starts when the person is brought before the appropriate judge and ends when the person is extradited or discharged: EA 2003 s44(2).

if an order for extradition has been made on the warrant under consideration.

7.70 The appropriate judge when deciding the above must take account of:

- the relative seriousness of the offence concerned;
- the place where each offence was committed (or was alleged to have been committed);
- the date on which each warrant was issued;
- whether in the case of each offence, the person is accused or alleged to be unlawfully at large after conviction.[26]

Removal where no application for permission to appeal is lodged

7.71 If there is no application for permission to appeal against the decision to order extradition, removal must take place within the ten days that follow the end of the seven-day period permitted for lodging an application for permission to appeal. This period can be extended if the judge and the judicial authority agree a later date. If the person is not removed within the required period then the person must be discharged if an application is made to the appropriate judge unless reasonable cause is shown for the delay.[27] See Crim PR 17.16(2) for the procedure to be followed where the failure to comply with this time limit gives rise to an application to discharge the requested person.

26 EA 2003 s44(7).
27 EA 2003 s35(3).

Figure 7.1 Procedure following arrest on a certified EAW

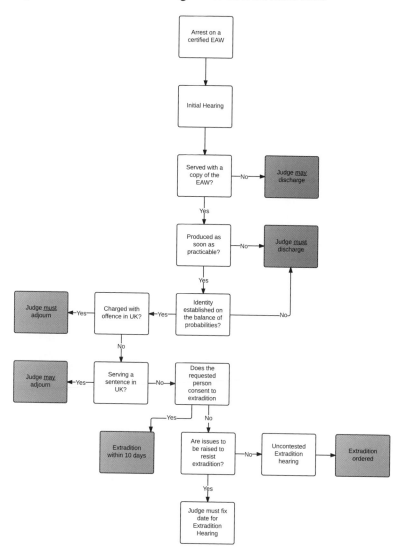

Figure 7.2 Extradition hearing procedure

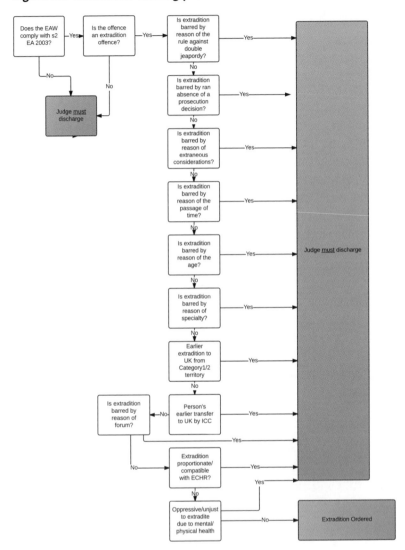

CHAPTER 8

Extradition requests from outside the European Union

continued

Introduction

8.1 This chapter looks at extradition requests from outside the European Union. Such requests are governed by Part 2 of the EA 2003 and are often referred to as 'Part 2 requests'. The procedure for dealing with Part 2 requests is very different from the procedure for dealing with EAW requests.

8.2 Part 2 requests can either be 'provisional' or 'full requests'. The procedure following arrest is different depending on whether it is a 'provisional' or 'full request' for extradition. This chapter will cover the following areas: the validity of Part 2 requests, the issue and execution of a Part 2 request, the initial hearing for provisional arrests and full requests, challenges at the extradition hearing, extradition offences, the requirement to show a prima facie case and the role of the SSHD.

Part 2 countries

8.3 The following countries have all been designated as category 2 territories as they have bilateral or multilateral extradition treaties with the United Kingdom or are non-EU countries that are signatories of the European Convention on Extradition ('ECE'). Requests for extradition from category 2 territories are made in accordance with Part 2 of the Act:

> Albania, Algeria, Andorra, Anguilla, Antigua and Barbuda, Argentina, Armenia, Aruba, Australia, Azerbaijan, The Bahamas, Bangladesh, Barbados, Belize, Bermuda, Bolivia, Bonaire, Bosnia and Herzegovina, Botswana, Brazil, British Antarctic Territory, British Indian Ocean Territory, Brunei, Canada, Cayman Islands, Chile, Colombia, Cook Islands, Cuba, Curaçao, Dominica, Ecuador, El Salvador, Falkland Islands, Faroe Islands, Fiji, The Gambia, Georgia, Ghana, Greenland, Grenada, Guatemala, Guyana, Hong Kong Special Administrative Region, Haiti, Iceland, India, Iraq, Israel, Jamaica, Kenya, Kiribati, Kosovo, Lesotho, Liberia, Libya, Liechtenstein, Macedonia (FYR), Malawi, Malaysia, Maldives, Mauritius, Mexico, Moldova, Monaco, Montenegro, Montserrat, Nauru, New Zealand, Nicaragua, Nigeria, Norway, Panama, Papua New Guinea, Paraguay, Peru, Philippines, Pitcairn, Henderson, Ducie and Oeno Islands, Republic of Korea, Russian Federation, Saba, Saint Christopher and Nevis, Saint Helena, Ascension and

Tristan da Cunha, Saint Lucia, Saint Vincent and the Grenadines, San Marino, Serbia, Seychelles, Sierra Leone, Singapore, Sint Eustatius, Sint Maarten, Solomon Islands, South Africa, South Georgia and the South Sandwich Islands, The Sovereign Base Areas of Akrotiri and Dhekalia, Sri Lanka, Swaziland, Switzerland, Tanzania, Thailand, Tonga, Trinidad and Tobago, Turkey, Turks and Caicos Islands, Tuvalu, Uganda, Ukraine, United Arab Emirates, United States, Uruguay, Vanuatu, Virgin Islands, Western Samoa, Zambia, Zimbabwe.

Ad hoc arrangements

8.4   A country that has not been designated a category 2 territory but is a party to an international convention to which the United Kingdom is also a party can request the extradition of a person under EA 2003 s193 if the SSHD has designated that international convention and specifies conduct to which the convention applies.[1] A country that is not an extradition treaty partner with the United Kingdom can also make extradition requests and be treated as if they were a category 2 territory. This can be achieved by the government of the United Kingdom and the government of the requesting state entering into an arrangement for the person's extradition and by the SSHD recognising that the two countries have entered into a 'special extradition arrangement'. Once this is done, the SSHD will issue a certificate under EA 2003 s194 and the extradition proceedings will be as for those of a category 2 request under Part 2 of the Act.

8.5   In recent years, ad hoc arrangements have been made in relation to individuals sought by the Government of Rwanda and the extradition of an individual from Scotland by the Republic of Taiwan.

Dealing with Part 2 extradition requests

8.6   The duty solicitor at WMC will from time to time have to deal with Part 2 requests. They are far less common than Part 1 (EAW) requests. In 2013 there were just 68 requests for extradition made to the United Kingdom from category 2 territories.[2]

---

1   Section 169 of the Anti-social Behaviour, Crime and Policing Act 2014 substituted a new EA 2003 s193.

2   www.gov.uk/government/publications/extradition-requests-received-and-made-by-the-uk-in-2013/extradition-requests-received-and-made-by-the-uk-from-january-to-december-2013.

8.7   On notification from the CPS extradition prosecutor or the court that a Part 2 extradition request is expected, the first question to ask will be 'is it a provisional or full request?' The answer to this question will determine how the case will proceed that day and how much time is likely to be spent with the client. If it is a full request, then it will be necessary to consider possible bars to extradition and human rights considerations. This is because the court will ask the representative to identify the issues in the case and will proceed to fix a date for the extradition hearing to take place. If it is a provisional warrant, only bail instructions will be required as, until the full request is received, it is likely to be premature to identify the possible challenges to extradition.

Issuing a provisional warrant

8.8   A provisional warrant of arrest can be issued if an appropriate judge is satisfied on information in writing or on oath that a person is accused of an offence in a category 2 territory or is alleged to be unlawfully at large after conviction[3] and that the person is believed to be in the United Kingdom or the person is on their way to the United Kingdom or is believed to be on their way to the United Kingdom.[4]

8.9   The appropriate judge may issue a warrant for a person's arrest if he has reasonable grounds for believing that:[5]

- The offence for which the person is accused of/convicted of is an extradition offence and;
- There is written evidence/information[6] about this.

8.10   The evidence/information is evidence/information that would justify the issue of a warrant for the arrest of a person accused of the offence within the judge's jurisdiction (if accused of an offence) or evidence/information that would justify the issue of a warrant for the arrest of a person unlawfully at large after conviction.[7]

8.11   The defence are not involved in the issuing of a provisional warrant of arrest. Applications are often made in camera and the first a

---

3   EA 2003 s73(2).

4   EA 2003 s73(1).

5   EA 2003 s73(3).

6   Evidence is required for those countries required to demonstrate a prima facie case, otherwise it is information only.

7   EA 2003 s73(4).

person will know about the issue of a Part 2 arrest warrant is when it is executed.

8.12   An example of where a provisional warrant may be used is where a person is in transit in the United Kingdom en route to another country via a connecting flight and the person has been identified as being wanted in another country (possibly by the existence of an Interpol Red Notice). In those circumstances a full request may not have been sent to the Home Office because the requesting state is not aware of the presence of the requested person in the United Kingdom.

Arrest following the issuing of a provisional warrant

8.13   Once a provisional warrant of arrest has been issued it will be circulated. Any police officer or customs officer can execute it even if neither the warrant nor a copy of it is in the possession of the person executing it.[8]

8.14   If the offence is very serious or the subject of the warrant is high profile, the extradition squad at New Scotland Yard may actively pursue the person.

8.15   A person arrested under a provisional warrant must be given a copy of it as soon as practicable after arrest.[9] The person will be cautioned in the following terms: 'You do not have to say anything. Anything you do say may be given in evidence.' This is the pre-1995 caution and does not contain the reference to failing to mention facts that are later relied upon.

8.16   Following arrest the requested person will be taken to the local police station where he or she will be booked into custody and have their detention authorised. Like all of those arrested and taken to a police station, those arrested under a provisional warrant will be entitled to speak to a solicitor. This will very often be the duty solicitor although it appears recently that those arrested under the EA 2003 are being referred straight to Criminal Defence Direct. There will be no interview and the sole purpose of the detention is to secure the requested person's attendance at WMC as soon as practicable.[10] Production as soon as practicable is not required if the person is granted bail by a constable following his arrest or the SSHD decides

8   EA 2003 s73(6)(b).
9   EA 2003 s74(2).
10   EA 2003 s74(3).

that the request for the person's extradition is not to be proceeded with because a competing extradition request exists.

8.17   The IJO at WMC will be notified of the person's arrest and arrangements will be made for production at the court. If the arrest is after the court 'referral time' for accepting prisoners (currently 12.30 pm) then the person will be kept at the police station for production the following day unless the judge agrees to accept the person into the cells after 12.30 pm.

Extradition request and certificate (full request)

8.18   If the SSHD receives a valid request for extradition she must issue a certificate pursuant to EA 2003 s70(1).[11] A valid request for extradition from a category 2 territory must be made in the approved way and also contain the statement referred to in section 70(4) or (4A).

- In relation to section 70(4) the statement is one that:
    - the person is accused in the category 2 territory of the commission of an offence specified in the request, and
    - the request is made with a view to his arrest and extradition to the category 2 territory for the purpose of being prosecuted for the offence.
- In relation to section 70(4A) the statement is one that:
    - the person has been convicted of an offence specified in the request by a court in the category 2 territory, and
    - the request is made with a view to his arrest and extradition to the category 2 territory for the purpose of being sentenced for the offence or of serving a sentence of imprisonment or another form of detention imposed in respect of the offence.

8.19   A request for extradition is made in the approved way if it is made by an authority of the territory that the SSHD believes has the function of making requests for extradition in that territory,[12] or by a person recognised by the SSHD as a diplomatic or consular representative of the territory.[13]

---

11 This is subject to section 70(2), which contains circumstances in which the SSHD may refuse to issue a certificate.
12 EA 2003 s70(7)(a).
13 EA 2003 s70(7)(b).

8.20 Once a full request for extradition has been certified the request and the certificate must be sent to the appropriate judge[14] at WMC for an arrest warrant to be issued.

Arrest on a full request

8.21 A person arrested under a 'full request' must be given a copy of the extradition request as soon as practicable after his or her arrest[15] and must be brought as soon as practicable before the appropriate judge.[16] If the warrant is not provided to the requested person as soon as practicable and he or she applies to the judge to be discharged, the judge *may* order his discharge. If the person is not brought to court as soon as practicable after arrest and an application for discharge is made, the judge *must* order his or her discharge.

8.22 The person need not be brought before the appropriate judge if he or she is granted bail by a constable following his arrest[17] or the SSHD decides that the request for the person's extradition is not to be proceeded with because there is a competing extradition request in existence (see EA 2003 s126 and paragraph 8.77 below).

Production at Westminster Magistrates' Court

8.23 WMC is the only court in England and Wales that deals with extradition cases at first instance. Requested persons must therefore be transported to that court following arrest.

8.24 There are often difficulties in getting a person to WMC as soon as practicable after arrest and practitioners must consider the reasons for any delay very carefully: it can sometimes result in the proceedings quickly coming to an end if the authorities have not managed to secure the attendance of the person at court as soon as practicable.

8.25 An arrest can take place anywhere in England and Wales. Unless it is a planned arrest, this can itself cause difficulties, as it may be the first time an officer has made an arrest under EA 2003. The officer may not be familiar with EA 2003 and may overlook the need to get the person to WMC as soon as practicable. The arrest may have

14 EA 2003 s70(9).
15 EA 2003 s72(2).
16 EA 2003 s72(3).
17 EA 2003 s72(4)(a). It is rare for a requested person to be granted bail after arrest to appear at court.

taken place over 300 miles from London and transport will need to be arranged.

8.26   Further complications can arise when a person has been arrested and charged with an offence in England and Wales and is then arrested under EA 2003 on a Part 2 request. If the person is denied bail on the domestic matter and taken to the local magistrates' court before being taken to WMC to be dealt with under EA 2003, it may not be deemed to be 'as soon as practicable'. A more detailed assessment of what is deemed to be 'as soon as practicable' can be found at paragraph 7.15.

First hearing – provisional arrest

8.27   At the first hearing the requested person will be produced from custody and, as in all court hearings, will be asked for his or her name and date of birth. Note that identity is not to be determined at the initial hearing although the person will be identified in the dock.

8.28   The appropriate judge must inform the person that he or she is either accused of the commission of an offence in a category 2 territory or that he or she is alleged to be unlawfully at large after conviction.[18] The required information about consent must then be given[19] unless the appropriate judge is informed that the person is charged with an offence in the United Kingdom or serving a sentence of imprisonment. The consent procedure is the same as that discussed in Part 1 cases (see paragraph 4.7).

Person charged with an offence in the UK or serving a sentence of imprisonment

8.29   If the person before the court is subject to a charge in the United Kingdom then the extradition hearing must be adjourned at this point pursuant to EA 2003 s76A until the charge is either disposed of, withdrawn, proceedings are discontinued or an order is made for the charge to lie on file. Consent will not be taken (although the requested person should be given the required information about consent)[20] and the court will proceed to deal with bail.

---

18   EA 2003 s74(7)(a).
19   EA 2003 s74(7)(b).
20   *Morozovs v Latvian Judicial Authority* [2013] EWHC 367 (Admin).

8.30   If the person before the court is subject to a sentence of imprisonment in the United Kingdom then the judge may adjourn the extradition hearing until the sentence of imprisonment has been served. A judge can adjourn the hearing for up to six months before the matter has to be brought back before the court. Again, under section 76B consent will not be taken.

8.31   Sections 76A and 76B were introduced into legislation in order to prevent a requested person escaping prosecution or having to serve a sentence in the United Kingdom by consenting to extradition and being removed from the United Kingdom before domestic proceedings are concluded.

8.32   If a requested person is subject to a lengthy sentence of imprisonment, the CPS will obtain instructions from the requesting state as to whether it wishes to seek the requested person's temporary extradition – this is known as 'temporary surrender'. The requesting state will be required to provide an undertaking stating that the requested person will be kept in custody pending their trial and returned to the United Kingdom after proceedings have concluded in that state. If the court agrees to temporary surrender, the requested person will be returned to the United Kingdom to serve the remainder of the sentence.

Date for service of the full extradition request

8.33   On a provisional arrest, neither the requested person nor the court will have the papers referred to in section 70(9) (certificate issued by the SSHD and the extradition request). The judge must therefore set a date by which he or she must have received the documents referred to in section 70(9).

8.34   The required period for service of the papers is 45 days, starting with the date of arrest. Certain countries are designated by the SSHD[21] for the purposes of section 74(11)(b) with a longer period for service of papers. Those countries and relevant periods are:

- Argentina – 65 days
- Bolivia – 65 days
- Bosnia and Herzegovina – 65 days
- Brazil – 65 days
- Chile – 65 days
- Colombia – 65 days
- Cuba – 65 days

21 Extradition Act 2003 (Designation of Part 2 Territories) Order 2003 SI No 3334.

- El Salvador – 65 days
- Guatemala – 95 days
- Haiti – 65 days
- Hong Kong Special Administrative Region – 65 days
- India – 65 days
- Iraq – 65 days
- Liberia – 95 days
- Libya – 65 days
- Mexico – 65 days
- Nicaragua – 65 days
- Panama – 95 days
- Paraguay – 95 days
- Peru – 95 days
- Saint Helena, Ascension and Tristan da Cunha – 65 days
- Thailand – 65 days
- United Arab Emirates – 65 days
- United States – 65 days.

8.35 The court will fix a date for the service of the papers and list the case for a review hearing a few days before the papers are due to be served. If the papers referred to in section 70(9) are not received by the judge by the date for service, the requested person must be discharged from the request upon his or her application.

8.36 The final matter for the court to determine at the first hearing after a person has been arrested under a provisional arrest warrant is the issue of bail.

Service of the full extradition request

8.37 A request for extradition is only valid if it contains a certificate issued by the SSHD that the extradition request has been made in the approved way and identifying the order by which the territory requesting extradition is designated as a category 2 territory. If a certificate has been issued by the SSHD, the request and certificate must be sent to the appropriate judge.[22]

8.38 The documents sent to the appropriate judge should include:

- certificate issued by the SSHD;
- particulars of the person whose extradition is requested;[23]

---

22 EA 2003 s70(9).
23 EA 2003 s78(2)(b).

- particulars of the offence specified in the request;[24]
- in an accusation case, a warrant for the person's arrest that has been issued in the category 2 territory;[25]
- in a conviction case, a certificate of the conviction issued in the category 2 territory and (if the person has been sentenced) of the sentence imposed.[26]

8.39   Once the papers have been received the judge must then proceed to fix a date within which the extradition hearing must begin. This period is two months starting from the date the papers are received.[27] In reality, the court will fix a date beyond the two-month deadline. In order to do this, the extradition hearing will be 'formally opened' and then adjourned with no decisions made. Opening or starting the extradition hearing and adjourning it in this way means that the two-month period set down in the Act has been complied with. There is no timeframe within which the extradition hearing must be concluded.

First hearing – full request

8.40   As with the first hearing under a provisional arrest, the judge must inform the person that he or she is either accused of the commission of an offence in a category 2 territory or that he or she is alleged to be unlawfully at large after conviction. The required information regarding consent must then be given (unless the requested person is subject to a charge in the United Kingdom or is serving a sentence of imprisonment) and then the judge must either remand the person in custody or on bail.

8.41   The judge must fix the date on which the extradition hearing is to begin. This must be within two months, starting from the date on which the person first appears before the court.[28] If the extradition hearing does not begin on or before the date fixed, the judge must order the discharge of that person if such an application is made.

8.42   The judge can fix a later date for the extradition hearing if he or she believes it is in the interests of justice to do so. This is predicated on

24   EA 2003 s78(2)(c).
25   EA 2003 s78(2)(d).
26   EA 2003 s78(2)(e).
27   EA 2003 s76(3).
28   EA 2003 s75(2).

the extradition hearing having been formally opened and adjourned with no substantive decisions having been made.

Case management forms

8.43 The case management forms discussed in chapter 7 do not need to be completed in Part 2 provisional warrant cases. However, the court will still expect the advocate to identify the issues at the initial hearing on a full request for extradition or when full papers have been served following arrest on a provisional warrant.

Initial stages of the extradition hearing

8.44 At the outset of the extradition hearing the appropriate judge must decide whether the documents sent by the SSHD consist of (or include) the information that is set out in paragraph 8.38 above.

8.45 If any of the documents referred to above are not before the appropriate judge he or she *must* order the person's discharge. If they are all present the appropriate judge must then consider whether:

- the person appearing or brought before him is the person whose extradition is requested;[29]
- the offence specified in the request is an extradition offence;[30]
- copies of the documents sent to the appropriate judge by the SSHD have been served upon the person whose extradition is sought.[31]

8.46 Identity – as in EAW cases – is to be determined by the appropriate judge on the balance of probabilities.[32]

8.47 If the judge decides any of the questions in paragraph 8.45 in the negative he or she must order the person's discharge.[33]

8.48 Once the preliminary stages of the extradition hearing have been conducted and the questions answered in the affirmative, the appropriate judge must then proceed under section 79 and consider whether the person's extradition is barred.

---

29 EA 2003 s78(4)(a).
30 EA 2003 s78(4)(b).
31 EA 2003 s78(4)(c).
32 EA 2003 s78(5).
33 EA 2003 s78(6).

Figure 8.1 Process following arrest under EA 2003 Part 2

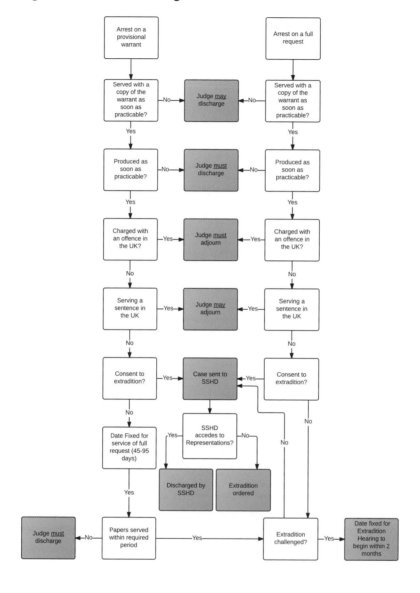

Challenges to extradition

8.49 Challenges to extradition are dealt with in chapter 5. In short, the following bars can be raised to resist extradition:

- section 80 –rule against double jeopardy;
- section 81 – extraneous considerations;
- section 82 – passage of time;
- section 83 – hostage-taking considerations;
- section 83A – forum;
- sections 84 and 86 – prima facie case;
- section 91 – physical or mental condition.

8.50 A challenge can also be brought on the basis that the warrant does not contain sufficient particulars of the offence. Although the wording in section 78(4)(c) is narrower than in section 2(4)(c) (for Part 1 cases) it was held in *Dudko v The Government of the Russian Federation*[34] by Thomas LJ that: '[...] the provision in s78(4)(c) should be interpreted to the same effect as that in s2(4)(c) using solely, as Dyson LJ suggested, the plain and ordinary meaning of that section without any gloss'.

8.51 The requested person may also seek to resist extradition on the basis that the conduct alleged would not amount to an extradition offence had the conduct occurred in England and Wales and that the request for extradition is not valid because it does not contain the papers referred to in section 70(9).

8.52 As with Part 1 requests, in a conviction case, the court must consider whether the person was convicted in his absence (EA 2003 s85). If he or she was, the court must consider whether the person deliberately absented him or herself from their trial. If he or she was not deliberately absent from his or her trial, the court must consider whether he or she would be entitled to a retrial or (on appeal) to a review amounting to a retrial.

8.53 The requested person also has the protection of the Human Rights Act 1998 and the appropriate judge must consider whether the person's extradition would be compatible with ECHR rights (EA 2003 s87): see chapter 6. Finally, the court has the power to stay proceedings as an abuse of process (see paragraph 5.113).

---

34 [2010] EWHC 1125 (Admin) at para 16.

Extradition offences

8.54 If the conduct alleged in the extradition request does not meet the requirements of 'dual criminality' then the judge must order the person's discharge. Section 137 of the Act deals with accusation cases and section 138 with conviction cases. The most common conduct that constitutes an extradition offence can be found in sections 137(3) and 138(3), although the representative should also be aware of the other subsections in sections 137 and 138.

8.55 Section 137 states that:

> The conduct constitutes an extradition offence in relation to the category 2 territory if these conditions are satisfied –
> (a) the conduct occurs in the category 2 territory;
> (b) the conduct would constitute an offence under the law of the relevant part of the United Kingdom punishable with imprisonment or another form of detention for a term of 12 months or a greater punishment if it occurred in that part of the United Kingdom;
> (c) the conduct is so punishable under the law of the category 2 territory.

8.56 The requirement in (b) is different from that which is required under Part 1. The conduct not only has to be an offence in the relevant part of the United Kingdom had it occurred there, it must also carry a sentence of at least 12 months' imprisonment. This means that conduct that would be extraditable under Part 1 of the Act – such as section 5 of the Public Order Act 1986 or assaulting a police constable in the execution of his duty – would not amount to an extradition offence under Part 2 because it would not satisfy the requirement that it is punishable with a form of detention of 12 months or greater in the United Kingdom.

8.57 The provisions for those convicted and sentenced also impose a similar requirement that the conduct carries a sentence of 12 months or greater in the United Kingdom. The sentence passed in the category 2 territory has to be for a term of four months or greater. Section 138 states that:

> The conduct constitutes an extradition offence in relation to the category 2 territory if these conditions are satisfied –
> (a) the conduct occurs in the category 2 territory;
> (b) the conduct would constitute an offence under the law of the relevant part of the United Kingdom punishable with imprisonment or another form of detention for a term of 12 months or a greater punishment if it occurred in that part of the United Kingdom;

(c) a sentence of imprisonment or another form of detention for a term of 4 months or a greater punishment has been imposed in the category 2 territory in respect of the conduct.

8.58 Conduct that occurs outside of the category 2 territory can also be an extradition offence if it would constitute an extraterritorial offence under the relevant part of the United Kingdom. For accusation cases the offence would have to provide for a sentence of 12 months' imprisonment or greater in the category 2 territory and in the United Kingdom.[35] For conviction cases the sentence imposed in the category 2 territory has to be four months' imprisonment or greater and punishable in the United Kingdom with at least 12 months' imprisonment.

8.59 Finally, conduct can amount to an extradition offence if it occurred outside the category 2 territory and no part of it occurred in the United Kingdom, is punishable under the law of the category 2 territory with 12 months' imprisonment (in accusation cases) or at least four months' imprisonment has been imposed (in conviction cases) and the conduct constitutes or if committed in the United Kingdom would constitute an offence as set out in sections 137(6) and 138(6).

8.60 The flowcharts below at figures 8.2 and figure 8.3 illustrate the various ways described above in which conduct may be an extradition offence under sections 137 and 138 respectively. These flowcharts should be used in conjunction with the legislation, bearing in mind the rule in *Osunta v The Public Prosecutor's Office in Dusseldorf*,[36] which allows for excision of conduct that would not amount to an extradition offence.

---

35 EA 2003 ss137(4) and 138(4).
36 [2007] EWHC 1562 (Admin).

Figure 8.2 Extradition offences (accusation cases)

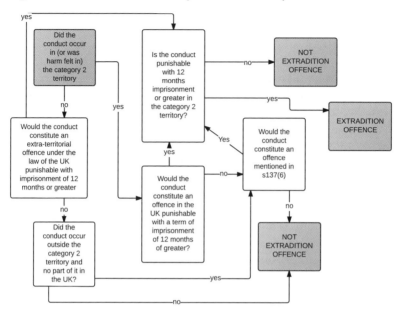

Figure 8.3 Extradition offences (conviction cases)

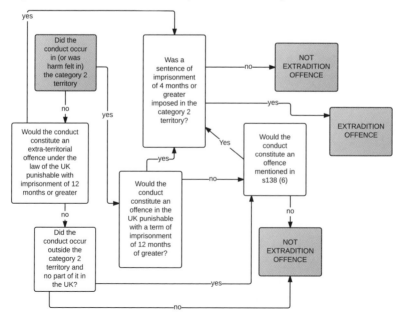

Prima facie case

8.61   One of the main differences between extradition requests from Part 1 and Part 2 is the requirement for the requesting state to establish a prima facie case. This is only applicable for the Part 2 countries that have *not* been designated by the SSHD. Signatories to the ECE, as well as Australia, Canada, New Zealand and the USA[37] have all been designated and are not required to establish a prima facie case. For those designated countries, they need only provide 'information' about the accusation or conviction. This requirement is often satisfied in an affidavit from the investigating police officer or the prosecutor.

8.62   The following countries are *not* required to provide evidence in support of their extradition requests:

> Albania, Andorra, Armenia, Aruba, Australia, Azerbaijan, Bonaire, Bosnia and Herzegovina, Canada, Curaçao, Faroe Islands, Georgia, Greenland, Iceland, Israel, Liechtenstein, Macedonia FYR, Moldova, Monaco, Montenegro, New Zealand, Norway, Russian Federation, Saba, San Marino, Serbia, Sint Eustatius, Sint Maarten, South Africa, Switzerland, Turkey, Ukraine and the United States.

8.63   Where required to do so a court must consider whether the requesting state can establish a prima facie case. Section 84 deals with cases where the requested person has not been convicted and section 86 where a person has been convicted. Sections 84 and 86 are in identical terms:

> (1) If the judge is required to proceed under this section he must decide whether there is evidence which would be sufficient to make a case requiring an answer by the person if the proceedings were the summary trial of an information against him.
> (2) In deciding the question in subsection (1) the judge may treat a statement made by a person in a document as admissible evidence of a fact if –
> (a) the statement is made by the person to a police officer or another person charged with the duty of investigating offences or charging offenders, and
> (b) direct oral evidence by the person of the fact would be admissible.

---

37 Australia, Canada, New Zealand and the USA are not signatories to the ECE but the prima facie requirement was removed on the basis they are democratic states and trusted extradition partners.

(3) In deciding whether to treat a statement made by a person in a document as admissible evidence of a fact, the judge must in particular have regard –

(a) to the nature and source of the document;

(b) to whether or not, having regard to the nature and source of the document and to any other circumstances that appear to the judge to be relevant, it is likely that the document is authentic;

(c) to the extent to which the statement appears to supply evidence which would not be readily available if the statement were not treated as being admissible evidence of the fact;

(d) to the relevance of the evidence that the statement appears to supply to any issue likely to have to be determined by the judge in deciding the question in subsection (1);

(e) to any risk that the admission or exclusion of the statement will result in unfairness to the person whose extradition is sought, having regard in particular to whether it is likely to be possible to controvert the statement if the person making it does not attend to give oral evidence in the proceedings.

(4) A summary in a document of a statement made by a person must be treated as a statement made by the person in the document for the purposes of subsection (2).

(5) If the judge decides the question in subsection (1) in the negative he must order the person's discharge.

(6) If the judge decides that question in the affirmative he must proceed under section 87.

(7) If the judge is required to proceed under this section and the category 2 territory to which extradition is requested is designated for the purposes of this section by order made by the Secretary of State –

(a) the judge must not decide under subsection (1), and

(b) he must proceed under section 87.[38]

8.64   The test to be applied by the court in order to determine whether there is a case to answer is whether the prosecution evidence, taken at its highest, is such that no jury properly directed could convict upon it.[39] In *R (Philip Harkins) v SSHD*,[40] Lloyd Jones J approved the test used by the judge in the magistrates' court. The test was expressed by the appropriate judge in the following terms:

> The evidence produced would, according to the Law of England and Wales, make a case requiring an answer by the defence if the proceedings were for trial here on these charges so there is sufficient evidence to justify an order for committal.

38 Subsections (8)–(9) omitted.
39 *R v Galbraith* [1981] 1 WLR 1039.
40 [2007] EWHC 639 (Admin) at para 31.

This is a slight variation of the test that applied in criminal committal proceedings pursuant to section 6(1) of the Magistrates' Courts Act 1980 where the court was required to consider whether: 'if the evidence stood alone at the trial, a reasonable jury, properly directed, could accept it and find a verdict of guilt.'[41]

8.65 It is generally accepted that if the court finds that there is a case to answer, the defence are entitled to call evidence in order to demonstrate that, in the light of all the evidence tendered by the requesting state, there is insufficient evidence to establish a case to answer.[42] For this reason, if a challenge is made under EA 2003 s84 or s86 it will allow the defence to properly test the case.

Role of the Secretary of State

8.66 In Part 1 cases it is the appropriate judge that orders a person's extradition. In Part 2 cases the SSHD performs this function.

8.67 Once a case is sent by the appropriate judge to the SSHD she has two months to make an order for extradition. The two-month period starts on the day on which the case is sent to the SSHD. Thus, if a case is sent to the SSHD on, for example, 17 May, she must order extradition by midnight on 16 July.[43] If she does not, the requested person *must* be discharged.[44] That time period can be extended on application by the SSHD to the appropriate judge and can be extended more than once. [45]

Person charged with an offence in the UK/sentenced to imprisonment

8.68 If a person is charged with an offence in the United Kingdom while the case is pending before the SSHD then the SSHD *must* not make a decision with regard to the person's extradition until the charge is disposed of; the charge is withdrawn; proceedings are discontinued or an order is made for the charge to lie on file.[46]

41 *Schtraks v Government of Israel* [1964] AC 556 at 580.
42 *Shankaran v The Government of the State of India and The Secretary of State for the Home Department* [2014] EWHC 957 (Admin).
43 Unless the end date happens to fall on a weekend or bank holiday in which case it will be the next working day.
44 *Zaporozhchenko v Westminster Magistrates' Court* [2011] EWHC 34 (Admin).
45 EA 2003 s99(4).
46 EA 2003 s97(2).

8.69   If a sentence of imprisonment has been imposed in respect of the offences charged then the SSHD *may* defer making a decision with regard to the person's extradition until the person is released from detention.[47]

8.70   If the case is sent to the SSHD by the appropriate judge and the person is serving a sentence of imprisonment, the SSHD may also defer making a decision with regards to the person's extradition until the person is released from detention.[48]

Representations to the SSHD

8.71   During the first four weeks following the case being sent to the SSHD, the SSHD cannot make an order for extradition. This is to allow for representations to be made by the requested person. If representations are not received in the four weeks following the case being sent, then the SSHD need not consider them.[49] This four-week period may be extended on application to the SSHD. The SSHD need not delay the making of a decision during the first four weeks if the person consented to extradition.[50]

8.72   The SSHD has a limited remit when considering representations. Representations can be made regarding:

- the death penalty;
- specialty;
- earlier extradition from a category 1 territory;
- earlier extradition from a category 2 territory.[51]

8.73   The SSHD is required to consider the above issues whether or not representations are received. If no issues are found, she will order extradition. If representations are received and rejected by the SSHD then an extradition order will be signed (unless the exceptions in s93(4) apply). An order for extradition (or discharge) must be made under the hand of one of the following:[52]

- the SSHD;
- a minister of state;

---

47   EA 2003 s97(3).
48   EA 2003 s98(2).
49   EA 2003 s93(5).
50   EA 2003 s93(7)(a).
51   EA 2003 s93(2).
52   EA 2003 s101.

- a parliamentary under-secretary of state;
- a senior official.[53]

8.74   If the representations are rejected, the requested person and his legal representatives will receive a response from the SSHD to the representations together with the order for extradition. If the representations are accepted the SSHD will order the person's discharge from the extradition request.

8.75   Once the extradition order is received the requested person has 14 days in which to lodge and serve an application for permission to appeal, from the date on which the SSHD informs the requested person (or his legal representatives) that an order for extradition has been made.[54] If no application for permission to appeal is lodged the person must be extradited to the category 2 territory within 28 days of the decision of the SSHD. This period can be extended on an application to the court.

8.76   If the requested person is not removed within the relevant period an application should be made to the appropriate judge at WMC for discharge.[55] Discharge must follow unless reasonable cause can be shown for the delay in removal.[56]

Competing extradition requests

8.77   There may be very rare occasions where two different category 2 territories make extradition requests for the same person. Under section 126 of the EA 2003, if the SSHD receives a valid request for extradition, the person is in the United Kingdom and before the person is extradited the SSHD receives another valid request for the person's extradition the SSHD may:

- order proceedings on one of the requests to be deferred until the other one has been disposed of, if neither of the requests has been disposed of;[57] or
- order the person's extradition to be deferred until the other request

---

53 A senior official is defined as a member of the senior civil service (grade 7 or above) or a member of the senior management structure of Her Majesty's Diplomatic Service.

54 EA 2003 s103(9).

55 EA 2003 s117(3).

56 *R (Tajik) v City of Westminster Magistrates' Court* [2012] EWHC 3347 (Admin).

57 EA 2003 s126(2)(a).

has been disposed of, if an order for extradition has already been made.[58]

8.78   The SSHD must take into account the following factors when applying section 126(2):

- the relative seriousness of the offences concerned;
- the place where each offence was committed (or alleged to have been committed);
- the date when each request was received;
- whether, in the case of each offence, the person is accused or unlawfully at large after conviction.[59]

Competing EAW and Part 2 requests for extradition

8.79   In even rarer scenarios there may be a situation where there are in existence an EAW and a Part 2 extradition request for the same person. Where there is a valid EAW in existence and a valid Part 2 request, and the person has not been extradited on either, the SSHD may:[60]

- order proceedings on either the EAW or the Part 2 request to be deferred until the other one has been disposed of;
- order the person's extradition in pursuance of the EAW to be deferred until the Part 2 request has been disposed of, if an order for extradition has been made on the EAW;
- order the person's extradition on the Part 2 request to be deferred until the EAW has been disposed of, if an order for extradition on the Part 2 request has been made.

8.80   The factors to be taken into consideration by the SSHD are:[61]

- the relative seriousness of the offences concerned;
- the place where each offence was committed (or alleged to have been committed);
- the date when the EAW was issued and the date when the Part 2 request was received;
- whether the person is accused or alleged to be unlawfully at large.

8.81   The SSHD is under no obligation to inform a requested person of a competing request and as a matter of policy the Home Office will not inform a requested person of the existence of a request until the person has been arrested.

58   EA 2003 s126(2)(b).
59   EA 2003 s126(3).
60   EA 2003 s179.
61   EA 2003 s179(3)(a)–(d).

Preparing for the contested hearing

continued

Introduction

9.1 Preparing even the most straightforward case for a contested hearing is likely to take some hours, particularly when time is factored in to allow for interpreters and travel to prisons to take instructions from those remanded in custody. It is important to consider these factors when setting a timetable for a contested hearing in court. This chapter will look at the casework that may need to be undertaken prior to any hearing.

Visiting the client in custody

9.2 It will often take time for a prison visit to be arranged, and the booking of a visit should therefore be prioritised. It can take over half an hour to gain entry to the visiting area, so it is always worth arriving at the prison well before the visit is due to start. The use of an interpreter will necessarily reduce the time available for the exchange of information, and a 'double visit' may be required.

9.3 While the relevant law and procedure will have been explained to the requested person at the first hearing, it will often be worth running through this again, in order to ensure the requested person has a proper understanding. In addition, lawyers will find that there are a large number of prisoners from Poland and the Baltic states on remand in extradition cases, many of whom have developed considerable knowledge about extradition. If the requested person has had an opportunity to speak to others in the prison, it may be necessary to deal with issues that other prisoners have advised him or her to raise, eg Article 3 in relation to prison conditions in Poland, or the impact of an asylum claim on extradition.

Use of interpreters

9.4 Criminal defence practitioners should be familiar with the Law Society practice note on 'Use of Interpreters in Criminal Cases',[1] which applies equally to extradition as to other types of criminal proceedings. The EU Directive on the right to interpretation and translation in criminal proceedings explicitly includes EAW proceedings (see

---

1 www.lawsociety.org.uk/advice/practice-notes/interpreters-in-criminal-cases/ (24 January 2012).

appendix L). The quality of interpreters provided by the court can vary greatly, and those representing requested persons will be aware of the need to ensure, as far as is possible, that the interpreter is competent.

9.5   Some requested persons may be confident in everyday speech, but not at a hearing that involves complicated legal concepts and terminology. It may be that he or she did not have an interpreter at the first hearing, but feels that one would be necessary for the extradition hearing. The court is familiar with such requests being made.

9.6   When seeing requested persons (or defence witnesses) outside court, the interpreter will need to be arranged by the solicitor. If the client is legally aided, the Legal Aid Agency will pay a maximum of £25 per hour for an interpreter (or £32 per hour outside London).[2] If the interpreter's fees fall within this rate, there will be no need to apply for prior authority. If, however, it proves impossible to find an interpreter who will work at this rate (in the case, for example, of a rare language), an application for prior authority should be made, demonstrating that the case is exceptional.

Case management and court directions

9.7   In most contested cases, the following documents will need to be prepared for service on the court and the prosecution:

- statement of issues;
- proof of evidence;
- witness statements;
- expert reports;
- objective evidence;
- skeleton argument.

9.8   This chapter will look at the preparation of each of these in turn. Prior to the extradition hearing, all documents in the case should be put together into a joint bundle with relevant paragraphs highlighted to be served on the court.

9.9   At the initial hearing, directions will be set for the service of the above documents, although in more complex cases (and in Part 2 cases) these directions may be made at a subsequent hearing. If the case is not straightforward (and most cases where there is an arguable point will not be) there may be one or indeed several case

2 Criminal Legal Aid (Remuneration) Regulations 2013 Sch 5.

management hearings. A review hearing may be listed at the initial hearing, or more commonly the case will be listed at the request of one of the parties prior to the extradition hearing.

9.10 If there are difficulties in complying with the directions, it is essential to make a written application to the court to extend time for service. Ignoring such directions may lead the court to exclude material served late or to consider wasted costs. Although it is possible to make applications administratively in criminal proceedings, the practice of the IJO is to list all such applications (including applications to vary bail) in court. Where the application is agreed by the other side or is not contentious, it is possible to request that attendance be excused; but where the application is disputed, attendance at court will obviously be preferable.

Taking instructions

9.11 Some basic instructions should already have been taken at the initial hearing, covering the areas set out in the checklists at appendices E and F. The requested person should be asked whether they have, or can get hold of, any documentary evidence (for example papers from the court in the requesting state). People often retain important documents and may not realise their significance. Those in custody will sometimes have friends or family who can assist in obtaining any documentation. Full background instructions should be taken when preparing for the contested hearing covering:

- family background and current circumstances;
- education;
- employment;
- health;
- immigration history;
- reason for coming to the UK;
- reason for leaving the requesting state;
- previous convictions in this or any other jurisdiction;
- concerns regarding extradition to the requesting state.

As with any client, the areas that will be covered will be led, to some extent, by the particular circumstances of that client. It is, of course, always important to foster a relationship with the client that encourages him or her to raise any issues that he or she thinks relevant, and it is good practice to ask the requested person whether there is anything that he or she can think of that has not been covered.

9.12 It may be necessary to take instructions directed towards the particular bar that the requested person wishes to raise. Clearly, there are some areas where a client's instructions will be of less importance. For example if a person is arguing that prison conditions in a particular country will result in a breach of his or her Article 3 rights, there may be little or indeed nothing that he or she can add to the expert reports, and it may be in such a case that no proof of evidence need be served. If, however, that person does have first-hand experience of prison conditions, or if he or she falls within a category of individual cited as being at risk in the reports (for example because of illness or race), this is something that should be covered when taking instructions. In view of the most commonly raised bars, suggested areas to discuss with the requested person are covered below.

Rule against double jeopardy

9.13 Full instructions should be taken on the circumstances of the previous conviction/acquittal, together with any sentence imposed and the extent to which it has been served. It will also be important to obtain any documentary evidence from the court in the requesting state that dealt with the case – a local lawyer will be able to facilitate this. A signed letter of consent to enable the gathering of such information from third parties should be obtained.

Absence of prosecution decision

9.14 Where there is a lack of clarity on the face of the warrant as to whether a decision to charge or try has been taken, it will be for the requested person to satisfy the appropriate judge that there are reasonable grounds for believing that this decision has not been taken; in looking at this the appropriate judge will be entitled to consider extraneous evidence. In appropriate circumstances, the requested person should therefore be asked whether or not she has any material which could support the contention that a decision to charge or try has not been made. In *Kandola*,[3] for example, in which a person's prosecution was sought for offences of tax evasion, the requested person adduced letters from tax authorities seeking payment of the outstanding tax which post-dated the issue of the EAW. It should be noted that the administrative court discouraged expert evidence

---

3 *Kandola and Others v Generalstaatwaltschaft Frankfurt, Germany and Others* [2015] EWHC 619 (Admin).

on this question. If this first hurdle can be overcome, the court will then go on to consider EA 2003 s12A(1)(a)(ii) viz. whether the sole reason for the decision to charge or try not having been made is the absence of the requested person. In considering this question, the court stated that 'it is likely that this could only be done by some sort of extraneous evidence from the requested person' but went on to say that, although the evidence need not be elaborate, mere assertion would be insufficient.[4]

Extraneous considerations

9.15 Relying on either limb, the requested person should be asked about any past experience of prejudice or punishment experienced by him or her on account of race, religion, nationality, gender, sexual orientation or political opinion.

Passage of time

9.16 It will be essential to take detailed instructions on the reasons why the requested person left the jurisdiction in order to deal with any assertion that the requested person has deliberately fled the jurisdiction. The warrant may give an indication as to whether the requesting state will assert that the requested person is a fugitive. If the person faces an accusation warrant, it will be necessary to probe her knowledge (if any) of the offence and its aftermath. If, for example, the person was arrested and later released, why did she subsequently leave the jurisdiction? Was she under any obligation to return or abide by any bail conditions? Similarly for a conviction warrant the requested person should be asked whether she knew that she had been convicted and, if so, why she left the jurisdiction. Was she given any assurance that led her to believe that she was allowed to leave? Documentary evidence in support will lend weight to the requested person's case.

9.17 The second area that should be covered in detail is the person's current circumstances as this will go to the question of oppression. How has his or her life changed since the time of the alleged offence, in particular with regards to family, employment and health? Does he or she now have familial responsibilities such that extradition would cause particular hardship to a vulnerable person? An expert report from, for example, a social worker may be helpful in such a case.

4 At para 33.

9.18   In addition to this, requested persons should be asked whether they know of any reason why their extradition would be unjust, ie whether there are essential witnesses who are no longer available.

Forum

9.20   It will often be clear from the warrant or request when looking at 'the gateway' of the forum test, whether a substantial measure of D's relevant activity was performed in the United Kingdom. Instructions on this question should, however, be carefully sought from the requested person. In addition to this, the specified matters that the appropriate judge can look at when considering the interests of justice test include a number of matters which the requested person should be asked about, including under EA 2003 ss19B/83A(3)(f) the jurisdictions in which co-defendants and other suspects are located and, importantly, under EA 2003 ss19B/83A(3)(g), D's connections with the United Kingdom.

Proportionality

9.21   In considering whether the extradition would be disproportionate, the appropriate judge is only permitted to take into account three specified matters, namely the seriousness of the offence, the likely penalty, and the possibility of the foreign authorities taking less coercive measures. In relation to the first of these, it will be noted that the LCJ's guidance suggests that previous offending history will be relevant to the seriousness of the offence. Instructions on the circumstances of previous convictions should therefore be taken. In relation to the third specified matter, that is, whether less coercive measures are available, this should be explored with the requested person given that there is an evidential burden on the requested person to identify these.[5] At the same time, the requested person should also be asked about any knowledge she might have of her obligations to the requesting state's authorities: if she is in breach of these obligations, it will be unlikely that the appropriate judge will find less coercive measures appropriate.[6]

---

5 *Miraszewski and Others v District Court in Torun, Poland and Others* [2014] EWHC 4261 (Admin) at para 41.

6 *Miraszewski* at para 41.

Human rights considerations

9.22   With regard to Articles 2, 3, 5 and 6, there will often be limited instructions that can be taken from the requested person (see paragraph 9.12 above) beyond his or her past experience of conditions in the requesting state. For Article 8, however, detailed instructions should be taken on the requested person's personal and family circumstances, covering areas similar to those set out in paragraph 9.16 above.

Conviction in absence

9.23   If the requested person was absent from his or her trial, instructions should be taken on his or her knowledge (or lack of knowledge) of the trial, covering the same areas as those set out in paragraph 9.13 above. If instructions establish that he or she was not deliberately absent and knew nothing of the criminal investigation, the requested person is unlikely to be able to provide any useful instructions on whether or not he or she will be entitled to a retrial: this will be a question for an expert to address. If the requested person was arrested or involved in the preliminary parts of the investigation, this should be covered.

Physical or mental health

9.24   While this is an area that will always require the commissioning of medical reports, it will often be the case (depending on the precise medical condition of the requested person) that useful instructions can be taken on the history of the requested person's medical complaints along with the effects that that condition has had on his or her life. In suicide risk cases, a full history of previous incidents of self-harm or attempts should be taken in addition to information on psychiatric diagnoses. Again, a signed authority for the release of medical records should be obtained from the client as well as details of the relevant GP, treating doctor and hospitals.

Statement of issues

9.25   A statement of issues will not be required in straightforward cases. Its purpose is to notify the court and primarily the prosecution of the grounds on which extradition is contested. A statement of issues should set out the very basic facts about the EAW or request, along with the challenges to be raised and an outline of the facts that support the grounds on which extradition is contested.

9.26   It is essential that it sets out any point on which the prosecution may wish to seek further information from the requesting state. If it does not, this may well lead to delay as the prosecution may seek time to obtain information to address issues that are raised late in proceedings. If it becomes apparent that an issue has arisen after the statement of issues has been served, it is good practice to notify the prosecution of this issue in writing at the first opportunity.

Drafting a proof of evidence

9.27   The proof of evidence is a crucial document in extradition proceedings. Particular time and care should be taken in its preparation. There are no rules or guidelines that dictate its form or content. While the court will direct that a 'proof of evidence' be served, this does not mean that a full statement setting out all of the client's instructions need necessarily be provided to the court. A proof of evidence in extradition cases is different from that which would be taken in usual criminal proceedings and that would be used by the defence team and not disclosed to the court or the other side. A proof of evidence for service in extradition proceedings will be more like a witness statement served in civil proceedings.

9.28   In terms of form, practice among solicitors varies – some favour serving the proof in the form of a section 9 statement;[7] others will serve it as a statement with numbered paragraphs signed and dated by the client. The authors prefer the latter approach. Given that there is no requirement to serve the statement in section 9 format,[8] there is no good reason for the requested person to provide a statement that carries a risk of prosecution for perjury if he or she does deviate from it under cross-examination. The proof should be set out in chronological order with subject headings at appropriate points. It is important that it is in the requested person's own words and that any comment that could be seen as legal argument is avoided.

9.29   The content of the proof should set out relevant background information, along with current circumstances and the particular

7 Criminal Justice Act 1967.
8 EA 2003 s 205 states that section 9 (proof by witness statement) and section 10 (proof by formal admission) apply to extradition proceedings as they do to proceedings for an offence.

detail pertaining to the grounds upon which extradition is contested (as set out in paragraphs 9.11–9.24). There is no need to serve a full statement setting out detail that is irrelevant, and district judges dealing with cases that are frequently document-heavy are unlikely to welcome lengthy biographical histories. Nevertheless, it is important that any fact that may be raised by the requested person in evidence is covered in the proof, and it may therefore be preferable to lean towards inclusion of detail if in doubt. Although no statutory inference will be drawn from failure to mention facts in a proof, requested persons should be aware that where facts not included are then elicited in live evidence, this may undermine their credibility. If there are parts of a client's case that are particularly problematic, it is tactically better to deal with this in the proof rather than to leave an obvious gap that will be exploited in cross-examination. Practitioners should be aware that some appropriate judges are reluctant to allow the defence advocate to ask questions that could have been covered in the proof of evidence.

Witness statements

9.30   Witnesses in extradition hearings range from friends and family of the requested person to professionals in the requesting state with, for example, knowledge of proceedings in that jurisdiction. Witness statements should be served in section 9 form, given that there will always be a possibility that the witness will not attend the extradition hearing.

Obtaining expert evidence

9.31   Expert evidence will usually be used in two areas. First, it is used in support of arguments about the situation (legal or political) in the requesting state, when challenging extradition on either extraneous considerations or human rights grounds. Second, experts are commonly relied upon to support cases where a requested person's personal circumstances are relevant to an issue in the case, for example doctors who can provide a report for the purposes of sections 25/81 or psychologists who can comment on the impact of a separation between parent and child for the purposes of an argument on ECHR

Article 8. An expert must have direct personal experience of, and proven expertise in, the issue upon which a report is sought.[9]

9.32   Where a requested person is legally aided, an application for prior authority should be made to cover the expert's costs. The hourly rates are set out in the Criminal Legal Aid (Remuneration) Regulations 2013 at Schedule 5. If it is impossible to find an expert who can produce a report at the rates set out in the Order the Legal Aid Agency may increase the rates in exceptional circumstances. Exceptional circumstances are defined by the LAA as:

> where the expert's evidence is key to the client's case and either –
> - the complexity of the material is such that an expert with a high level of seniority is required; or
> - the material is of such a specialised and unusual nature that only very few experts are available to provide the necessary evidence.[10]

9.33   If prior authority is refused, legally aided clients can, in certain circumstances, pay for experts' reports.[11]

9.34   As in other proceedings, an expert's duty is to the court, and he or she must be objective. Part 33 of the Criminal Procedure Rules applies to expert witnesses in extradition cases and a copy of this should be provided to any expert along with the letter of instruction. Rule 33.4 sets out information that all expert reports should contain. Compliance with the rules should be verified upon receipt of the report. It is important that the statement includes enough detail for a court to be able to establish that the expert has complied with his or her duties.

9.35   Letters of instruction should enclose the warrant or request along with any further information received from the prosecution, the proof of evidence and any pertinent witness statements. It may be useful in some cases for the expert to be provided with relevant case-law. The letter of instruction should set out a brief background before going through the questions to be addressed. These questions should be as specific as possible, and should direct the expert towards answering questions that are not addressed in the objective evidence. Funding matters and the timeframe should also be covered. It is advisable to require experts to submit reports at least a week prior to the deadline in order to allow sufficient time to address any issues. In drafting a

---

9   *Brazuks and Others v Prosecutor General's Office, Latvia* [2014] EWHC 1021 (Admin).

10 See LAA *Guidance on Remuneration of Expert Witnesses*, April 2015 www.gov. uk/government/uploads/system/uploads/attachment_data/file/420106/expert-witnesses-fees-guidance.pdf.

11 2010 Standard Criminal Contract Specification Part A para 8.52.

letter of instruction, it is important to bear in mind that the letter and enclosures, as well as any correspondence between the solicitor and the expert, may be seen by the court and/or the prosecution.

Solicitors will be responsible for paying the costs of the commissioning of expert reports. Where a client is legally aided and the expert's attendance at court is required, this will be covered by the court. The rates for travel and attendance for expert witnesses are minimal,[12] and can only be claimed after attendance. It can take the court many months to process the expert's claim for payment. For this reason it is frequently impossible to secure the attendance of experts based in other jurisdictions and the use of video link evidence is becoming more frequent.

Evidence via the internet hearings (EVie)

9.36   It is possible to arrange with the court for evidence to be given via the internet. This can be done in two ways. The first is by SCOPIA, which is a secure video link. In order for evidence to be given via SCOPIA an application must be made to the court in accordance with Crim PR 29.24 and must be granted by an appropriate judge. Once granted, the proposed expert or witness will be sent a link to download the software onto their computer or electronic device.

9.37   The second way to facilitate video evidence is by using the Prison Video Link network. The majority of magistrates' and Crown courts in England and Wales are connected to this network and the expert/witness will need to attend their local court to access the video link network. The local court should therefore be contacted in advance to ensure that they have a booth available for the time that the evidence is to be given. This way of giving evidence is not available for witnesses based abroad.

9.38   An application for a live link must (unless the court otherwise directs) identify the place from which the witness will give evidence.[13] If the place is in the United Kingdom, the application must explain why it would be in the interests of the efficient and effective administration of justice for the witness to give evidence by live link.[14] If the witness is to be accompanied by another person whilst giving

---

12 See the Guide to Allowances under Part V of the Costs in Criminal Cases (General) Regulations 1986 SI No 1335, available at www.justice.gov.uk, for the applicable rates of payment.

13 Crim PR 24.24(a).

14 Crim PR 24.24(b).

evidence (such as an interpreter) then the application must name that other person[15] (if possible) and explain why it is appropriate for the witness to be accompanied.[16]

9.39   Once granted, the court will provide details of the advocate of the relevant person to liaise with at the court to facilitate the link. In order to ensure that the SCOPIA link works with the expert/witness, a test should be carried out five working days before the date of the hearing where the video evidence is to be given. Tests are carried out between 09:00 and 09:45 and 13:15 and 13:45. A representative of the defence firm should be in attendance during the test in case there are any difficulties.

Objective evidence

9.40   Reports from international organisations, if available, should be served as part of the bundle in appropriate cases. If, for example, a requested person is arguing that his or her extradition will result in a breach of his or her human rights, reports from such organisations as Amnesty International, the US State Department or the European Committee for the Prevention of Torture will reinforce other evidence. Although criticism from independent international bodies may carry some weight, the court will also require expert evidence that is tailored to the specific facts of the case.

Further information from the issuing state

9.41   The court in this country cannot compel the requesting state to provide further information. It may, however, direct that further information, if it is to be provided, should be served by a particular date. While there is no obligation on the requesting state to serve further information, it is sometimes provided following service of defence documents where the requesting state 'wishes to resist the implications of evidence advanced and proffered by an appellant ...'.[17] Note, however, that a requesting state may well rely on the presumption that it will comply with its Convention obligations and serve no information in

---

15 Crim PR 24.24(c)(i).
16 Crim PR 24.24(c)(ii).
17 *Baksys v Ministry of Justice of the Republic of Lithuania* [2007] EWHC 2838 (Admin) at para 11.

response.[18] When it is provided, further information is frequently served very late in the proceedings. Even if the CPS has acted diligently in communicating requests for information, the requesting state itself can be dilatory in responding. In some cases, there will be no comment that the requested person can usefully make on the further information, but he or she should nevertheless be provided with the opportunity to do so. If it is a case in which expert reports have been commissioned, the expert's views on the further information should also be solicited – this may require a further application for prior authority if an addendum report is necessary.

Disclosure

9.42   The CPS does not have a general duty of disclosure as it does when conducting prosecutions in English criminal proceedings. However, the CPS owes the court a duty of candour and good faith.[19] It is accepted that, while it is for the requesting state to determine which evidence to put forward in support of its request for extradition, the CPS in accordance with its duty to the court must disclose evidence (but only if such material is brought to the attention of the CPS by the requesting state) which destroys, renders worthless or very severely undermines the evidence on which it relies.[20] In *R (Raissi) v Secretary of State for the Home Department*[21] the court said that the CPS's duty to the court includes a duty to ensure that the requesting state complies with its duty of disclosure.

Closed material hearings and secret evidence

9.43   A closed material hearing is often used in immigration cases. It is a hearing in which the evidence is considered by the judge but not seen or disclosed to the other side. Closed material hearings are not permitted in extradition proceedings[22] and the judge at the extradition hearing has no power to limit disclosure to the requesting state of evidence relied upon by the requested person. All material

---

18 If the court has been satisfied that the 'presumption' has been rebutted in a case concerning a Council of Europe or EU state, an 'assurance' or 'guarantee' is a legitimate means by which such a state can 'dispel doubts' – *Ilia v Appeal Court in Athens, Greece* [2015] EWHC 547 (Admin) at para 38. See para 6.21.

19 *Knowles Jr v United States of America and Another* [2006] UKPC 38 at para 35.

20 At para 35.

21 [2008] EWCA Civ 72.

22 *VB and Others v Westminster Magistrates' Court* [2014] UKSC 59.

relied upon must be served upon the CPS with the expectation that it will be disclosed to the requesting state. The requested person must be made aware of this.

Drafting a skeleton argument

9.44   A skeleton argument is usually served well in advance of the extradition hearing. Those used to drafting skeleton arguments in usual criminal proceedings will recognise the format: in short, it should set out the facts, followed by the law, then the submissions. The headings below provide a suggested structure for a skeleton argument:

- introduction and procedural chronology:
  - details of the EAW (relevant dates, accusation/conviction, offence);
  - court proceedings since initial hearing;
- issues for the court to determine:
  - set out the challenges to be raised;
- the law:
  - set out the statutory provisions and relevant case-law relied upon. It may be necessary to set out more of the case-law than in criminal proceedings;
- submissions:
  - apply the law to the facts;
- conclusion.

Preparation of the bundle

9.45   A bundle, preferably indexed with tabs and page numbering, should be served on the court prior to the extradition hearing. It should include all the documents set out in paragraph 9.7, along with the documents relied upon by the prosecution (usually EAW/extradition request, further information and skeleton argument) and the relevant statutory provisions and case-law. If a joint bundle is to be prepared it should be properly paginated and indexed. The general running order for such a joint bundle will be:

- opening note/skeleton argument of the judicial authority;
- EAW/extradition request;
- witness statements from the judicial authority;
- expert reports;
- further information from judicial authority;

- defence skeleton argument;
- proof of requested person;
- witness statements;
- expert reports;
- authorities (highlighting key passages).

9.46 Current practice at WMC is to assign a specific district judge to hear a case prior to the extradition hearing. When sending the bundle to the court, it should be accompanied by a covering letter requesting that it be placed before the relevant district judge so that he or she has time to read it prior to the extradition hearing. The court and the CPS should be served with the bundle electronically (as a PDF) where possible.

Certificate for counsel

9.47 Where a case is publicly funded, a certificate for counsel (including, in appropriate cases, Queen's Counsel) can be granted for extradition proceedings in the magistrates' court. The relevant legislation is the Criminal Legal Aid (Determinations by a Court and Choice of Representative) Regulations 2013. Regulation 16 reads:

Criminal proceedings before a magistrates' court

16(1) Subject to paragraph (2), in relation to any criminal proceedings before a magistrates' court, the right of an individual conferred by section 27(4) of the Act does not include a right to select an advocate.

(2) The relevant court may determine that the individual can select an advocate if –

(a) the proceedings relate to an extradition hearing under the Extradition Act 2003 or an indictable offence; and

(b) the relevant court determines that because there are circumstances which make the proceedings unusually grave or difficult, representation by an advocate would be desirable.

9.48 It is important to note that the Regulations use the word 'desirable' rather than, for example, 'necessary'. In order to apply for a certificate for counsel, a written application should be submitted to the LAA setting out the facts of the case and the reason that the proceedings are unusually grave or difficult. The application can be supplemented by a written advice from counsel. The application can be submitted to the LAA via its email address: extraditionapplica@legalaid.gsi.gov.uk. Once the application has been logged by the LAA they will send the application to the IJO at WMC for it to be listed before an appropriate judge. An application that has been refused on the papers can be renewed at an oral hearing. If granted, the representation order will be amended accordingly from the date of grant.

CHAPTER 10

The contested extradition hearing

continued

Introduction

10.1 The extradition hearing can vary in length depending on the complexity of the issues to be argued and the amount of evidence that is to be called. Straightforward issues can be argued in 30 minutes whereas complex Part 2 cases may require several days of the court's time.

Criminal Procedure Rules

10.2 The general rule is that the magistrates' court must hold hearings in public, however the Criminal Procedure Rules state that that is subject to the court's power to impose reporting restrictions, withhold information from the public or order a hearing in private.[1] Hearings should be held in the defendant's presence unless either (1) the case is being discharged or (2) the requested person is represented, and her presence is impracticable because of her ill health or disorderly conduct.[2]

Receivable and admissible documents

10.3 An EAW is a receivable document that is admissible in proceedings under the Act.[3] But what about other documents adduced by the judicial authority/requesting state in the course of the proceedings?

10.4 Section 202(2) and (3) state that any other document issued in a category 1 or 2 territory may be received in evidence if it has been 'duly authenticated'. Duly authenticated is defined in subsection (4). A document is duly authenticated if one of the following apply; it purports to be:

- signed by a judge, magistrate or officer of the territory;
- certified, whether by seal or otherwise, by the ministry or department of the territory responsible for justice or for foreign affairs;
- authenticated by the oath or affirmation of a witness.

---

1 Criminal PR 17.3(1).
2 Criminal PR 17.3(2).
3 EA 2003 s202(1).

10.5 A document that is not duly authenticated is not precluded from being admitted into evidence in extradition proceedings.[4] However, less weight may be attached to it.

10.6 Closed material hearings are not permitted in extradition proceedings and the judge at the extradition hearing has no power to limit the disclosure of evidence relied upon by the requested person to the requesting state.[5] All material relied upon must be served upon the CPS with the expectation that it will be disclosed to the requesting state. The requested person must be made aware of this.

Burden and standard of proof

10.7 Unless any express provisions in the Act apply, the burden and standard of proof must be applied as if the person who is facing extradition is accused of an offence and the judicial authority/requesting state is the prosecution.[6] That is to say, it is for the requesting state to prove to the criminal standard.

Requests for further information

10.8 The CPS decides what will be disclosed. Domestic rules of disclosure do not apply to extradition proceedings.[7] However, the CPS owes the court a duty of candour and good faith.

10.9 Although the appropriate judge can request further information from the CPS acting on behalf of the judicial authority/requesting state, he or she cannot compel them to provide it. Failure to provide a response could, however, lead to an inference being drawn as to why it has not been produced.

---

4 In *Prendi (aka Aleks Kola) v The Government of the Republic of Albania* [2015] EWHC 1809 (Admin), the court stated that the correct test to be applied as to the admissibility of an authenticated document is: 'is this document, which has not been authenticated in accordance with section 202(3), admissible as evidence of the facts stated in it, according to the English rules of criminal evidence?'.

5 *VB and Others v Westminster Magistrates' Court* [2014] UKSC 59.

6 EA 2003 s206.

7 *R (Raissi) v Secretary of State for the Home Department* [2008] EWCA Civ 72, [2008] QB 836.

Applications to adjourn

10.10   The Criminal Procedure Rules set out a non-exhaustive list of the reasons for which an adjournment may be sought as follows:

- to allow information that the court requires to be obtained;
- following a provisional arrest under Part 1 of the Extradition Act 2003, pending receipt of the warrant;
- following a provisional arrest under Part 2 of the Act, pending receipt of the extradition request;
- if the court is informed that the defendant is serving a custodial sentence in the UK;
- if it appears to the court that the defendant is not fit to be extradited, unless the court discharges the defendant for that reason;
- where a court dealing with a warrant to which Part 1 of the Act applies is informed that another such warrant has been received in the UK; or
- where a court dealing with a warrant to which Part 1 of the Act applies is informed of a request for the temporary transfer of the defendant to the territory to which the defendant's extradition is sought.

10.11   Under Crim PR 17.3(5), the general rule is that, before exercising a power to adjourn, the court must give each party an opportunity to make representations, unless that party is absent deliberately.

10.12   Applications to adjourn should not be left until the day of the extradition hearing unless unavoidable. The court will be reluctant to lose court time, especially given the courts' listing difficulties. The court is unlikely to consider sympathetically an application to adjourn the extradition hearing if it is made on the day of the hearing. However, if an application to adjourn on the day of the extradition hearing is essential, it must be made on notice.

10.13   The CPS acting on behalf of the judicial authority/requesting state should be put on notice of an intention to seek an adjournment as soon as the need arises. The reasons that an adjournment is sought, and the proposed timetable for the case going forward should the court grant the application to adjourn, should be set out. If the CPS do not oppose the application or is 'neutral' to it, the application is more likely to be granted. In that case, the court will expect the parties to have agreed directions.

10.14   Ordinarily, the court should be notified in writing of an application to adjourn the extradition hearing. This can be done by emailing the international office (Westminster.ij@hmcts.gsi.gov.uk) and should clearly outline the reason an adjournment is required and state why it is in the interests of justice for the case to be adjourned. The court will be referred to any previous applications to adjourn and will consider whether the parties have complied with directions set by the court. It is therefore important to apply to vary the directions where they cannot be complied with.

10.15   Where an application to adjourn is made on the day of the extradition hearing, advocates should be prepared for the application to be refused and for the hearing to proceed. Challenges to the refusal to grant adjournments are made by way of judicial review but the Administrative Court will be slow to interfere in a decision by the appropriate judge.

Housekeeping

10.16   Before the extradition hearing begins the advocate should ensure that both the court and the CPS have all the documents that are to be relied upon. Ideally, these should all be in an indexed and paginated joint bundle (see chapter 9). If the judge has not had sight of the bundle or has not read it, the court should be invited to rise to allow the judge to read the skeleton arguments.

10.17   If the judge has considered the skeleton arguments, he or she should be taken through the bundle. The relevance of each document in the bundle should be explained.

10.18   The order in which live witnesses are to be called should be outlined. If there is a witness who is to be called 'out of turn', the reason for this should be explained to the court.

10.19   Finally, if the time estimate does not appear sufficient, the court should be informed so that the judge can decide whether to begin to hear the case and adjourn the proceedings part-heard or to adjourn to a day when the hearing can be heard in full.

Who goes first?

10.20   Those acting on behalf of the judicial authority/requesting state will open the hearing and take the court through the EAW/extradition request. They will outline the issues that are raised by the requested person and invite the court to find matters not contested in their favour.

10.21   If the burden is on the judicial authority to prove the issue under EA 2003 (for example, the burden is on the judicial authority to prove to the criminal standard that the conduct contained in the EAW/ extradition request is an extradition offence) then they will go first in making their submission to the court.

10.22   In all other situations, it will be the requested person's case that is heard first, with his or her evidence called first.

10.23   The structure of the EA 2003 envisages a 'step-by-step' approach by the judge to particular questions[8] and the answer to each particular question will determine the next question that has to be considered. Arguments should therefore be presented in sequence as a failure to do so could lead the court 'into error.'[9] The prescribed sequence is set out in Crim PR 17.6(2) for Part 1 cases and Crim PR 17.13(2) for Part 2.

Calling your client – evidence in chief

10.24   Before the requested person gives evidence it is important to ensure that no other witness of fact is sitting in the courtroom. Any witness of fact should be asked to leave while the requested person is giving his or her testimony. This does not apply to expert witnesses who can sit in court throughout the proceedings while other evidence is being heard.

10.25   If the requested person is in custody he or she will be brought to the witness box by the gaolers. If the requested person is on bail he or she will be asked to make his or her way to the witness box by the court usher.

10.26   It is important that the requested person has with him or her the proof of evidence and any other documents that will be referred to. If the court has a bundle of evidence for the hearing the requested person should also be provided with one.

10.27   As with many types of proceeding, the requested person will be asked to affirm or to swear on oath. If the requested person is assisted by an interpreter the interpreter will also be sworn in.

10.28   The advocate should ask the requested person to adopt his or her proof of evidence as part of his or her evidence-in-chief. In order for this to be done, the requested person should be asked if the proof of evidence that is before the court is his or her statement and confirm that it is true to the best of his or her knowledge and belief. The

---

8   *Sonea v Mehedinti* [2009] EWHC 89 (Admin).

9   *Bagri v Public Prosecutor Bordeaux Court of First Instance* [2014] EWHC 4066 (Admin).

requested person should be asked to confirm that it is his or her signature on each page of the statement.

10.29   Depending on the issues raised, there may be no supplementary questions for the requested person or he or she may be asked to address issues that have arisen subsequent to the proof of evidence being served. For example, the requested person may need to address further information served on behalf of the judicial authority.

10.30   The advocate should be careful not to frustrate the court by asking questions where the answers are clearly contained in the proof of evidence: the judge should have read the papers ahead of the extradition hearing. If it is clear that the judge has not had an opportunity to read the papers in advance of the hearing, it may be necessary to summarise the main points covered in the proof of evidence with the requested person. If there is information that has been served by the judicial authority/requesting state subsequent to the proof of evidence being served, then this will need to be addressed by the requested person in oral evidence.

10.31   If there is a break in the proceedings and the requested person is in the middle of giving evidence it is important to remember that the evidence cannot be discussed.

10.32   Once the requested person has finished giving his evidence in chief he or she will be exposed to cross-examination from the judicial authority and is also likely to be questioned by the judge. Re-examination follows should there be a need for it.

Expert evidence

10.33   If relying upon expert evidence, the report of such experts should have been served ahead of the hearing to allow the judicial authority an opportunity to respond and adduce its own evidence in rebuttal.

10.34   The reports of experts can be adopted into evidence – in the same manner as that presented by the requested person – and this can drastically reduce the time an expert spends in the witness box. The expert should have a copy of the report when giving evidence and any other documents that he or she will be asked to consider. If there is a bundle, this should be provided to the expert before giving evidence.

10.35   With the permission of the court it is possible to lead experts through their qualifications and experience before addressing the main conclusion and findings of a report. If the judicial authority/requesting state does not contest the expertise of an expert there will be no need to go through their qualifications.

10.36   It is important that the expert addresses any points made by the judicial authority/requesting state in further information served in the proceedings if this has not been addressed in an addendum report. Once the expert has finished giving their evidence in chief he or she may be subjected to questions from both the court and the judicial authority/requesting state.

Adducing other evidence

10.37   If other evidence is to be adduced, the time to do it is after the requested person and expert (if applicable) have given their evidence.

10.38   Other evidence could take the form of section 9 witness statements[10] to be read, or objective reports. If the court admits written statements from a witness or expert as evidence, each relevant part of the statement must be read or summarised aloud[11] or the court must read the statement and its gist must be summarised aloud.[12]

10.39   If lengthy objective reports are being relied upon, relevant passages in the judge's bundle should be highlighted to ensure that they are easily found when reference is made to them. Relevant passages should be read out to the court.

Submissions

10.40   Once all the evidence has been called/adduced then it is time for submissions to be made. The skeleton argument that has already been served should address the submissions on behalf of the requested person. This is an opportunity to expand upon the main arguments and address the evidence that has been heard.

10.41   The court should be addressed on the relevant law. If the applicability of the law is agreed between the requested person and the judicial authority/requesting state then this could be agreed in a section 10 admission.[13]

10.42   The advocate should apply the facts of the case to the law. It may be necessary to distinguish the facts of the current case from the reported case-law. When referring to reported cases the court should

10 Criminal Justice Act (CJA) 1967.
11 Crim PR 17.15(2)(a).
12 Crim PR 17.15(2)(b).
13 CJA 1967.

be taken to the relevant passages. If the passage relied upon is not too lengthy, it should be read to the court. Again, highlighting key passages in the authorities in the bundle will bring them to the judge's attention in pre-hearing reading.

10.43   Very often judges will be careful to avoid making decisions that will 'open the floodgates'. It is therefore important not to make general sweeping assertions (ie 'a fair trial is not possible in Malta') but rather to emphasise the points in the case being presented that are unique (ie 'a fair trial in Malta is not possible for this particular requested person because …').

Judgment

10.44   After both the requested person and the judicial authority have made submissions, the judge will give his or her ruling. Current practice is to allow for time for writing a judgment to be built into the hearing time and the judge will therefore rise to draft his or her ruling.

10.45   If judgment is reserved to another date, the parties will have to return to court for a written ruling to be handed down. This is normally read out in full in open court. However, it is the practice of some judges to read the findings of fact and the conclusion rather than the whole judgment.

10.46   If there are any factual errors in the judgment these should be noted and brought to the attention of the judge once it has been read out in full. The amendments (if any) can then be made by hand.

10.47   A copy of the written ruling in a reserved judgment will be provided to the parties and there is therefore no need to take a detailed note.

Ex tempore judgments

10.48   If the issue raised at the contested extradition hearing is straightforward the judge may give an *ex tempore* judgment.[14] This will not be in writing; therefore as full a note as possible should be taken. If the matter is to be appealed a summary of the judgment should be agreed between the parties so that it can be provided to the Administrative Court Office with the application for permission to appeal (see chapter 11 on appeals).

14 Practitioners should note that the LCJ in *Polish Judicial Authorities v Celinski and Others* stated that the practice of giving oral judgments in Article 8 cases was 'unacceptable' as no official transcript of it would be available to the appellate court.

Information provided to the requested person after judgment

10.49 After reading out the judgment, the judge will then explain to the requested person the effect of his or her decision. If the result is to order the person's extradition (in a Part 1 case) or to send the case to the SSHD (in a Part 2 case) the judge will explain the timeframe for appealing. He or she will then remand the person in custody or on bail.

10.50 If the decision of the judge is to order the person's discharge, and the CPS gives an indication to the judge of an intention to appeal the decision, then the judge must continue to remand the person in custody or on bail. If no such indication is given, and the requested person is in custody he or she will be released. If the requested person was subject to bail conditions then those conditions will cease to apply.

10.51 Whether the court's decision is to order extradition or to discharge, the Criminal Procedure Rules state that the court must also consider any ancillary application, such as those relating to reporting restrictions or costs.[15]

Costs where extradition ordered

10.52 If the judge orders extradition, in the vast majority of cases the CPS will make an application for costs pursuant to section 60 of the Act. The costs sought by the CPS should be limited to the 'expenses reasonably incurred in conducting extradition proceedings' and can include:

- costs incurred through the preparation of the case by the CPS;
- counsel's fees and disbursements; and
- witness expenses.

10.53 However, the CPS internal memo on applying for costs states that 'it is impractical to maintain detailed time and costs records and in any event the requested person is generally only able to make a contribution to costs'. The contribution in 'standard cases' usually amounts to the following:

- £100 where extradition is ordered at the first hearing;
- £100 per interim and review hearing;
- £165 for a contested extradition hearing (each day).

---

15 Crim PR 17.6(3) and (4).

10.54   The High Court has urged caution on the magistrates' court regarding the imposition of costs. Collins J in *Mencwel v Regional Court in Poznan, Poland*,[16] stated:

> The District Judge took a robust view of the circumstances put before him which were said to be a bar to extradition. He said it was a typical case of non-existent grounds and very flimsy arguments to resist it. He made a point that the court as from April this year will consider ordering costs against requested persons who pointlessly resist extradition in this way. I note that. It is a jurisdiction which no doubt the court has but it is one which on the face of it should be exercised with the greatest possible care.

10.55   The appropriate route for challenging a costs order is by way of judicial review. In *Bizunowicz and Others v Poland*[17] the Divisional Court concluded that the High Court had no jurisdiction to determine an appeal from a costs order where a person has challenged that order as part of an unsuccessful extradition appeal. However, the court does have jurisdiction to vary or quash a costs order where the appellant has successfully appealed the extradition order.

Costs in Part 2 cases

10.56   Section 133 of the Act allows the appropriate judge to award costs where extradition is ordered. In Part 2 cases, it is not the appropriate judge that orders extradition and therefore at the time the case is still with the appropriate judge he has no power to award costs.

Costs where discharge ordered

10.57   When discharge is ordered, the requested person is able to make an application for a costs order pursuant to sections 61/134 of the Act for their out of pocket expenses (usually travel costs).

10.58   A requested person who has funded his case privately will be able to seek a costs order for a recovery of costs from central funds subject to the rules of determination which state that the costs are capped at legal aid rates.

---

16 [2013] EWHC 1513 (Admin).

17 *Bizunowicz and Florea v Koszalin District Court, Poland and Plzen Regional Court, Czech Republic* [2014] EWHC 3238 (Admin).

Appeals

continued

Introduction

11.1 The Sir Scott Baker report of October 2011 recommended that 'appeals under Part 1 and Part 2 of the 2003 Act should only be allowed to proceed with the leave either of the extradition judge or the court which considers the appeal'.[1]

11.2 A permission to appeal stage became effective from 15 April 2015 by virtue of the coming into force of Anti-social Behaviour, Crime and Policing Act 2014 s160. As of that date, both the requested person whose extradition has been ordered and the issuing state can appeal against adverse decisions made at the extradition hearing but subject to being granted permission to appeal by the High Court.

11.3 In EAW cases the appeal is against the decision of the appropriate judge who either ordered extradition or ordered the person's discharge.

11.4 In Part 2 cases the appeal can be against the decision of the appropriate judge to send the case to the SSHD and/or the decision of the SSHD to order extradition or a decision by either to order the person's discharge from the extradition request.

11.5 The timeframe in which an application for permission to appeal must be lodged and served differs depending on the part of the Act under which proceedings are brought.

11.6 Appeals to the High Court under EA 2003 are also governed by the Criminal Procedure Rules 2015 (Crim PR) and Rule 17 of the Criminal Practice Directions (Crim PD).

Appeals under Part 1 of the Act

11.7 If a person's extradition is ordered then that person has *seven days* in which to apply for permission to appeal to the High Court. The seven days start with the day the extradition order is made. If, for example, the order is made on a Tuesday, the appeal must be filed and served by the following Monday. If the decision is made on a Monday the deadline will be the following Monday as the seventh day falls on a Sunday when the Administrative Court Office (ACO) is closed. Similarly, if the seventh day falls on a bank holiday or a day when the ACO is shut, the deadline moves to the next working day.[2]

---

1 *A Review of the United Kingdom's Extradition Arrangements* – 30 September 2011.

2 *Mucelli v The Government of Albania* [2009] UKHL 2.

Preparing the permission to appeal application

11.8   The following documents should be put together in a bundle to be lodged at the High Court:

- Form EXN161 – appellant's notice – application for permission to appeal;
- grounds of appeal;
- EAW;
- judgment of the appropriate judge;
- any other documents relied upon (witness statements, expert reports, further information).

It is prudent to include all documents that the appropriate judge had before him at the extradition hearing.

11.9   In total, four bundles should be prepared. The court will require three copies and one master copy should be retained by the defence so that it can be served upon the CPS and the NCA. If numerous 'other documents' are being relied on, then it may be appropriate to submit the bundles with dividers and an index.

11.10   The appellant will be covered by the representation order in the lower court for the preparation and filing of the application for permission to appeal. The CRM14 and a copy of the representation order from the magistrates' court (if applicable) should also accompany the appeal documents.

Legal aid

11.11   In order to apply for legal aid in extradition proceedings before the High Court, a fully completed form CRM14 must be submitted to the ACO. There is no means testing in the High Court for extradition appeals and therefore the delays that are sometimes experienced in the magistrates' court do not occur once the case reaches the appeal stage.

11.12   CRM14s that were previously submitted to the magistrates' court will not be accepted.

11.13   The CRM14 should be submitted at the same time that the appeal notice is lodged so that the issuing fee of £240 can be recovered as a disbursement. The representation order only takes effect from the date on which the form, properly completed, is received. The case-lawyers at the ACO have delegated powers to grant a representation order. A copy of the representation order will usually be received by the legal representative two to three days after a CRM14 is submitted.

11.14   Although the Criminal Practice Direction states that 'a representation order will be granted for a solicitor and junior counsel and will cover the preparation of the Notice of Appeal to the determination of the appeal'[3], practitioners should be aware that it will only cover preparation of the notice of appeal after the grant of the representation order (for example, if the notice of appeal is perfected in the ten business days after service). Preparation of the notice of appeal prior to the grant of the High Court representation order will be covered by the magistrates' court representation order.

11.15   In order to obtain a representation order for leading counsel alone or for leading counsel and junior counsel, an application must be made to extend the representation order (see paragraph 11.71 below).

11.16   The representation order can also be extended to cover disbursements such as experts' fees and translation fees (see paragraphs 11.72–11.76 below).

Court fees

11.17   Court fees are payable in extradition appeals before the Administrative Court and practitioners are referred to the applicable fees table available on the ACO website[4]. Where a court fee is due, a party lodging the application must pay that fee when lodging the application[5]. However, unless the court directs otherwise, failure to pay the relevant fee will not result in the High Court refusing to accept the application in respect of which the court fee is due or dismiss an application for permission to appeal. Instead, the High Court must serve a notice on the defaulting party requiring payment of the fee within a period specified in the notice[6]. A party must then comply with the notice by the expiry of the period specified in the notice or risk having the application dismissed.

---

3 Crim PD 17C.1.

4 www.justice.gov.uk/downloads/courts/administrative-court/aco-fees-22-apr-2014.doc.

5 Crim PR 17.31(2).

6 Crim PR 17.31(3)(a).

Appellant's Notice – application for permission to appeal – Form EXN161

11.18   Form EXN161 can be completed online[7] and then printed. The form itself is relatively straightforward and an example can be found at appendix I. Guidance for its completion is provided on the ACO website.

11.19   Form EXN161 should be signed either by the appellant or a solicitor of the firm lodging the leave to appeal application.

11.20   Any documents not included at the time of lodging that should ordinarily be included (such as a copy of the EAW or a copy of the judge's ruling) should be provided as soon as possible to the court and the respondents if they do not already have a copy.

Grounds of appeal

11.21   The grounds of appeal must be attached to the Form EXN161 and contain the information provided for in the Crim PR 17.20. Form EXN161 states that the grounds of appeal must:

- specify the date of arrest;[8]
- specify the date of the decision that is being appealed;[9]
- specify whether the appellant is in custody and if so where the appellant is detained, their prison number, date of birth and the date the appellant was remanded into custody;
- specify the issues raised in the court below;
- provide an explanation if the appellant is raising an issue not raised at the extradition hearing or seeking to adduce evidence which was not available at the extradition hearing;
- identify each ground of appeal on which the appellant relies, numbering them consecutively (if there is more than one) and concisely outlining each argument in support;[10]
- summarise the relevant facts;[11]
- identify any relevant authorities;
- identify any other document or information that the appellant

---

7   http://hmctsformfinder.justice.gov.uk/HMCTS/GetForm.do?court_forms_id=4734.
8   Crim PR 17.20(3)(a)(i).
9   Crim PR 17.20(3)(a)(ii).
10   Crim PR 17.20(3)(b).
11   Crim PR 17.20(3)(c).

thinks the court will need to decide the permission to appeal and the appeal, if the court grants permission;[12]

- include or attach a list of those on whom the appellant has served the notice of appeal and the date of service;[13]
- where an appellant is in custody, include an application for
  - bail pending appeal, or
  - a direction that an unrepresented appellant be produced for the hearing of the appeal.

11.22 Where the appeal is against the decision of the magistrates' court and the ground is that the court ought to have decided a question of fact or law at the extradition hearing differently, the notice must:

- identify that question;[14]
- explain what decision the magistrates' court should have made, and why;[15] and
- explain why the magistrates' court would have been required not to make the order under appeal, if that question had been decided differently.[16]

11.23 If the grounds of appeal are that there is an issue which was not raised at the extradition hearing or that there is evidence now available that was not before the appropriate judge at the extradition hearing then the appeal notice must also:

- identify that issue or evidence;[17]
- explain why the issue was not raised or the evidence not available at the extradition hearing;[18]
- explain why that issue or evidence would have resulted in the magistrates' court deciding a question differently at the extradition hearing;[19] and
- explain why, if the court had decided that question differently, the court would have been required not to make the order it made.[20]

11.24 The EXN161 states that the grounds of appeal, if drafted by counsel, must be signed by counsel with the name of counsel printed

---

12 Crim PR 17.20(3)(d).
13 Crim PR 17.20(2)(e).
14 Crim PR 17.20(6)(a)(i).
15 Crim PR 17.20(6)(a)(ii).
16 Crim PR 17.20(6)(a)(iii).
17 Crim PR 17.20(6)(b)(i).
18 Crim PR 17.20(6)(b)(ii).
19 Crim PR 17.20(6)(b)(iii).
20 Crim PR 17.20(6)(b)(iv).

underneath their signature. This does not appear to be a requirement of the Crim PR or Crim PD and it is also unclear if solicitors will have to comply with the same requirement if the grounds of appeal have been prepared by them.

Lodging and service of the leave to appeal application

11.25   The EXN161 and grounds of appeal must be served on the CPS and the NCA prior to it being lodged with the ACO[21] and a declaration of service must be completed on the form. It is best to serve these documents by fax (0203 357 0055/0056) or email (scd.extradition@cps.gsi.gov.uk – Manchester@nca.x.gsi.gov.uk) to ensure service the same day. When serving by fax, it is important to ensure that a 'transmission ok' receipt is received.

11.26   There is no need to serve any other document on the CPS or NCA as the grounds of appeal will identify the documents which the appellant thinks the court will need to decide the permission to appeal stage.

11.27   Once the bundles have been prepared they should then be taken to the Royal Courts of Justice on the Strand, London and lodged with the ACO. A directions map at the enquiries counter is available to help those unfamiliar with the court to navigate to the fees office and on to the ACO.

11.28   Before the appeal is lodged at the ACO, the fee must be paid at the fees office. The fee for lodging the application is £240. The fee can be paid in cash, by debit/credit card or by cheque made payable to 'HMCTS'.

11.29   On paying the fee, the EXN161 will be stamped to show the fee has been paid. A receipt will also be provided. The documents should then be taken to the ACO where the staff will issue the appeal and 'seal' the EXN161 by stamping it with the court seal and retain three copies of the bundles. The ACO can become very busy at certain times and in particular on a Friday afternoon. It is therefore important to allow plenty of time to lodge the appeal.

11.30   Once the EXN161 has been sealed it, together with the grounds of appeal, should be served upon the CPS and the NCA within the same seven-day period.[22]

---

21 Crim PR 17.20(2)(e).

22 Although there is no requirement for this, the authors believe it is best practice for this to be done, despite the unsealed EX161 and grounds of appeal having to be served prior to the appeal being issued by the ACO.

Lodging out of time

11.31 Unlike the previous appeal system, the amendments to the 2003 Act[23] allow for an out of time application for permission to appeal to be made. The Act now states that where a person gives notice of application for leave to appeal after the end of the permitted period, the High Court must not for that reason refuse to entertain the application if the person did everything reasonably possible to ensure that the notice was given as soon as it could be given. Reasons must be provided when an application for permission to appeal is lodged out of time. On receipt of the application, it will be sent to a single judge within 24 hours for a decision on whether the court has jurisdiction to hear the application. If the court refuses to grant an extension, it appears that there is no route of appeal against that decision.

Extension of time for service of Form EXN161

11.32 If an extension of time for service of the EXN161 is required, detailed reasons for the delay must be provided and attached to the grounds of appeal under a separate heading explaining what was done to ensure that the notice was served as soon as it could be.[24]

Amendments to the leave to appeal notice

11.33 An application for leave to appeal can be amended by serving an amended application on the High Court and the respondents by no later than ten business days after the service of the original appeal notice.[25] If the ten-business-day period has expired then the application for permission to appeal notice may not be amended without the permission of the court.[26] If the application to amend is made prior to permission to appeal being determined then the application will be determined without a hearing.[27]

---

23 EA 2003 s26(5) as inserted by Anti-social Behaviour, Crime and Policing Act 2014 s160(1)(c).
24 Crim PR 17.20(4)(a).
25 Crim PR 17.20(5)(a) and (b) and Crim PD 17B.18.
26 Crim PD 17B.18(i).
27 Crim PD 17B.18(ii).

Applying for leave to appeal in Part 2 cases

11.34   Under Part 2 of the Act it is the appropriate judge that sends the case to the Secretary of State for the Home Department (SSHD) who then has a two-month period in which to make the extradition order, starting on the day on which the case is sent to the SSHD.[28] Once the extradition order has been signed by the SSHD, the requested person has *14 days* in which to lodge the application for permission to appeal starting from the date he is informed of the SSHD's decision.

11.35   An appeal can be against either the decision of the appropriate judge or the SSHD or both.

11.36   The following documents should be put together in a bundle to be lodged at the High Court:

- Form EXN161 – appellant's notice – application for permission to appeal;
- grounds of appeal;
- extradition request;
- judgment of the appropriate judge;
- decision of the SSHD (if the decision has been made);
- any other documents relied upon (witness statements, expert reports, further information).

The appellant's notice (EXN161) and grounds of appeal are to take the same form as that outlined at paragraphs 11.18–11.24 above.

Lodging out of time

11.37   As with Part 1 appeals (see paragraph 11.31), EA 2003 (as amended) states that the High Court must not refuse to entertain the application where notice is given after the end of the permitted period if the person did everything reasonably possible to ensure that the notice was given as soon as it could be given.

11.38   The notes to Part 17.19 of the Criminal Procedure Rules 2014 go further and state that 'a defendant may apply out of time for permission to appeal to the High Court on human rights grounds against an order for extradition made by the Secretary of State.'[29]

---

28 See *Zaporozhchenko and Another v Westminster Magistrates' Court and Others* [2011] EWHC 34 (Admin).

29 Crim PR 17.20(4)(b).

Respondent's notice – Form EXN162

11.39 Rule 17.21 Crim PR imposes an obligation upon a party to file a respondent's notice if they wish to make representations to the High Court or if the court so directs. The respondent's notice must be served on the High Court, the appellant and any other person on whom the appellant served the appeal notice and must be served no more than *five business days*[30] after receipt of either:

- the appeal notice;
- an appellant's notice renewing an application for permission to appeal; or
- a direction by the High Court to serve a respondent's notice.

11.40 The respondent's notice should be completed using Form EXN162 which can be found at appendix K. Guidance for the completion of Form EXN162 can also be found on the ACO website.[31]

11.41 The respondent's notice must provide the information contained within Rule 17.21(4), namely:

- the date on which the respondent was served with, as appropriate –
  (i) the appeal notice;
  (ii) the appellant's notice renewing the application for permission to appeal;
  (iii) a direction to serve a respondent's notice;
- each ground of opposition on which the respondent relies, identifying the grounds of appeal to which each relates;
- summary of any relevant facts not already summarised in the appeal notice; and
- identification of any other document or material that the appellant thinks the court will need to decide the permission to appeal and the appeal, if the court grants permission.

11.42 Amendments to a respondent's notice cannot be made without permission of the court.[32]

---

30 Practitioners should note that on 15 July 2015, Sir Brian Leveson (President, QBD) directed that, until such time as the Criminal Procedure Rules are amended, respondents will be granted an automatic extension of 15 business days to submit a respondent's notice. Therefore, the time limit for lodging a respondent's notice will be 20 business days from the date of service/lodging of the application for permission to appeal.

31 http://hmctsformfinder.justice.gov.uk/HMCTS/GetForms.do?court_forms_category=administrative%20court.

32 Crim PD 17B.19(i).

Consideration of the application for permission to appeal

11.43　An application for permission to appeal will usually be considered on the papers without a hearing[33] by a single judge of the High Court. There may be occasions where leave to appeal is determined at an oral hearing. The court has the power to refuse or grant permission to appeal, or to give permission, but not on every ground identified in the appeal notice.

11.44　　The test applied to the permission stage is whether the ground(s) of appeal are 'reasonably arguable'.[34]

11.45　　There does not appear to be any requirement on the High Court to give reasons for its decision.

11.46　　If permission is granted then the court must give directions as are required for the preparation and hearing of the appeal.[35] In Part 2 cases, the court may direct that a case management hearing takes place (see paragraph 11.60).

Renewing an application for permission to appeal

11.47　If the decision to refuse to give permission to appeal is made at an oral hearing, there is no right to renew that application.[36]

11.48　　If the decision is made on the papers then the appellant may renew the application to the High Court to be determined by a single judge of the High Court[37] (other than by the judge who determined permission) or a Divisional Court.[38]

11.49　　The renewal notice must be in the prescribed format and explain the grounds for renewal. No fee applies to the lodging of a renewed application for permission to appeal.

11.50　　If the court decides to give permission to appeal, but not on every ground identified in the appeal notice, then any application to renew must specify which ground or grounds are renewed and explain the grounds for renewal.

33　Crim PR 17.17(1)(b)(i).
34　Crim PR 17.17(4)(b).
35　Crim PR 17.17(4)(c).
36　Crim PR 17.22(1), (2).
37　Crim PR 17.30(3)(a).
38　Crim PR 17.30(3)(b).

11.51 An application to renew is given by serving notice on the High Court, the respondent and the NCA in a Part 1 case or the High Court, CPS and SSHD in a Part 2 case. This must be done no later than five business days after service of the court's decision on the appellant.[39]

11.52 Crim PR 17.17 gives the High Court the power to extend or shorten the time limits specified for renewing an application for permission to appeal. This is likely to be applied to cases where the issue is suicide risk of the requested person.[40]

Permission granted – the appeal

11.53 Under EA 2003 s31 an appeal under Part 1 of the Act must begin to be heard within 40 days of the person's arrest.[41]

11.54 Appeals under Part 2 of the Act should begin within 76 days[42] after the later of:

- service of the appeal notice; or
- the day on which the SSHD informs the appellant of the SSHD's order, in a case in which –
  - the appeal is by the appellant against an order by the magistrate's court sending the case to the SSHD; and
  - the appeal notice is served before the SSHD decides whether the appellant should be extradited.

11.55 The above prescribed time limits for the hearing of appeals may be extended if the High Court believes it to be in the interests of justice to do so and the court may make such an order even if the time limit for the hearing of the appeal has expired.[43] The power to extend time may be exercised by a Lord Justice of Appeal, a single judge of the High Court, a Master of the Administrative Court or a nominated legal officer of the court.[44]

---

39 Crim PR 17.22(2).
40 In January 2013 the President of the Queen's Bench Division (PQBD) stated in *Wolkowicz v Polish Judicial Authority* [2013] EWHC 102 (Admin) that an appeal in a case where the risk of suicide is an issue should be heard within as short a timescale as practicable. He stated that such appeals should be listed for hearing within 2–3 weeks of the notice of appeal being lodged at the ACO.
41 Crim PR 17.23(1).
42 Crim PR 17.23(2).
43 Crim PD 17B.8.
44 Crim PD 17B.9.

11.56   An appeal may be determined by a single judge of the High Court or a Divisional Court.[45]

Date for hearing

11.57   The Listing Office is responsible for the listing of appeal hearings under the guidance of the judge with overall responsibility for supervision of extradition appeals.[46]

11.58   If a party disagrees with a time estimate given by the court for a hearing then they must, within five business days of the notification of the listing, inform the Listing Office and provide their time estimate.[47]

11.59   Regard will not usually be given to counsel's existing commitments.[48]

Case management conference

11.60   If the court so directs, a case management conference will be listed after leave to appeal has been granted.

11.61   The case management conference will be held before a master or deputy master of the Administrative Court. The purpose of the case management hearing is to provide effective management of the appeal to ensure that the appeal takes place on the date fixed for hearing. Five days before the case management conference the parties will be expected to send to the court office a document marked for the attention of the master providing the following information:

- a time estimate for the appeal hearing including delivery of the judgment;
- names of counsel and a list of dates to avoid for listing of the substantive appeal;
- a list of issues for the case management conference (if any);
- a list of the legal points to be taken at the appeal (together with any relevant authorities, with page references to passages relied on);
- a chronology of events;

---

45 Crim PR 17.30(4)(a).
46 Currently Lord Justice Aikens.
47 Crim PD 17B.14.
48 Crim PD 17B.13.

- a list of the essential documents for the advance reading of the court;
- the case for any further evidence to be adduced, having regard to the provisions set out in *The Szombathely City Court v Fenyvesi*;[49]
- a date for the exchange of evidence that the parties may be permitted to rely upon;
- a date for replies following exchange of evidence;
- a date for the parties to provide joint bundles;
- any further directions necessary for the appeal to proceed without delay that the master ought to consider.

11.62 The purpose of providing dates to avoid and a time estimate five days in advance of the case management conference is to enable the list office to fix a date for the appeal so that all parties at the conference have an opportunity to consider whether it allows sufficient time for the preparation of the appeal. If insufficient time has been set aside for the appeal hearing an application should be made at the case management conference for the date to be vacated and re-fixed. The reason that more time is required should be identified in the documents to be provided to the master ahead of the conference.

11.63 The court will expect the parties to the appeal to reach agreement (as far as is possible) as to the directions to be applied that are necessary to ensure that the appeal will be heard on the date fixed.

11.64 Case management conferences take place in open court and therefore only barristers or solicitors with higher rights of audience may appear. The case management conference will usually be listed to commence at 9.30 am.

Compliance with directions made by the High Court

11.65 It is important to comply with all directions made by the High Court (as with any court). Where a direction cannot be complied with, the court should be notified of the reasons why and an extension sought in a formal application by lodging form EX244 – application notice together with the relevant fee (see para 11.78).

11.66 Any application to vary directions should be made promptly before the deadline for compliance has passed in order to seek fur-

---

49 [2009] EWHC 231 (Admin).

ther directions. An application to vary directions attracts a fee and the application must:

- provide full and proper explanations as to why the current directions have not been complied with;
- set out the views of the other parties to the appeal; and
- include a draft order with the timetable for directions going forward.[50]

11.67   A failure to seek a variation in directions before the expiry of the deadline will generally result in the refusal of the application unless good reasons are shown.[51] It is therefore important to provide a detailed application setting out the reasons why the directions could not be complied with and saying why no application to vary was made prior to the expiry of the deadline. Practitioners' attention is specifically drawn to Crim PD 17F.2 and 17F.3 which states:

> 17F.2 Judges dealing with extradition appeals will seek full and proper explanations for any breaches of the rules and the provisions of this Practice Direction.
>
> 17F.3 If no good explanation can be given immediately by counsel or solicitors, the senior partner of the departmental head responsible is likely to be called to court to explain any failure to comply with a court order. Where counsel or solicitors fail to obey orders of the Court and are unable to provide proper and sufficient reasons for their disobedience they may anticipate the matter being formally referred to the President of the Queen's Bench Division with a recommendation that the counsel or solicitors involved be reported to their professional bodies.

11.68   Whenever corresponding with the ACO it is important to ensure that the case reference number is included so that court staff can identify the case more easily. Misspelt names can cause delays and result in misfiling. If documents are to be sent to the judge's clerk these should be copied to the extradition team by email: administrativecourtoffice.crimex@hmcts.gsi.gov.uk.

Applying to extend the representation order

11.69   The representation order covers the work of a solicitor and junior counsel. Applications to extend the representation order for a QC and junior, QC alone, translation of documents or the cost of an expert,

---

50 Crim PD 17D.7.
51 Crim PD 17D.8.

must be made in writing to the Administrative Court Office. Applications to extend representation orders are not subject to any court fee[52] and can be sent via email to administrativecourtoffice.crimex@hmcts.gsi.gov.uk .

11.70 The applications will be considered by a Lord Justice of Appeal, a single judge of the High Court, a master of the Administrative Court or a nominated Court Officer on the papers although he or she may order that the matter be dealt with at a case management conference. In Part 2 cases the applications should be included in the information to be provided to the master ahead of the case management conference so that the issue(s) can be determined at the conference.

Application to instruct a QC

11.71 An application can be made to extend the representation order to cover a QC and junior counsel or a QC alone. The application must include the following information:[53]

- the substantial novel or complex issues of law or fact in the case;
- why these may only be adequately presented by a Queen's Counsel;
- whether a Queen's Counsel has been instructed on behalf of the respondent;
- an explanation for any delay in making the request.

The application must be supported by an advice from junior or leading counsel.

Expert evidence

11.72 An application to extend the representation order to include the cost of obtaining expert evidence must include[54] (where applicable):

- confirmation that the evidence sought has not been considered in any previous appeals determined by the appellate courts;
- an explanation of why the new evidence was not called at the extradition hearing in WMC and what evidence can be produced to support that;

52 Crim PD 17B.27.
53 Crim PD 17C.3.
54 In accordance with Crim PD 17C.4.

- an explanation of why the new evidence would have resulted in the District Judge deciding a question at the extradition hearing differently and whether, if so, the District Judge would have been required to make a different order as to discharge of the requested person;
- an explanation of why the evidence was not raised when the case was being considered by the SSHD or information was available that was not available at the time;
- an explanation of why the new evidence would have resulted in the SSHD deciding a question differently, and why, had the question had been decided differently, the SSHD would not have ordered the person's extradition;
- an indication of when the need for the new evidence first became known;
- an explanation of any delay in making the request;
- an explanation of what relevant factual, as opposed to expert evidence, is being given by whom to create the factual basis for the expert's opinion;
- an explanation of why this particular area of expertise is relevant: for example, why a child psychologist should be appointed as opposed to a social worker;
- an indication of whether the requested person has capacity;
- a full breakdown of all costs involved including any VAT or other tax payable, including alternative quotes or explaining why none are available;
- a list of all previous extensions of the representation order and the approval of expenditure to date;
- a timetable for the production of the evidence and its anticipated effect on the time estimate and hearing date;
- an indication of the level of compliance to date with any directions order.

Expert status

11.73   Only experts that have direct personal experience of and proven expertise in the issue upon which a report is sought will be considered for expert status. In *Brazuks and Others v Prosecutor General's Office, Latvia*[55] Collins J provided guidance for expert reports and experts. He stated at para 42:

55 [2014] EWHC 1021 (Admin).

I should say a word about the experts' reports which have been put forward. No doubt it is helpful to identify the material available in reports on prison conditions in any requesting state. That material can then be produced to the court and any relevant matters referred to in support of any submissions. The views of an expert are not relevant and probably not admissible since it is for the judge to decide on the evidence produced whether there is a real risk of any material ill-treatment. Approval should not be given to pay such experts who have no direct personal experience of the conditions in a particular country. If they do have such experience and it is relevant, they can of course give evidence of what they have observed. They may also have knowledge of the economic situation or of any views expressed by government officials which may mean that any shortcomings will not be likely to be dealt with. Thus their knowledge of the existing situation and their added knowledge of the prospects of improvements may entitle them to put forward expert opinions. But if they do not have any such expertise, they will be doing no more than giving factual evidence.

11.74 The fact that the court has extended a representation order to include the costs of an expert does not necessarily mean the expert report will be admitted into evidence. The normal rules of having new evidence admitted on appeal apply (see paragraph 11.84).

Other disbursements

11.75 Other reasons for applying to extend the representation order could be to cover the cost of disbursements such as the translation of long documents. Such an application to the court will act as 'prior authority' but will not enable the solicitors to obtain an interim payment.

11.76 The application must:[56]

- explain the importance of the document for which a translation is being sought and the justification for obtaining it;
- explain the contents of the document and the issues those contents will address to assist the court in hearing the appeal;
- confirm that the evidence sought has not been considered in any previous appeals determined by the appellate courts;
- confirm that the evidence sought was not called at the extradition hearing;
- explain why the evidence sought would have resulted in the district judge deciding a question at the extradition hearing differently

56 Crim PD 17C.7.

and, if this were the case, whether the district judge would have been required to make a different order as to discharge the requested person;
- confirm that the new evidence was not raised when the case was being considered by the SSHD (Part 2 cases only);
- explain why the new evidence would have resulted in the SSHD deciding a question differently, and if the question had been decided differently, that the SSHD would not have ordered the person's extradition (Part 2 cases only);
- confirm when the need for the new evidence first became known;
- explain any delay in making the request;
- explain fully the evidential basis for incurring the expenditure;
- explain why the appellant cannot produce the evidence himself or herself in the form of a statement of truth;
- set out a full breakdown of all costs involved including any VAT or other tax payable, including alternative quotes or explaining why none are available;
- provide a list of all previous extensions of the representation order and the approval of expenditure to date.

Applications to adjourn

11.77   Once a date has been fixed, it can only be vacated on written application to the court. Any application to adjourn should be made on form EX244 and be accompanied by a signed witness statement. If the issue is relatively straightforward the witness statement can be contained within the EX244. The application must comply with Crim PD 17D.4 and must therefore explain the reasons why the application to vacate the hearing is being made and detail the views of the other parties to the appeal. A draft order must also be attached to the application notice setting out the orders sought.

11.78   A fee is applicable if the application to vacate is made within 14 days of the hearing date[57]. If the other party consents then a fee of £50 is due. If the other party does not consent, a fee of £155 is payable.

11.79   The application notice should be lodged with the ACO and served upon the CPS, or the CPS and Home Office for Part 2 matters.

11.80   An application to adjourn will normally be dealt with on the papers by a nominated court officer unless the papers are already with the

---

57 Crim PD 17D.4.

single judge or Divisional Court, in which case the decision will be made by the single judge or the presiding judge of the Divisional Court.

Applications to amend the appeal notice/grounds of appeal

11.81 An application to amend the appeal notice or grounds of appeal after permission has been granted will normally be dealt with at the hearing unless there is any risk that the proposed amendment may lead to the hearing being adjourned.[58]If the application to amend is likely to lead to the other party having to seek time to answer the proposed amendment, then the application to amend must be made as soon as practicable and in any event, well in advance of the appeal hearing. A failure to make the application as soon as possible may lead to a refusal to amend.

11.82 Practitioners must inform the court at the time the application to amend is made if the time estimate is likely to be affected by the proposed amendment[59] and must attempt to agree a revised time estimate with the other party no later than five business days after service of the application.[60]

11.83 Applications to amend the appeal notice and/or the grounds of appeal must be made using form EX244 and be accompanied by the relevant fee.

Introduction of new evidence

11.84 Strict rules apply to the introduction of new evidence being adduced on appeal. The introduction of fresh evidence was considered in *The Szombathely City Court v Fenyvesi*.[61]

11.85 The Divisional Court considered the provisions in EA 2003 s29(4), in particular where evidence was available on appeal that was not available at the extradition hearing. The court held that 'not available at the extradition hearing' was to be interpreted as evidence that either did not exist at the time of the extradition hearing, or that was

58 Crim PD 17B.18(iii).
59 Crim PD 17B.18(iv)(a).
60 Crim PD 17B.18(iv)(b).
61 [2009] EWHC 231 (Admin).

not at the disposal of the party wishing to adduce it and that he or she could not with reasonable diligence have produced.

11.86 Following the case of *Fenyvesi* a party wishing to adduce fresh evidence must submit a witness statement explaining why the evidence was not available at the extradition hearing.

11.87 When considering whether to admit fresh evidence the court must consider it to be decisive; in other words the court must be satisfied that the evidence would have resulted in the appropriate judge deciding the relevant question differently.

11.88 Appellants should not 'keep their powder dry' and adduce evidence on appeal or raise new issues that could have been presented before the appropriate judge at first instance. However, there is a material difference between seeking to adduce fresh evidence on appeal that could have been available before the appropriate judge and raising a new issue that was not argued at first instance. In *Hoholm v Government of Norway*[62] Stanley Burnton LJ held:

> ... it seems to me to be significant that section 104 distinguishes between a new issue and new evidence. I would therefore hold that where an issue was available to be raised by an appellant on the evidence adduced at the extradition hearing, she is in general, if not always, entitled to raise that issue on appeal to this Court, even though the issue was not raised at that hearing. In any event, I see no good reason why the Appellant should not be permitted to argue the issue before this Court. Extradition is an infringement of liberty, and while the Court is concerned to ensure that those who are the subject of conforming requests for extradition are lawfully extradited, the legal requirements for extradition are safeguards that must be observed.

11.89 It is therefore possible to raise an issue on appeal (such as dual criminality, validity of the warrant) that was not raised at the extradition hearing, provided no new evidence is to be adduced. However, practitioners should be aware of the opposing views proffered in *Khan v Government of the United States of America*[63] and *Koziel v Poland*[64] and take note of the ruling of Bean, J in *R (Soltysiak) v Judicial Authority of Poland*[65] in which he said:[66] 'I am also in no doubt that until or unless this issue is resolved authoritatively, possibly by a three judge Divisional Court or perhaps by a still higher court, *it is the duty of advocates to ensure that this court, when it is sought to raise a point of law*

---

62 [2009] EWHC 1513 (Admin).
63 [2010] EWHC 1127 (Admin).
64 [2011] EWHC 3781 (Admin).
65 [2011] EWHC 1338 (Admin).
66 At para 18.

not taken below, is made aware of both Hoholm *and* Khan' (emphasis added).

11.90 If new evidence is to be adduced then the criteria in *Fenyvesi* must be satisfied.

11.91 If a new issue and/or fresh evidence are to be raised on appeal that was not raised at the extradition hearing by previous legal representatives and if specific criticism of the previous legal representatives is being levelled, then the guidance set out in *Sondy v Crown Prosecution Service*[67] should be followed. Openshaw J stated:

> In my judgment, the practice commonly followed in the Court of Appeal Criminal Division should have been followed here; the appellant should have been formally invited to waive his privilege and, whether he did so or not, the lawyers should have been asked by the court to deal with the points made against them, having regard to whether privilege has been waived or not. If the appellant did not waive privilege, then of course an adverse inference could in any event be drawn against him.

Withdrawing the appeal

11.92 If the appellant wishes to withdraw an appeal, the solicitor must notify the High Court, other parties to the appeal and any other person on whom the appeal notice was served.[68]

11.93 When serving notice of withdrawal of the appeal on form EX244, a joint notice consenting to the dismissal of the appeal must be included (as set out overleaf) that sets out an agreement between the parties about costs. The fee for the application (if by consent) will be £50.

Applying to come off the record

11.94 It may sometimes be necessary for the solicitors instructed to withdraw from the case for professional reasons, for example if the client wishes to pursue an appeal against the advice of the solicitor.

---

67 [2010] EWHC 108 (Admin).
68 Crim PR 17.24(2).

IN THE HIGH COURT OF ENGLAND and WALES:
QUEEN'S BENCH DIVISION
ADMINISTRATIVE COURT   CASE NO

BETWEEN

THE REQUESTED PERSON

Appellant

v

THE REQUESTING STATE

Respondent

CONSENT ORDER

UPON CONSIDERATION OF THE DOCUMENTS LODGED BY
THE APPELLANT WITHDRAWING THE APPEAL

AND IT BEING DECLARED THAT NEITHER THE APPELLANT
NOR THE RESPONDENT IS A CHILD OR PATIENT

IT IS ORDERED THAT:

1. The appeal be dismissed

2. [The appellant be remanded in custody/remanded on bail pending his removal]

3. There be no order for costs save for a detailed assessment of the legally aided party's public funding certificate

---

11.95   Any application made to come off the record must be made at least seven business days before the hearing of the appeal.[69]

11.96   Crim PD 17D.3 states that an application to come off the record must be accompanied by a statement of truth and contain:

- proper and sufficient reasons why the solicitor wishes to come off record (without breaching client confidentiality);

69   Crim PD 17D.2.

- confirmation that the solicitor has complied with orders made by the High Court before the application to come off-record was made or an explanation as to why there has been non-compliance;
- confirmation that where the appellant is on bail, he or she has been advised of the time and date of the appeal hearing and the need to attend in person;
- identifying, where the appellant is in custody, the prison in which he or she is held, their prison number and date of birth.

11.97 Once submitted with the relevant fee, the application will be determined by a Lord Justice of Appeal, a single judge of the High Court, a master of the Administrative Court or a nominated legal officer of the court.

Preparing the appeal

Skeleton arguments

11.98 Skeleton arguments will normally be drafted by instructed counsel but should be considered (and amended where necessary, by agreement with counsel) by the solicitor before it is submitted. Skeleton arguments can be submitted electronically to administrativecourtlondon. skeletonarguments@hmcts.gsi.x.gov.uk

11.99 Crim PD 17E.1 sets out guidance as to the format of the skeleton argument. A skeleton argument must:

- not normally exceed 25 pages (excluding front sheets and back sheets) and be concise;
- be printed on A4 paper in not less than 12 point font and 1.5 line spacing;
- define the issues in the appeal;
- be set out in numbered paragraphs;
- be cross-referenced to any relevant document in the bundle;
- be self-contained and not incorporate by reference material from previous skeleton arguments;
- not include extensive quotations from documents or authorities.

11.100 Where skeleton arguments refer to an authority, they must also:

- state the proposition of law the authority demonstrates; and
- identify but not quote the parts of the authority that support the proposition.

If more than one authority is cited in support of a given proposition, the skeleton argument must state why.

11.101   A chronology of relevant events will be necessary in most appeals and should be incorporated into the skeleton argument.

11.102   If a skeleton argument has been submitted in support of the application for leave to appeal then it may be relied upon in the appeal upon notice being given to the court. Alternatively, a replacement skeleton argument may be lodged not less than 10 business days before the hearing of the appeal.[70]

11.103   Practitioners should take note that the court may refuse to hear submissions on a point if it is not included in the skeleton argument served within the prescribed time.[71]

Bundles

11.104   A joint bundle should be provided to the court that has been agreed between the parties. If the appeal is to be heard by a single judge two bundles should be provided to the court. If the case has been allocated to a Divisional Court, three bundles will be required.

11.105   Court rules state that the bundle should be paginated and indexed[72] and should include the following documents:

- a copy of the appellant's notice;
- a copy of any respondent's notice;
- a copy of any appellant's or respondent's skeleton argument;
- a copy of the order under appeal;
- a copy of any order made by the court in the exercise of its case management powers;
- any judgment of the court made in a previous appeal involving the party or parties which is relevant to the present proceedings.

11.106   Where the bundle of papers in the joint bundle exceeds more than 200 pages, the parties must agree a core appeal[73] bundle that must include the documents set out above at paragraph 11.105.

11.107   Authorities relied upon should also be included in the bundle. If there is a law report of the authority, that should be provided to the court as opposed to the transcript of judgment.

---

70 Crim PD 17E.6
71 Crim PD 17E.7
72 Crim PD 17E.9.
73 Crim PD 17E.10(g).

Role of the appellate court in proportionality cases

11.108 In determining the statutory provisions relating to an appeal (see below), the single question for the appellate court to answer is whether or not the appropriate judge made the wrong decision. Lord Neuberger in *Re B (A Child) (FC)*[74] set out at paras 93–94 the ways in which an appellate court might consider a trial judge's conclusions:

> 93. There is a danger in over-analysis, but I would add this. An appellate judge may conclude that the trial judge's conclusion on proportionality was (i) the only possible view, (ii) a view which she considers was right, (iii) a view on which she has doubts, but on balance considers was right, (iv) a view which she cannot say was right or wrong, (v) a view on which she has doubts, but on balance considers was wrong, (vi) a view which she considers was wrong, or (vii) a view which is unsupportable. The appeal must be dismissed if the appellate judge's view is in category (i) to (iv) and allowed if it is in category (vi) or (vii).

> 94. As to category (iv), there will be a number of cases where an appellate court may think that there is no right answer, in the sense that reasonable judges could differ in their conclusions. As with many evaluative assessments, cases raising an issue on proportionality will include those where the answer is in a grey area, as well as those where the answer is in a black or a white area. An appellate court is much less likely to conclude that category (iv) applies in cases where the trial judge's decision was not based on his assessment of the witnesses' reliability or likely future conduct. So far as category (v) is concerned, the appellate judge should think very carefully about the benefit the trial judge had in seeing the witnesses and hearing the evidence, which are factors whose significance depends on the particular case. However, if, after such anxious consideration, an appellate judge adheres to her view that the trial judge's decision was wrong, then I think that she should allow the appeal.

11.109 This approach was endorsed in an extradition context by the Lord Chief Justice in *Celinski*:[75]

> It is only if the court concludes that the decision was wrong, applying what Lord Neuberger said [in *Re B (A Child)*], that the appeal can be allowed. Findings of fact, especially if evidence has been heard, must ordinarily be respected. In answering the question whether the district judge, in the light of those findings of fact, was wrong to decide that extradition was or was not proportionate, the focus must be on the outcome that is on the decision itself. Although the district judge's

---

74 [2013] UKSC 33.
75 At para 23.

reasons for the proportionality decision must be considered with care, errors and omissions do not of themselves necessarily show that the decision on proportionality itself was wrong.

11.110 The LCJ reiterated that findings of fact, especially if live evidence has been heard and evaluated by the appropriate judge, should ordinarily be respected. This is in keeping with the dictum of Lord Neuberger in *Re B (A Child)*.

11.111 Therefore, the appellate court should not overturn the decision of the appropriate judge 'simply because it takes a different view overall of the value-judgment that the District Judge has made or even the weight that he has attached to one or more individual factors which he took into account in reaching that overall value-judgment.'[76] If fresh evidence is admitted into evidence on appeal, then the appellate court may have to conduct the balancing exercise itself so as to determine whether it would have altered the appropriate judge's decision. Note however the comments of the Divisional Court in *Belbin* in which the court refused to admit fresh evidence as it would not have resulted in the appropriate judge deciding the question differently.[77] Any fresh evidence submitted must be decisive (see paragraph 11.87 above).

11.112 At the time of publication it is a moot point as to whether the above approach is applicable to all appeals under the EA 2003, or whether it is just restricted to considerations of proportionality.

Court's powers on appeal in Part 1 cases

11.113 On appeal under section 26 the High Court may either allow or dismiss the appeal. The court can only allow the appeal if the conditions in section 27(3) or (4) are satisfied.

11.114 The conditions in section 27(3) are that:

(a) the appropriate judge ought to have decided a question before him at the extradition hearing differently;

(b) if he had decided the question in the way he ought to have done, he would have been required to order the person's discharge.

11.115 The conditions in section 27(4) are that:

(a) an issue is raised that was not raised at the extradition hearing or evidence is available that was not available at the extradition hearing;

---

76 *Belbin v The Regional Court in Lille, France* [2015] EWHC 149 (Admin) at para 66.
77 At para 70.

(b) the issue or evidence would have resulted in the appropriate judge deciding a question before him at the extradition hearing differently;

(c) if he had decided the question in that way, he would have been required to order the person's discharge.

11.116 On allowing the appeal the court must order the person's discharge and quash the order for his or her extradition.[78]

Appeal against discharge at extradition hearing

11.117 If the judicial authority has appealed the decision of the appropriate judge to discharge the requested person then the appeal is brought under section 28. On appeal under section 28 the High Court may either allow the appeal or dismiss it. Section 29 subsections (3) and (4) set out the powers of the court on appeal.

11.118 If the appeal is allowed the court must quash the order discharging the requested person and remit the case back to the judge, directing the judge to proceed, as he or she would have been required to had he or she decided the relevant question differently at the extradition hearing.[79]

Court's powers on appeal in Part 2 cases

11.119 On appeal under section 103 (appeal against the decision of the appropriate judge) the court may:

- allow the appeal;
- direct the judge to decide again a question (or questions) which he or she decided at the extradition hearing; or
- dismiss the appeal.[80]

11.120 The court may only allow the appeal if the conditions in section 104(3) or subsection (4) are satisfied. The conditions in subsection (3) are:

- the judge ought to have decided a question before him or her at the extradition hearing differently;
- if the judge had decided the question in the way he or she ought

---

78 EA 2003 s27(5).
79 EA 2003 s29(5)(a)–(c).
80 EA 2003 s104(1)(a)–(c).

to have done, he or she would have been required to order the person's discharge.

11.121   The conditions in subsection (4) are:

- an issue is raised that was not raised at the extradition hearing or evidence is available that was not available at the extradition hearing;
- the issue or evidence would have resulted in the judge deciding a question before him or her at the extradition hearing differently;
- if the judge had decided the question in that way, he or she would have been required to order the person's discharge.

11.122   If the court allows the appeal then it must make an order for the person's discharge and quash the order for his or her extradition.[81]

11.123   If the court directs the judge to decide again a question (or questions) which he decided at the extradition hearing, then the case will be remitted back to the appropriate judge to consider the case again on the point remitted. If the judge comes to a different decision on any question that is the subject of a direction under EA 2003 s104(1)(b) he must order the person's discharge.[82] If the judge comes to the same decision as he did at the extradition hearing on the question that is (or all the questions that are) the subject of a direction under EA 2003 s104(1)(b) the appeal must be taken to have been dismissed by a decision of the High Court.[83]

Appeal against discharge at extradition hearing

11.124   On appeal under section 105 the High Court may allow the appeal, direct the judge to decide the relevant question again or dismiss the appeal.[84] The court may allow the appeal only if the conditions in subsection (4) or the conditions in subsection (5) are satisfied.

11.125   If the appeal is allowed the court must quash the order discharging the person; remit the case to the judge; and direct the judge to proceed as he or she would have been required to do if he or she had decided the relevant question differently at the extradition hearing.

11.126   If the court makes a direction that the judge is to decide the relevant question again and the judge subsequently decides the relevant

---

81   EA 2003 s104(5).
82   EA 2003 s104(6).
83   EA 2003 s104(7).
84   EA 2003 s106(1)(a)–(c).

question differently he or she must proceed, as he or she would have been required to do had he or she decided that question differently at the extradition hearing. If the court makes a direction that the judge is to decide the relevant question again and the judge does not subsequently decide the relevant question differently, the appeal must be taken to have been dismissed by a decision of the High Court.

Appeal against decision of the SSHD to order extradition

11.127 The requested person may also appeal against the decision of the SSHD to order extradition and the category 2 territory can appeal the decision of the SSHD to discharge the person from the extradition request.

11.128   Under section 109(1) the High Court may either allow the requested persons appeal or dismiss the appeal

11.129   The court may allow the appeal only if the conditions in section 109(3) or the conditions in subsection (4) are satisfied.

11.130   The conditions in subsection (3) are that:

- the SSHD ought to have decided a question before her differently;
- if the SSHD had decided the question in the way she ought to have done, she would not have ordered the person's extradition.

11.131 The conditions in subsection (4) are that:

- an issue is raised that was not raised when the case was being considered by the SSHD or information is available that was not available at that time;
- the issue or information would have resulted in the SSHD deciding a question before her differently;
- had the SSHD decided the question in that way, she would not have ordered the person's extradition.

11.132 If the court allows the appeal it must order the person's discharge and quash the order for extradition.[85]

11.133   The same conditions apply to an appeal against the decision of the SSHD under section 110 to order the person's discharge. If the appeal is allowed against the decision to discharge the person the

---

85 EA 2003 s109(5).

court must quash the order discharging the person and order the person's extradition.[86]

Reserved judgments

11.134   In many cases, the court will make its decision at the conclusion of the hearing (known as an *ex tempore* judgment). In other cases, judgment will be reserved and handed down at a later date that will be notified to the parties. The parties to the appeal will receive a draft copy of the judgment about a week before it is due to be handed down. The parties must provide any amendments to the judgment by a specified date and nil returns[87] will be required. It is important to note that draft copies of the judgment will be embargoed and disclosure of its content could constitute a contempt of court. This means that the client cannot be informed of the decision unless express provision is given by the court.

11.135   Attendance is not usually required at the handing down of judgment.

11.136   Once the court has adjourned for judgment, no further submissions or evidence should be submitted without the consent of the court. In *Ilia v Appeal Court in Athens, Greece*,[88] Aikens LJ held at para 15:

> We appreciate that the circumstances of this case are unusual, but we strongly deprecate the practice adopted by the appellant and her advisers in this case …of serving further evidence and submissions after the hearing has been completed, without asking the court whether it wished or permitted such further evidence to be adduced. When a hearing has been concluded, unless there is a particular matter that has been left outstanding, that must be the end of submitting further materials or observations to the court, unless the court specifically asks for, or agrees to accept, further submissions.

11.137   Practitioners should therefore enquire with the court whether it wishes to receive further submissions and/or evidence should the need to serve arise and should not just serve the additional submissions and/or evidence without the court's agreement. If the court invites further submissions they should be sent to the judge via the

---

86   EA 2003 s111(5).
87   A reply of zero to a request for a quantified reply.
88   [2015] EWHC 547 (Admin).

ACO using the administrativecourtoffice.crimex@hmcts.gsi.x.gsi.gov.uk email address.

Appeals to the Supreme Court

11.138 If permission to appeal is refused following an oral renewal hearing, that is the end of the appeal process and there is no possibility of applying to the court to certify a point of law of general public importance.

11.139   In order to appeal to the Supreme Court, the High Court must have certified that there is a point of law of general public importance involved in the decision and it must appear to the court granting leave that the point is one that ought to be considered by the Supreme Court.[89]

11.140   An application to certify a point of law must be made within *14 days* starting with the day on which the High Court makes its decision on the appeal.[90] Such an application can be made orally after judgment has been handed down but where an application is made orally, there has to be an application in writing filed with the court. The usual course is for an application to certify to be made in writing within the permitted period and then dealt with on the papers. Only in exceptional circumstances would the court agree to an oral hearing to determine certification. However, the decision will always be pronounced in open court (no attendance required) so there is no confusion as to when time runs from for removal/appeal to the Supreme Court.

11.141   A refusal to certify a point of law of general public importance does not make the High Court's decision final or abridge the 14-day period.[91] Theoretically, it would therefore be possible to submit additional points of law for certification, provided that such application was made within the permitted period.

11.142   If the High Court certifies that there is a point of law of general public importance it can then also grant or refuse leave to appeal. If the High Court refuses leave to appeal then an application for leave can be made to the Supreme Court within 14 days starting with the

---

89 EA 2003 s114(4).

90 EA 2003 s114(5).

91 *Ownes v City of Westminster Magistrates' Court and Others* [2009] EWHC 1343 (Admin) at paras 31 and 32.

day on which the High Court refuses to grant leave.[92] It is rare for the High Court to grant leave to appeal to the Supreme Court.

11.143   The Supreme Court has no power to grant a representation order. If a point of law of general public importance is certified, an application for a representation order to be extended to cover an application to the Supreme Court for leave to appeal should be made at the time of certification.

Making the application to certify a point of law

11.144   A formal application must be submitted (form EX244) with the fee of £155. It is usual for counsel to draft the application to certify and for it to be attached to the application notice.

11.145   Although the application must be lodged and served within 14 days, there is no time limit within which the application must be determined by the High Court.

11.146   If leave is granted by the High Court then the appeal must be lodged with the Supreme Court within 28 days of the date on which the High Court granted leave.[93]

11.147   If leave to appeal is granted by the Supreme Court the appeal must also be lodged with them within 28 days of leave being granted.

11.148   The Supreme Court has strict rules and Practice Directions relating to appeals brought before it and the reader is referred to the Supreme Court website for further information.[94]

11.149   The Supreme Court has the power to allow an appeal, dismiss an appeal or remit[95] the matter back to the appropriate judge.[96]

Re-opening the appeal

11.150   An application to re-open an appeal must be referred to the court that determined the appeal. Applications are made in accordance with

---

92   EA 2003 s114(6).
93   EA 2003 s114(7).
94   www.supremecourt.gov.uk/procedures/index.html.
95   In *Norris v Government of the United States of America* [2008] UKHL 16, their Lordships stated at para 110: 'we have no doubt that the House has an inherent power to remit determination of an issue to an inferior tribunal where the interests of justice so require, and that is a power which nothing in the 2003 Act purports to abrogate.'
96   EA 2003 s115(7).

Crim PR 17.27. A party wishing to apply for permission to re-open an appeal must do so in writing, as soon as practicable after becoming aware of the grounds for doing so. The application must specify the decision which the party wishes to re-open and give reasons why:

- it is necessary for the court to reopen that decision in order to avoid real injustice;
- the circumstances are exceptional and make it appropriate to reopen the decision; and
- there is no alternative effective remedy.

11.151 Each party must have an opportunity to make representations before the court determines permission to re-open an appeal.

Judge informed after extradition hearing or order that the person is charged with offence in UK

11.152 The Anti-social Behaviour, Crime and Policing Act 2014 inserts a new section 36A in Part 1 of the Act and section 118A in Part 2 of the Act.

11.153 If the requested person is charged with an offence in the United Kingdom after an order for extradition has been made, but before removal is effected, then on application, the appropriate judge *must* order the extradition not to be carried out until:

- the charge is disposed of;
- the charge is withdrawn;
- proceedings in respect of the charge are discontinued; or
- an order is made for the charge to lie on the file.

11.154 If the requested person has appealed the decision of the appropriate judge to order extradition then the application is made to the High Court.[97] If a requested person has been charged with an offence in the United Kingdom after the High Court's decision to dismiss the application for permission/appeal has become final, but before removal takes place, then the application is made to the appropriate judge.

---

97 Section 36A(4) (Part 1); s118A(4) (Part 2).

Judge informed after extradition hearing or order that person is serving a sentence in the UK

11.155   Section 36B was inserted by the Anti-social Behaviour, Crime and Policing Act 2014 to deal with cases where a person has been sentenced to a term of imprisonment after an extradition order has been made but who has yet to be removed.

11.156   On being informed of such, the appropriate judge (or High Court if the matter is on appeal) *may* order that the extradition is not carried out until the person is released from detention (on licence or otherwise).

Extradition (or not) following appeal

11.157   Practitioners should familiarise themselves with the provisions in the Act that deal with extradition following appeal. It is not unusual for the authorities to fail to remove the requested person within the statutory timeframe and in such situations a judge must discharge the requested person unless reasonable cause can be shown for the delay. Practitioners should therefore diarise the date by which their client should be extradited and if the deadline is missed (and no application has been made to extend the time for removal) then an application for discharge should be made without delay.

11.158   EA 2003 s36 (section 118 for Part 2 cases) provides the basis for such an application to be made and also allows the judicial authority an opportunity to agree a later starting date for removal than that set out in the legislation.

11.159   Applications for discharge must be made in accordance with the Criminal Procedure Rules that state that the application must be in writing[98] and served upon the court officer[99] and the prosecutor.[100] The application must explain the grounds on which it is made.[101] The hearing of the application should be listed as soon as practicable and in any event no later than the second business day after the application has been served.[102]

11.160   Section 36(3) sets out the 'required period' within which a requested person is to be extradited:

98 Crim PR 17.16(2)(a).
99 Crim PR 17.16(2)(a)(i).
100 Crim PR 17.16(2)(a)(ii).
101 Crim PR 17.16(2)(b).
102 Crim PR 17.16(2)(c).

(a) 10 days starting with the day on which the decision of the relevant court on the appeal becomes final or proceedings on the appeal are discontinued, or

(b) if the relevant court and the authority which issued the Part 1 warrant agree a later date, ten days starting with the later date.

11.161 Where section 36(3) is not complied with, section 36(8) provides a mechanism for the requested person's discharge:

If sub-section (2) is not complied with, and the person applies to the appropriate judge to be discharged, the judge must order his discharge, unless reasonable cause is shown for the delay.

11.162 The reference in section 36(8) to 'appropriate judge' means a judge sitting at Westminster Magistrates' Court. Therefore, despite the High Court having been seized of the appeal, the section 36(8) application for discharge is dealt with at the magistrates' court.

11.163 Applications for the required period to be extended are made 'ex parte' by the NCA and the Administrative Court (if there have been appeal proceedings). The ten-day period then starts on a date nominated by the NCA and agreed by the court. The defence do not have any part to play in this application process.

11.164 The Divisional Court in *Netecza v The Governor of Holloway Prison, CPS and NCA*[103] held that when the required period of ten days had expired, there was no statutory basis upon which the NCA could apply for a later date of surrender. In other words, it held that the required period cannot be revived once it has expired. This would prevent the NCA circumventing the provisions that allow the requested person to apply for discharge by simply making an ex parte application to the court to agree a later date of surrender.

11.165 Later on in 2014, a Divisional Court was constituted with three judges to reconsider the decision in *Netecza*. In *Desai v City of Westminster Magistrates' Court*[104] Laws LJ (with whom Ouseley LJ and Simon J agreed) held that the conclusion in *Netecza* was 'erroneous'. Ouseley LJ stated:

I would only add that in the light of a conclusion that *Netecza* was wrongly decided, the NCA should nonetheless not lessen their current efforts to obtain agreement under s36(3)(b) for a new 10 day period before the expiry of the previous one.

---

103 [2014] EWHC 2098 (Admin).
104 [2014] EWHC 4631 (Admin).

Reasonable cause for delay?

11.166   If an application under section 36(8) is made, the appropriate judge must discharge unless 'reasonable cause' is shown for the delay.

11.167   An administrative error[105] can amount to a reasonable cause as can negligence,[106] but not in all cases. Each case will turn on its own facts. The seriousness of the offence is not a factor the appropriate judge is entitled to take into account when determining whether reasonable cause has been shown.

11.168   Judicial review is the preferred way of challenging a decision of the appropriate judge not to discharge rather than habeas corpus, unless the requested person is remanded in custody. However, since 6 April 2015, the Civil Procedure Rules covering writs of habeas corpus changed[107] and, like applications for judicial review, a paper permission stage has been added. In practice, there will be little difference whether the challenge is by way of judicial review or by applying for a writ of habeas corpus.

Application to the European Court of Human Rights for rule 39 interim measures

11.169   On exhaustion of all domestic avenues of appeal, an appellant can apply to the ECtHR under rule 39 of the Rules of Court. The ECtHR will only grant rule 39 relief in exceptional circumstances. In 2014, 833 applications for rule 39 relief were made from the United Kingdom and only four of these applications were granted.[108] If an application is granted, the ECtHR will issue interim measures against the United Kingdom against the removal of the person until the ECtHR directs otherwise.

11.170   The ECtHR will only impose interim measures where, having reviewed all the relevant information, it considers that the applicant

---

105   *Owens* [2009] EWHC 1343 (Admin) at para 50.
106   In *Desai* [2014] EWHC 4631 (Admin), Laws, LJ stated that 'Administrative error may be covered and in my judgment may, I emphasise the word may, encompass cases where there has been negligence: not, of course, any negligence.'
107   Schedule 2 to Civil Procedure (Amendment No 8) Rules 2014 inserted a new Part 87 into the Civil Procedure Rules.
108   Figures provided by the ECtHR website: www.echr.coe.int/Documents/Stats_art_39_01_ENG.pdf.

faces a real risk of serious, irreversible harm if the measure is not applied.

11.171 Any application for a rule 39 interim measure must state reasons and, in particular, must specify in detail the grounds on which the applicant's particular fears are based, the nature of the alleged risks and the Convention provisions that are alleged to have been violated or will be violated if the measures are not imposed.

11.172 The application must be accompanied by the final decision of the domestic court (if available).

11.173 The expected date and time of removal must be provided in the application together with the applicant's place of detention, if in custody. If the final decision of the court is imminent and there is a risk of immediate removal, an application for rule 39 interim measures can be made without the need to await the final decision of the domestic court, but the application must indicate that the request is subject to an adverse decision of the domestic court.

11.174 The ECtHR recommends that an application for rule 39 interim measures should be sent by fax and all requests should be marked in bold on the face of the request:

> **Rule 39 – Urgent**
> **Person to contact (name and contact details)**
> **Date and time of removal and destination**

11.175 The ECtHR has a dedicated fax number for sending requests for rule 39 interim measures: + 33 (0)3 88 41 39 00.[109]

11.176 Applications are only received between Monday to Friday from 8 am to 4.30 pm.[110] Requests sent after 4.30 pm will normally be dealt with the next working day.

11.177 The result of the application will be communicated to the parties relatively quickly and, if such application is refused, there are no further steps that can be taken to prevent removal unless a supervening event occurs.

---

109 Correct as of 31 May 2015. Those wishing to apply for rule 39 interim measures from the ECtHR should check the court website for up-to-date contact information: www.echr.coe.int/ECHR.

110 The times given are local time (GMT+1).

CHAPTER 12

Ancillary matters

Introduction

12.1　This chapter seeks to deal with matters that are generally outside the scope of EA 2003, but nonetheless are matters that practitioners need to be aware of when conducting (and concluding) extradition proceedings.

Compromising the extradition request

12.2　As the preceding pages show, resisting extradition is notoriously difficult. Very often a requested person will be more likely to avoid extradition by attempting to persuade the requesting state to withdraw the request for extradition. In order to do this, it will be necessary to secure the assistance of a lawyer in the requesting state. This lawyer can then apply to the court for the case to be dealt with without the requested person having to return. For example on an 'accusation warrant' it may be possible for the requested person to plead guilty and be sentenced to a non-custodial sentence in his or her absence. In a conviction case, it may be possible for a lawyer in the requesting state to apply to the court to suspend or defer a sentence of imprisonment.

12.3　A lawyer in the requesting state will not be funded by the representation order: it is very often the requested person or his or her family who fund this. Very occasionally lawyers may agree to carry out the work on a *pro bono* basis, particularly where the requested person is a former client.

12.4　Practitioners may sometimes be asked to assist in finding a lawyer in the requesting state. Given the likelihood of language difficulties, it is unlikely that a lawyer in this country will be able to offer any real help unless he or she has had previous dealings with a lawyer in the issuing state. It is therefore worth retaining details of those lawyers who have been effective in securing the withdrawal of a warrant for future use.

12.5　The court is often reluctant to adjourn extradition proceedings while attempts are being made to compromise a warrant. In order to persuade the court to adjourn, the defence will have to demonstrate that the attempt to compromise is at an advanced stage and stands a chance of success. Evidence from the lawyer instructed in the requesting state will assist such an application.

Temporary transfer

12.6   Section 21B of the Act was inserted by section 159 of the Anti-social Behaviour, Crime and Policing Act 2014 and provides a mechanism, at the request of the judicial authority[1] or requested person,[2] for either temporary transfer to the requesting territory or arrangements to be made for discussions with investigators/prosecutors from the requesting territory. It applies only to Part 1 cases and those who are accused within the meaning of section 2(3) of the Act.

12.7   Section 21B can be invoked at any time before or in the extradition hearing.[3] A request is made to the appropriate judge by either the judicial authority or the requested person.

12.8   If such a request is made then the appropriate judge must order the extradition proceedings to be adjourned if he or she thinks it necessary to do so to enable the judicial authority or requested person to consider whether to consent to the request.[4] However, an adjournment must not be for more than seven days.

12.9   Once consent is given, the appropriate judge must make whatever orders and directions are appropriate to give effect to the request.[5] The judge must also adjourn the extradition proceedings for however long seems necessary to enable the orders and directions to be carried out.[6]

12.10   If a request is made before the extradition hearing has been fixed then the proceedings will be adjourned and when they resume, the permitted period for fixing the date of the hearing is extended by the same number of days for which the extradition proceedings have been adjourned.[7]

12.11   A requested person cannot make a further request if the request is withdrawn or the judicial authority does not consent.[8] Furthermore, a requested person cannot make a request if the judicial authority has made a counter-request that has been dealt with.[9]

1 EA 2003 s21B(2).
2 EA 2003 s21B(3).
3 EA 2003 s21B(1)(b).
4 EA 2003 s21B(4).
5 EA 2003 s21B(5)(a).
6 EA 2003 s21B(5)(b).
7 EA 2003 s21B(9).
8 EA 2003 s21B(8).
9 EA 2003 s21B(7).

'Iron letters'

12.12   Some jurisdictions will withdraw an extradition request on an application by the requested person to a court upon payment of a security to guarantee the requested person's return. This is known as an 'iron letter'. Although it can result in the withdrawal of the extradition request it requires the requested person to appear voluntarily at the court in the requesting state when summoned to appear (unlike the scenarios at paragraph 12.2). Arranging for an iron letter to be issued will require close liaison with a lawyer in the requesting state – it will only be issued after a bail security has been deposited in the requesting state. After this has been paid in, the extradition request will be withdrawn resulting in the discharge of the requested person in the United Kingdom.

Transfer of prisoners

12.13   It is, in some cases, possible for a sentence to be transferred across jurisdictions. Where, for example, a British person is serving a sentence of imprisonment in another state, the Repatriation of Prisoners Act 1984 (RPA 1984) will in some cases allow that person to be repatriated to complete that sentence in the United Kingdom. Using these provisions, it is possible to transfer a sentence of a requested person prior to his or her extradition, thus obviating the need for return.

12.14   Currently there are significant practical difficulties involved in negotiating such a transfer of a sentence; however, with increasing judicial co-operation between EU member states it is anticipated that this alternative to extradition will become more common. It should be noted that Article 4(6) of the Framework Decision provides an optional bar to extradition 'where the requested person is staying in, or is a national or a resident of the executing member state and that state undertakes to execute the sentence or detention order in accordance with its domestic law'. The United Kingdom has not however implemented this bar.

12.15   RPA 1984 s1(1) sets out the circumstances in which a transfer can take place as follows:

>   (a) the United Kingdom is a party to international arrangements providing for the transfer between the United Kingdom and a country or territory outside the British Islands of persons [...]; and

(b) the relevant Minister and the appropriate authority of that country or territory have each agreed to the transfer under those arrangements of a particular person (in this Act referred to as 'the prisoner'); and

(c) the prisoner has consented to being transferred in accordance with those arrangements.

12.16 The international arrangements referred to under RPA 1984 s1(1)(a) are as follows:

- Council of Europe Convention on the Transfer of Sentenced Persons and the Additional Protocol;[10]
- Commonwealth Scheme for the Transfer of Convicted Offenders;
- bilateral agreements;
- EU Framework Decision 2008/909/JHA. This replaced the Europe Convention referred to above in relation to the repatriation of prisoners between EU member states from 5 December 2011.

12.17 EU Framework Decision 2008/909/JHA aims to facilitate the transfer of prisoners across EU member states[11] and those representing requested persons facing a custodial sentence should, in appropriate cases, make efforts for a sentence to be transferred to this country. While RPA 1984 envisages the transfer of British nationals, the Framework Decision expands the scope of those who can be transferred to residents as well.[12] This will inevitably require the assistance of a lawyer in the requesting state, along with negotiations with 'the relevant minister' as set out in RPA 1984 s1(1)(b), ie the Secretary of State for Justice. Requests for transfer are dealt with by the Cross Border Transfer Section of the National Offender Management Service (NOMS), an executive agency of the Ministry of Justice.

EU measures in the field of Justice and Home Affairs

12.18 Whilst the United Kingdom has the right to opt out of EU measures in the field of Justice and Home Affairs, there are certain measures that do apply, including of course the EAW. It is important for those practising in this area to have an awareness of the measures which

---

10 ETS 112.
11 Poland has a five-year derogation from 6 December 2011.
12 Article 4(1).

do apply and the particular way in which cases in which a person's rights under the measures are affected can be litigated.

12.19 Those measures affecting defence rights and to which the United Kingdom has opted in include:

- Directive of the European Parliament and of the Council on the right to interpretation and translation in criminal proceedings;[13]
- Directive of the European Parliament and of the Council on the right to information in criminal proceedings;[14]
- Mutual recognition of pre-trial supervision orders (the European Supervision Order).[15]

12.20 These measures are included in the appendices (see appendices L, M and N). Lawyers working in this area should also be familiar with the Charter of Fundamental Rights of the European Union[16] which protects rights also set out in the European Convention on Human Rights but in some respects goes further. See for example Article 49 of the Charter in which proportionality of sentence is articulated as a right under the principle of legality. Other measures to which the United Kingdom has opted in in the field of Justice and Home Affairs include those covering the following areas:

- taking account of previous criminal convictions;[17]
- transfer of prisoners – mutual recognition of judgments imposing a custodial sentence;[18]
- exchange of information on criminal records (ECRIS);[19]
- Schengen Information System (SIS II).[20]

12.21 Where a requested person's case raises a question of interpretation of a matter of EU law, the court can refer the matter to the Court of Justice of the European Union (CJEU) for a 'preliminary ruling'. For further information, see the excellent free online training module entitled *A Guide to the Court of Justice of the EU* available on the Fair Trials website.[21]

---

13 2010/64/EU.
14 2012/13/EU.
15 Framework Decision 2009/829/JHA.
16 2010/C 83/02.
17 Framework Decision 2008/675/JHA.
18 Framework Decision 2008/909/JHA.
19 Framework Decision 2009/315/JHA and Council Decision 2009/316/JHA.
20 Council Decision 2007/533/JHA.
21 www.fairtrials.org/publications/a-guide-to-the-court-of-justice-of-the-eu/.

Funding and billing

12.22   Where a case is privately funded, for all cases commencing after 1 October 2012, it will be possible to obtain an order for costs from central funds if the requested person is discharged; but costs will be capped at legal aid rates.[22]

12.23   All extradition cases conducted in the magistrates' court that are the subject of public funding are to be submitted for taxation to the Legal Aid Agency within three months of conclusion. A CRM7 must be completed for all cases and lodged with the file of papers. If a certificate for counsel has been granted in the proceedings then counsel's claim for costs must be completed on a CRM8 and submitted at the same time as the CRM7.

12.24   Given that the claim will be for a non-standard fee, it is possible to apply for an uplift in costs.[23] An enhancement to the hourly rate will be allowed if:

- the work was done with exceptional competence, skill or expertise; or
- the work was done with exceptional dispatch; or
- the case involved exceptional circumstances or complexity.

12.25   In deciding whether to grant an enhancement in fees, and in determining the appropriate percentage enhancement, the LAA will have regard to:

- the degree of responsibility;
- the care, speed and economy with which the case was prepared;
- the novelty, weight and complexity of the case.

12.26   The percentage enhancement is capped at 100 per cent, except where proceedings relate to serious or complex fraud, where the relevant hourly rate will not be enhanced by more than 200 per cent.

12.27   If applying for an enhancement, a covering letter stating why the case meets the above criteria should be sent to the LAA when the claim is submitted.

12.28   Cases that have concluded before the Administrative Court must be submitted for taxation to the Senior Courts Cost Office (SCCO) at the Royal Courts of Justice (DX 44454 Strand). It is usual for a bill of costs to be drafted by an experienced costs draftsman. The bill of

---

22   Schedule 7 to the Legal Aid, Sentencing and Punishment of Offenders Act 2012.
23   Criminal Contract Specification Part B para 10.100.

costs, representation order and disbursement invoices are the only documents that need to be sent to the SCCO.

12.29   Again, an uplift can be applied to the solicitor's costs. Counsel instructed in these cases are able to submit their bills directly to the SCCO and need not submit them at the same time as the solicitor submits his or her bill.

12.30   Publicly funded judicial review proceedings will be funded under a civil legal aid certificate. Firms without a civil legal aid contract but holding a 2010 Standard Crime Contract are entitled to apply for community legal services certificates for this work: judicial review and habeas corpus are classified as 'associated Civil Work carried out under the provisions governing civil legal aid in Part 1 of the Act [LASPO]'.[24]

12.31   Practitioners must ensure that they adhere to the Funding Code criteria as set out on the LAA website. Applications should be made using forms CIV APP1 and the relevant means form (usually CIV MEANS 1 or 2) and sent to the regional LAA office. An advice from counsel setting out the merits of the case will usually be required. It can take many weeks for such applications to be processed. If the application is urgent, the form CIV APP 6 should be faxed or emailed to the Special Cases Unit of the Legal Aid Agency, currently based in Brighton.

12.32   The more detailed CIV APP1 must be submitted to the regional office within five working days of the grant of a certificate. A certificate will then be issued that permits work to a given stage of the case and with a limitation on costs. If the work is to proceed beyond that permitted in the funding certificate, a further application should be made to the LAA using form CIV APP8. This form should also be used to apply to extend funding to cover the cost of experts or leading counsel.

---

24   See 2010 Standard Crime Contract – Specification para 1.5.

APPENDICES

Framework Decision on the European Arrest Warrant and the surrender procedures between member states

2002/584/JHA: Council Framework Decision of 13 June 2002 on the European arrest warrant and the surrender procedures between member states: statements made by certain member states on the adoption of the Framework Decision[1]

THE COUNCIL OF THE EUROPEAN UNION,

Having regard to the Treaty on European Union, and in particular Article 31(a) and (b) and Article 34(2)(b) thereof,

Having regard to the proposal from the Commission,

Having regard to the opinion of the European Parliament,

Whereas:

(1) According to the Conclusions of the Tampere European Council of 15 and 16 October 1999, and in particular point 35 thereof, the formal extradition procedure should be abolished among the Member States in respect of persons who are fleeing from justice after having been finally sentenced and extradition procedures should be speeded up in respect of persons suspected of having committed an offence.

(2) The programme of measures to implement the principle of mutual recognition of criminal decisions envisaged in point 37 of the Tampere European Council Conclusions and adopted by the Council on 30 November 2000, addresses the matter of mutual enforcement of arrest warrants.

(3) All or some Member States are parties to a number of conventions in the field of extradition, including the European Convention on extradition of 13 December 1957 and the European Convention on the suppression of terrorism of 27 January 1977. The Nordic States have extradition laws with identical wording.

(4) In addition, the following three Conventions dealing in whole or in part with extradition have been agreed upon among Member States and form part of

---

1 *Official Journal* L 190 , 18/07/2002 P. 0001–0020. Available at http://eur-lex.europa. eu/LexUriServ/LexUriServ.do?uri=CELEX:32002F0584:en:HTML.

the Union acquis: the Convention of 19 June 1990 implementing the Schengen Agreement of 14 June 1985 on the gradual abolition of checks at their common borders (regarding relations between the Member States which are parties to that Convention), the Convention of 10 March 1995 on simplified extradition procedure between the Member States of the European Union and the Convention of 27 September 1996 relating to extradition between the Member States of the European Union.

(5) The objective set for the Union to become an area of freedom, security and justice leads to abolishing extradition between Member States and replacing it by a system of surrender between judicial authorities. Further, the introduction of a new simplified system of surrender of sentenced or suspected persons for the purposes of execution or prosecution of criminal sentences makes it possible to remove the complexity and potential for delay inherent in the present extradition procedures. Traditional cooperation relations which have prevailed up till now between Member States should be replaced by a system of free movement of judicial decisions in criminal matters, covering both pre-sentence and final decisions, within an area of freedom, security and justice.

(6) The European arrest warrant provided for in this Framework Decision is the first concrete measure in the field of criminal law implementing the principle of mutual recognition which the European Council referred to as the 'cornerstone' of judicial cooperation.

(7) Since the aim of replacing the system of multilateral extradition built upon the European Convention on Extradition of 13 December 1957 cannot be sufficiently achieved by the Member States acting unilaterally and can therefore, by reason of its scale and effects, be better achieved at Union level, the Council may adopt measures in accordance with the principle of subsidiarity as referred to in Article 2 of the Treaty on European Union and Article 5 of the Treaty establishing the European Community. In accordance with the principle of proportionality, as set out in the latter Article, this Framework Decision does not go beyond what is necessary in order to achieve that objective.

(8) Decisions on the execution of the European arrest warrant must be subject to sufficient controls, which means that a judicial authority of the Member State where the requested person has been arrested will have to take the decision on his or her surrender.

(9) The role of central authorities in the execution of a European arrest warrant must be limited to practical and administrative assistance.

(10) The mechanism of the European arrest warrant is based on a high level of confidence between Member States. Its implementation may be suspended only in the event of a serious and persistent breach by one of the Member States of the principles set out in Article 6(1) of the Treaty on European Union, determined by the Council pursuant to Article 7(1) of the said Treaty with the consequences set out in Article 7(2) thereof.

(11) In relations between Member States, the European arrest warrant should replace all the previous instruments concerning extradition, including the provisions of Title III of the Convention implementing the Schengen Agreement which concern extradition.

(12) This Framework Decision respects fundamental rights and observes the principles recognised by Article 6 of the Treaty on European Union and reflected in the Charter of Fundamental Rights of the European Union, in particular Chapter VI thereof. Nothing in this Framework Decision may be interpreted as prohibiting refusal to surrender a person for whom a European arrest warrant has been issued when there are reasons to believe, on the basis of objective elements, that the said arrest warrant has been issued for the purpose of prosecuting or punishing a person on the grounds of his or her sex, race, religion, ethnic origin, nationality, language, political opinions or sexual orientation, or that that person's position may be prejudiced for any of these reasons.

This Framework Decision does not prevent a Member State from applying its constitutional rules relating to due process, freedom of association, freedom of the press and freedom of expression in other media.

(13) No person should be removed, expelled or extradited to a State where there is a serious risk that he or she would be subjected to the death penalty, torture or other inhuman or degrading treatment or punishment.

(14) Since all Member States have ratified the Council of Europe Convention of 28 January 1981 for the protection of individuals with regard to automatic processing of personal data, the personal data processed in the context of the implementation of this Framework Decision should be protected in accordance with the principles of the said Convention,

HAS ADOPTED THIS FRAMEWORK DECISION:

CHAPTER 1
GENERAL PRINCIPLES

Article 1
Definition of the European arrest warrant and obligation to execute it

1. The European arrest warrant is a judicial decision issued by a Member State with a view to the arrest and surrender by another Member State of a requested person, for the purposes of conducting a criminal prosecution or executing a custodial sentence or detention order.

2. Member States shall execute any European arrest warrant on the basis of the principle of mutual recognition and in accordance with the provisions of this Framework Decision.

3. This Framework Decision shall not have the effect of modifying the obligation to respect fundamental rights and fundamental legal principles as enshrined in Article 6 of the Treaty on European Union.

Article 2
Scope of the European arrest warrant

1. A European arrest warrant may be issued for acts punishable by the law of the issuing Member State by a custodial sentence or a detention order for a maximum period of at least 12 months or, where a sentence has been passed or a detention order has been made, for sentences of at least four months.

2. The following offences, if they are punishable in the issuing Member State

by a custodial sentence or a detention order for a maximum period of at least three years and as they are defined by the law of the issuing Member State, shall, under the terms of this Framework Decision and without verification of the double criminality of the act, give rise to surrender pursuant to a European arrest warrant:

- participation in a criminal organisation,
- terrorism,
- trafficking in human beings,
- sexual exploitation of children and child pornography,
- illicit trafficking in narcotic drugs and psychotropic substances,
- illicit trafficking in weapons, munitions and explosives,
- corruption,
- fraud, including that affecting the financial interests of the European Communities within the meaning of the Convention of 26 July 1995 on the protection of the European Communities' financial interests,
- laundering of the proceeds of crime,
- counterfeiting currency, including of the euro,
- computer-related crime,
- environmental crime, including illicit trafficking in endangered animal species and in endangered plant species and varieties,
- facilitation of unauthorised entry and residence,
- murder, grievous bodily injury,
- illicit trade in human organs and tissue,
- kidnapping, illegal restraint and hostage-taking,
- racism and xenophobia,
- organised or armed robbery,
- illicit trafficking in cultural goods, including antiques and works of art,
- swindling,
- racketeering and extortion,
- counterfeiting and piracy of products,
- forgery of administrative documents and trafficking therein,
- forgery of means of payment,
- illicit trafficking in hormonal substances and other growth promoters,
- illicit trafficking in nuclear or radioactive materials,
- trafficking in stolen vehicles,
- rape,
- arson,
- crimes within the jurisdiction of the International Criminal Court,
- unlawful seizure of aircraft/ships,
- sabotage.

3. The Council may decide at any time, acting unanimously after consultation of the European Parliament under the conditions laid down in Article 39(1) of the Treaty on European Union (TEU), to add other categories of offence to the list contained in paragraph 2. The Council shall examine, in the light of the report submitted by the Commission pursuant to Article 34(3), whether the list should be extended or amended.

4. For offences other than those covered by paragraph 2, surrender may be subject to the condition that the acts for which the European arrest warrant has

been issued constitute an offence under the law of the executing Member State, whatever the constituent elements or however it is described.

Article 3
Grounds for mandatory non-execution of the European arrest warrant

The judicial authority of the Member State of execution (hereinafter 'executing judicial authority') shall refuse to execute the European arrest warrant in the following cases:

1. if the offence on which the arrest warrant is based is covered by amnesty in the executing Member State, where that State had jurisdiction to prosecute the offence under its own criminal law;

2. if the executing judicial authority is informed that the requested person has been finally judged by a Member State in respect of the same acts provided that, where there has been sentence, the sentence has been served or is currently being served or may no longer be executed under the law of the sentencing Member State;

3. if the person who is the subject of the European arrest warrant may not, owing to his age, be held criminally responsible for the acts on which the arrest warrant is based under the law of the executing State.

Article 4
Grounds for optional non-execution of the European arrest warrant

The executing judicial authority may refuse to execute the European arrest warrant:

1. if, in one of the cases referred to in Article 2(4), the act on which the European arrest warrant is based does not constitute an offence under the law of the executing Member State; however, in relation to taxes or duties, customs and exchange, execution of the European arrest warrant shall not be refused on the ground that the law of the executing Member State does not impose the same kind of tax or duty or does not contain the same type of rules as regards taxes, duties and customs and exchange regulations as the law of the issuing Member State;

2. where the person who is the subject of the European arrest warrant is being prosecuted in the executing Member State for the same act as that on which the European arrest warrant is based;

3. where the judicial authorities of the executing Member State have decided either not to prosecute for the offence on which the European arrest warrant is based or to halt proceedings, or where a final judgment has been passed upon the requested person in a Member State, in respect of the same acts, which prevents further proceedings;

4. where the criminal prosecution or punishment of the requested person is statute-barred according to the law of the executing Member State and the acts fall within the jurisdiction of that Member State under its own criminal law;

5. if the executing judicial authority is informed that the requested person has been finally judged by a third State in respect of the same acts provided that, where there has been sentence, the sentence has been served or is currently

being served or may no longer be executed under the law of the sentencing country;

6. if the European arrest warrant has been issued for the purposes of execution of a custodial sentence or detention order, where the requested person is staying in, or is a national or a resident of the executing Member State and that State undertakes to execute the sentence or detention order in accordance with its domestic law;

7. where the European arrest warrant relates to offences which:
   (a) are regarded by the law of the executing Member State as having been committed in whole or in part in the territory of the executing Member State or in a place treated as such; or
   (b) have been committed outside the territory of the issuing Member State and the law of the executing Member State does not allow prosecution for the same offences when committed outside its territory.

Article 4a
Decisions rendered following a trial at which the person did not appear in person

1. The executing judicial authority may also refuse to execute the European arrest warrant issued for the purpose of executing a custodial sentence or a detention order if the person did not appear in person at the trial resulting in the decision, unless the European arrest warrant states that the person, in accordance with further procedural requirements defined in the national law of the issuing Member State:
   (a) in due time:
      (i) either was summoned in person and thereby informed of the scheduled date and place of the trial which resulted in the decision, or by other means actually received official information of the scheduled date and place of that trial in such a manner that it was unequivocally established that he or she was aware of the scheduled trial;
      and
      (ii) was informed that a decision may be handed down if he or she does not appear for the trial;
   or
   (b) being aware of the scheduled trial, had given a mandate to a legal counsellor, who was either appointed by the person concerned or by the State, to defend him or her at the trial, and was indeed defended by that counsellor at the trial;
   or
   (c) after being served with the decision and being expressly informed about the right to a retrial, or an appeal, in which the person has the right to participate and which allows the merits of the case, including fresh evidence, to be re-examined, and which may lead to the original decision being reversed:
      (i) expressly stated that he or she does not contest the decision;
      or
      (ii) did not request a retrial or appeal within the applicable time frame;
   or

(d) was not personally served with the decision but:

    (i) will be personally served with it without delay after the surrender and will be expressly informed of his or her right to a retrial, or an appeal, in which the person has the right to participate and which allows the merits of the case, including fresh evidence, to be re-examined, and which may lead to the original decision being reversed;

    and

    (ii) will be informed of the time frame within which he or she has to request such a retrial or appeal, as mentioned in the relevant European arrest warrant.

2. In case the European arrest warrant is issued for the purpose of executing a custodial sentence or detention order under the conditions of paragraph 1(d) and the person concerned has not previously received any official information about the existence of the criminal proceedings against him or her, he or she may, when being informed about the content of the European arrest warrant, request to receive a copy of the judgment before being surrendered. Immediately after having been informed about the request, the issuing authority shall provide the copy of the judgment via the executing authority to the person sought. The request of the person sought shall neither delay the surrender procedure nor delay the decision to execute the European arrest warrant. The provision of the judgment to the person concerned is for information purposes only; it shall neither be regarded as a formal service of the judgment nor actuate any time limits applicable for requesting a retrial or appeal.

3. In case a person is surrendered under the conditions of paragraph (1)(d) and he or she has requested a retrial or appeal, the detention of that person awaiting such retrial or appeal shall, until these proceedings are finalised, be reviewed in accordance with the law of the issuing Member State, either on a regular basis or upon request of the person concerned. Such a review shall in particular include the possibility of suspension or interruption of the detention. The retrial or appeal shall begin within due time after the surrender.

Article 5
Guarantees to be given by the issuing Member State in particular cases

The execution of the European arrest warrant by the executing judicial authority may, by the law of the executing Member State, be subject to the following conditions:

1. if the offence on the basis of which the European arrest warrant has been issued is punishable by custodial life sentence or life-time detention order, the execution of the said arrest warrant may be subject to the condition that the issuing Member State has provisions in its legal system for a review of the penalty or measure imposed, on request or at the latest after 20 years, or for the application of measures of clemency to which the person is entitled to apply for under the law or practice of the issuing Member State, aiming at a non-execution of such penalty or measure;

2. where a person who is the subject of a European arrest warrant for the purposes of prosecution is a national or resident of the executing Member State, surrender may be subject to the condition that the person, after being heard, is returned to the executing Member State in order to serve there the custodial

sentence or detention order passed against him in the issuing Member State.

Article 6
Determination of the competent judicial authorities

1. The issuing judicial authority shall be the judicial authority of the issuing Member State which is competent to issue a European arrest warrant by virtue of the law of that State.

2. The executing judicial authority shall be the judicial authority of the executing Member State which is competent to execute the European arrest warrant by virtue of the law of that State.

3. Each Member State shall inform the General Secretariat of the Council of the competent judicial authority under its law.

Article 7
Recourse to the central authority

1. Each Member State may designate a central authority or, when its legal system so provides, more than one central authority to assist the competent judicial authorities.

2. A Member State may, if it is necessary as a result of the organisation of its internal judicial system, make its central authority(ies) responsible for the administrative transmission and reception of European arrest warrants as well as for all other official correspondence relating thereto.

Member State wishing to make use of the possibilities referred to in this Article shall communicate to the General Secretariat of the Council information relating to the designated central authority or central authorities. These indications shall be binding upon all the authorities of the issuing Member State.

Article 8
Content and form of the European arrest warrant

1. The European arrest warrant shall contain the following information set out in accordance with the form contained in the Annex:
   (a) the identity and nationality of the requested person;
   (b) the name, address, telephone and fax numbers and e-mail address of the issuing judicial authority;
   (c) evidence of an enforceable judgment, an arrest warrant or any other enforceable judicial decision having the same effect, coming within the scope of Articles 1 and 2;
   (d) the nature and legal classification of the offence, particularly in respect of Article 2;
   (e) a description of the circumstances in which the offence was committed, including the time, place and degree of participation in the offence by the requested person;
   (f) the penalty imposed, if there is a final judgment, or the prescribed scale of penalties for the offence under the law of the issuing Member State;
   (g) if possible, other consequences of the offence.

2. The European arrest warrant must be translated into the official language or

one of the official languages of the executing Member State. Any Member State may, when this Framework Decision is adopted or at a later date, state in a declaration deposited with the General Secretariat of the Council that it will accept a translation in one or more other official languages of the Institutions of the European Communities.

CHAPTER 2
SURRENDER PROCEDURE

Article 9
Transmission of a European arrest warrant

1. When the location of the requested person is known, the issuing judicial authority may transmit the European arrest warrant directly to the executing judicial authority.

2. The issuing judicial authority may, in any event, decide to issue an alert for the requested person in the Schengen Information System (SIS).

3. Such an alert shall be effected in accordance with the provisions of Article 95 of the Convention of 19 June 1990 implementing the Schengen Agreement of 14 June 1985 on the gradual abolition of controls at common borders. An alert in the Schengen Information System shall be equivalent to a European arrest warrant accompanied by the information set out in Article 8(1).

For a transitional period, until the SIS is capable of transmitting all the information described in Article 8, the alert shall be equivalent to a European arrest warrant pending the receipt of the original in due and proper form by the executing judicial authority.

Article 10
Detailed procedures for transmitting a European arrest warrant

1. If the issuing judicial authority does not know the competent executing judicial authority, it shall make the requisite enquiries, including through the contact points of the European Judicial Network, in order to obtain that information from the executing Member State.

2. If the issuing judicial authority so wishes, transmission may be effected via the secure telecommunications system of the European Judicial Network.

3. If it is not possible to call on the services of the SIS, the issuing judicial authority may call on Interpol to transmit a European arrest warrant.

4. The issuing judicial authority may forward the European arrest warrant by any secure means capable of producing written records under conditions allowing the executing Member State to establish its authenticity.

5. All difficulties concerning the transmission or the authenticity of any document needed for the execution of the European arrest warrant shall be dealt with by direct contacts between the judicial authorities involved, or, where appropriate, with the involvement of the central authorities of the Member States.

6. If the authority which receives a European arrest warrant is not competent to act upon it, it shall automatically forward the European arrest warrant to the competent authority in its Member State and shall inform the issuing judicial authority accordingly.

Article 11
Rights of a requested person

1. When a requested person is arrested, the executing competent judicial authority shall, in accordance with its national law, inform that person of the European arrest warrant and of its contents, and also of the possibility of consenting to surrender to the issuing judicial authority.

2. A requested person who is arrested for the purpose of the execution of a European arrest warrant shall have a right to be assisted by a legal counsel and by an interpreter in accordance with the national law of the executing Member State.

Article 12
Keeping the person in detention

When a person is arrested on the basis of a European arrest warrant, the executing judicial authority shall take a decision on whether the requested person should remain in detention, in accordance with the law of the executing Member State. The person may be released provisionally at any time in conformity with the domestic law of the executing Member State, provided that the competent authority of the said Member State takes all the measures it deems necessary to prevent the person absconding.

Article 13
Consent to surrender

1. If the arrested person indicates that he or she consents to surrender, that consent and, if appropriate, express renunciation of entitlement to the 'speciality rule', referred to in Article 27(2), shall be given before the executing judicial authority, in accordance with the domestic law of the executing Member State.

2. Each Member State shall adopt the measures necessary to ensure that consent and, where appropriate, renunciation, as referred to in paragraph 1, are established in such a way as to show that the person concerned has expressed them voluntarily and in full awareness of the consequences. To that end, the requested person shall have the right to legal counsel.

3. The consent and, where appropriate, renunciation, as referred to in paragraph 1, shall be formally recorded in accordance with the procedure laid down by the domestic law of the executing Member State.

4. In principle, consent may not be revoked. Each Member State may provide that consent and, if appropriate, renunciation may be revoked, in accordance with the rules applicable under its domestic law. In this case, the period between the date of consent and that of its revocation shall not be taken into consideration in establishing the time limits laid down in Article 17. A Member State which wishes to have recourse to this possibility shall inform the General Secretariat of the Council accordingly when this Framework Decision is adopted and shall specify the procedures whereby revocation of consent shall be possible and any amendment to them.

Article 14
Hearing of the requested person

Where the arrested person does not consent to his or her surrender as referred to in Article 13, he or she shall be entitled to be heard by the executing judicial authority, in accordance with the law of the executing Member State.

Article 15
Surrender decision

1. The executing judicial authority shall decide, within the time-limits and under the conditions defined in this Framework Decision, whether the person is to be surrendered.

2. If the executing judicial authority finds the information communicated by the issuing Member State to be insufficient to allow it to decide on surrender, it shall request that the necessary supplementary information, in particular with respect to Articles 3 to 5 and Article 8, be furnished as a matter of urgency and may fix a time limit for the receipt thereof, taking into account the need to observe the time limits set in Article 17.

3. The issuing judicial authority may at any time forward any additional useful information to the executing judicial authority.

Article 16
Decision in the event of multiple requests

1. If two or more Member States have issued European arrest warrants for the same person, the decision on which of the European arrest warrants shall be executed shall be taken by the executing judicial authority with due consideration of all the circumstances and especially the relative seriousness and place of the offences, the respective dates of the European arrest warrants and whether the warrant has been issued for the purposes of prosecution or for execution of a custodial sentence or detention order.

2. The executing judicial authority may seek the advice of Eurojust when making the choice referred to in paragraph 1.

3. In the event of a conflict between a European arrest warrant and a request for extradition presented by a third country, the decision on whether the European arrest warrant or the extradition request takes precedence shall be taken by the competent authority of the executing Member State with due consideration of all the circumstances, in particular those referred to in paragraph 1 and those mentioned in the applicable convention.

4. This Article shall be without prejudice to Member States' obligations under the Statute of the International Criminal Court.

Article 17
Time limits and procedures for the decision to execute the European arrest warrant

1. A European arrest warrant shall be dealt with and executed as a matter of urgency.

2. In cases where the requested person consents to his surrender, the final

decision on the execution of the European arrest warrant should be taken within a period of 10 days after consent has been given.

3. In other cases, the final decision on the execution of the European arrest warrant should be taken within a period of 60 days after the arrest of the requested person.

4. Where in specific cases the European arrest warrant cannot be executed within the time limits laid down in paragraphs 2 or 3, the executing judicial authority shall immediately inform the issuing judicial authority thereof, giving the reasons for the delay. In such case, the time limits may be extended by a further 30 days.

5. As long as the executing judicial authority has not taken a final decision on the European arrest warrant, it shall ensure that the material conditions necessary for effective surrender of the person remain fulfilled.

6. Reasons must be given for any refusal to execute a European arrest warrant.

7. Where in exceptional circumstances a Member State cannot observe the time limits provided for in this Article, it shall inform Eurojust, giving the reasons for the delay. In addition, a Member State which has experienced repeated delays on the part of another Member State in the execution of European arrest warrants shall inform the Council with a view to evaluating the implementation of this Framework Decision at Member State level.

Article 18
Situation pending the decision

1. Where the European arrest warrant has been issued for the purpose of conducting a criminal prosecution, the executing judicial authority must:
   (a) either agree that the requested person should be heard according to Article 19;
   (b) or agree to the temporary transfer of the requested person.

2. The conditions and the duration of the temporary transfer shall be determined by mutual agreement between the issuing and executing judicial authorities.

3. In the case of temporary transfer, the person must be able to return to the executing Member State to attend hearings concerning him or her as part of the surrender procedure.

Article 19
Hearing the person pending the decision

1. The requested person shall be heard by a judicial authority, assisted by another person designated in accordance with the law of the Member State of the requesting court.

2. The requested person shall be heard in accordance with the law of the executing Member State and with the conditions determined by mutual agreement between the issuing and executing judicial authorities.

3. The competent executing judicial authority may assign another judicial authority of its Member State to take part in the hearing of the requested person in order to ensure the proper application of this Article and of the conditions laid down.

Article 20
Privileges and immunities

1. Where the requested person enjoys a privilege or immunity regarding jurisdiction or execution in the executing Member State, the time limits referred to in Article 17 shall not start running unless, and counting from the day when, the executing judicial authority is informed of the fact that the privilege or immunity has been waived.

   The executing Member State shall ensure that the material conditions necessary for effective surrender are fulfilled when the person no longer enjoys such privilege or immunity.

2. Where power to waive the privilege or immunity lies with an authority of the executing Member State, the executing judicial authority shall request it to exercise that power forthwith. Where power to waive the privilege or immunity lies with an authority of another State or international organisation, it shall be for the issuing judicial authority to request it to exercise that power.

Article 21
Competing international obligations

This Framework Decision shall not prejudice the obligations of the executing Member State where the requested person has been extradited to that Member State from a third State and where that person is protected by provisions of the arrangement under which he or she was extradited concerning speciality. The executing Member State shall take all necessary measures for requesting forthwith the consent of the State from which the requested person was extradited so that he or she can be surrendered to the Member State which issued the European arrest warrant. The time limits referred to in Article 17 shall not start running until the day on which these speciality rules cease to apply. Pending the decision of the State from which the requested person was extradited, the executing Member State will ensure that the material conditions necessary for effective surrender remain fulfilled.

Article 22
Notification of the decision

The executing judicial authority shall notify the issuing judicial authority immediately of the decision on the action to be taken on the European arrest warrant.

Article 23
Time limits for surrender of the person

1. The person requested shall be surrendered as soon as possible on a date agreed between the authorities concerned.

2. He or she shall be surrendered no later than 10 days after the final decision on the execution of the European arrest warrant.

3. If the surrender of the requested person within the period laid down in paragraph 2 is prevented by circumstances beyond the control of any of the Member States, the executing and issuing judicial authorities shall immediately

contact each other and agree on a new surrender date. In that event, the surrender shall take place within 10 days of the new date thus agreed.

4. The surrender may exceptionally be temporarily postponed for serious humanitarian reasons, for example if there are substantial grounds for believing that it would manifestly endanger the requested person's life or health. The execution of the European arrest warrant shall take place as soon as these grounds have ceased to exist. The executing judicial authority shall immediately inform the issuing judicial authority and agree on a new surrender date. In that event, the surrender shall take place within 10 days of the new date thus agreed.

5. Upon expiry of the time limits referred to in paragraphs 2 to 4, if the person is still being held in custody he shall be released.

Article 24
Postponed or conditional surrender

1. The executing judicial authority may, after deciding to execute the European arrest warrant, postpone the surrender of the requested person so that he or she may be prosecuted in the executing Member State or, if he or she has already been sentenced, so that he or she may serve, in its territory, a sentence passed for an act other than that referred to in the European arrest warrant.

2. Instead of postponing the surrender, the executing judicial authority may temporarily surrender the requested person to the issuing Member State under conditions to be determined by mutual agreement between the executing and the issuing judicial authorities. The agreement shall be made in writing and the conditions shall be binding on all the authorities in the issuing Member State.

Article 25
Transit

1. Each Member State shall, except when it avails itself of the possibility of refusal when the transit of a national or a resident is requested for the purpose of the execution of a custodial sentence or detention order, permit the transit through its territory of a requested person who is being surrendered provided that it has been given information on:
   (a) the identity and nationality of the person subject to the European arrest warrant;
   (b) the existence of a European arrest warrant;
   (c) the nature and legal classification of the offence;
   (d) the description of the circumstances of the offence, including the date and place.

   Where a person who is the subject of a European arrest warrant for the purposes of prosecution is a national or resident of the Member State of transit, transit may be subject to the condition that the person, after being heard, is returned to the transit Member State to serve the custodial sentence or detention order passed against him in the issuing Member State.

2. Each Member State shall designate an authority responsible for receiving transit requests and the necessary documents, as well as any other official cor-

respondence relating to transit requests. Member States shall communicate this designation to the General Secretariat of the Council.

3. The transit request and the information set out in paragraph 1 may be addressed to the authority designated pursuant to paragraph 2 by any means capable of producing a written record. The Member State of transit shall notify its decision by the same procedure.

4. This Framework Decision does not apply in the case of transport by air without a scheduled stopover. However, if an unscheduled landing occurs, the issuing Member State shall provide the authority designated pursuant to paragraph 2 with the information provided for in paragraph 1.

5. Where a transit concerns a person who is to be extradited from a third State to a Member State this Article will apply mutatis mutandis. In particular the expression 'European arrest warrant' shall be deemed to be replaced by 'extradition request'.

CHAPTER 3
EFFECTS OF THE SURRENDER

Article 26
Deduction of the period of detention served in the executing Member State

1. The issuing Member State shall deduct all periods of detention arising from the execution of a European arrest warrant from the total period of detention to be served in the issuing Member State as a result of a custodial sentence or detention order being passed.

2. To that end, all information concerning the duration of the detention of the requested person on the basis of the European arrest warrant shall be transmitted by the executing judicial authority or the central authority designated under Article 7 to the issuing judicial authority at the time of the surrender.

Article 27
Possible prosecution for other offences

1. Each Member State may notify the General Secretariat of the Council that, in its relations with other Member States that have given the same notification, consent is presumed to have been given for the prosecution, sentencing or detention with a view to the carrying out of a custodial sentence or detention order for an offence committed prior to his or her surrender, other than that for which he or she was surrendered, unless in a particular case the executing judicial authority states otherwise in its decision on surrender.

2. Except in the cases referred to in paragraphs 1 and 3, a person surrendered may not be prosecuted, sentenced or otherwise deprived of his or her liberty for an offence committed prior to his or her surrender other than that for which he or she was surrendered.

3. Paragraph 2 does not apply in the following cases:
   (a) when the person having had an opportunity to leave the territory of the Member State to which he or she has been surrendered has not done so within 45 days of his or her final discharge, or has returned to that territory after leaving it;

(b) the offence is not punishable by a custodial sentence or detention order;

(c) the criminal proceedings do not give rise to the application of a measure restricting personal liberty;

(d) when the person could be liable to a penalty or a measure not involving the deprivation of liberty, in particular a financial penalty or a measure in lieu thereof, even if the penalty or measure may give rise to a restriction of his or her personal liberty;

(e) when the person consented to be surrendered, where appropriate at the same time as he or she renounced the speciality rule, in accordance with Article 13;

(f) when the person, after his/her surrender, has expressly renounced entitlement to the speciality rule with regard to specific offences preceding his/her surrender. Renunciation shall be given before the competent judicial authorities of the issuing Member State and shall be recorded in accordance with that State's domestic law. The renunciation shall be drawn up in such a way as to make clear that the person has given it voluntarily and in full awareness of the consequences. To that end, the person shall have the right to legal counsel;

(g) where the executing judicial authority which surrendered the person gives its consent in accordance with paragraph 4.

4. A request for consent shall be submitted to the executing judicial authority, accompanied by the information mentioned in Article 8(1) and a translation as referred to in Article 8(2). Consent shall be given when the offence for which it is requested is itself subject to surrender in accordance with the provisions of this Framework Decision. Consent shall be refused on the grounds referred to in Article 3 and otherwise may be refused only on the grounds referred to in Article 4. The decision shall be taken no later than 30 days after receipt of the request.

For the situations mentioned in Article 5 the issuing Member State must give the guarantees provided for therein.

Article 28
Surrender or subsequent extradition

1. Each Member State may notify the General Secretariat of the Council that, in its relations with other Member States which have given the same notification, the consent for the surrender of a person to a Member State other than the executing Member State pursuant to a European arrest warrant issued for an offence committed prior to his or her surrender is presumed to have been given, unless in a particular case the executing judicial authority states otherwise in its decision on surrender.

2. In any case, a person who has been surrendered to the issuing Member State pursuant to a European arrest warrant may, without the consent of the executing Member State, be surrendered to a Member State other than the executing Member State pursuant to a European arrest warrant issued for any offence committed prior to his or her surrender in the following cases:

(a) where the requested person, having had an opportunity to leave the territory of the Member State to which he or she has been surrendered, has not done so within 45 days of his final discharge, or has returned to that territory after leaving it;

(b) where the requested person consents to be surrendered to a Member State other than the executing Member State pursuant to a European arrest warrant. Consent shall be given before the competent judicial authorities of the issuing Member State and shall be recorded in accordance with that State's national law. It shall be drawn up in such a way as to make clear that the person concerned has given it voluntarily and in full awareness of the consequences. To that end, the requested person shall have the right to legal counsel;

(c) where the requested person is not subject to the speciality rule, in accordance with Article 27(3)(a), (e), (f) and (g).

3. The executing judicial authority consents to the surrender to another Member State according to the following rules:

(a) the request for consent shall be submitted in accordance with Article 9, accompanied by the information mentioned in Article 8(1) and a translation as stated in Article 8(2);

(b) consent shall be given when the offence for which it is requested is itself subject to surrender in accordance with the provisions of this Framework Decision;

(c) the decision shall be taken no later than 30 days after receipt of the request;

(d) consent shall be refused on the grounds referred to in Article 3 and otherwise may be refused only on the grounds referred to in Article 4.

For the situations referred to in Article 5, the issuing Member State must give the guarantees provided for therein.

4. Notwithstanding paragraph 1, a person who has been surrendered pursuant to a European arrest warrant shall not be extradited to a third State without the consent of the competent authority of the Member State which surrendered the person. Such consent shall be given in accordance with the Conventions by which that Member State is bound, as well as with its domestic law.

Article 29
Handing over of property

1. At the request of the issuing judicial authority or on its own initiative, the executing judicial authority shall, in accordance with its national law, seize and hand over property which:

(a) may be required as evidence, or

(b) has been acquired by the requested person as a result of the offence.

2. The property referred to in paragraph 1 shall be handed over even if the European arrest warrant cannot be carried out owing to the death or escape of the requested person.

3. If the property referred to in paragraph 1 is liable to seizure or confiscation in the territory of the executing Member State, the latter may, if the property is needed in connection with pending criminal proceedings, temporarily retain it or hand it over to the issuing Member State, on condition that it is returned.

4. Any rights which the executing Member State or third parties may have acquired in the property referred to in paragraph 1 shall be preserved. Where such rights exist, the issuing Member State shall return the property without charge to the executing Member State as soon as the criminal proceedings have been terminated.

Article 30
Expenses

1. Expenses incurred in the territory of the executing Member State for the execution of a European arrest warrant shall be borne by that Member State.

2. All other expenses shall be borne by the issuing Member State.

CHAPTER 4
GENERAL AND FINAL PROVISIONS

Article 31
Relation to other legal instruments

1. Without prejudice to their application in relations between Member States and third States, this Framework Decision shall, from 1 January 2004, replace the corresponding provisions of the following conventions applicable in the field of extradition in relations between the Member States:
   (a) the European Convention on Extradition of 13 December 1957, its additional protocol of 15 October 1975, its second additional protocol of 17 March 1978, and the European Convention on the suppression of terrorism of 27 January 1977 as far as extradition is concerned;
   (b) the Agreement between the 12 Member States of the European Communities on the simplification and modernisation of methods of transmitting extradition requests of 26 May 1989;
   (c) the Convention of 10 March 1995 on simplified extradition procedure between the Member States of the European Union;
   (d) the Convention of 27 September 1996 relating to extradition between the Member States of the European Union;
   (e) Title III, Chapter 4 of the Convention of 19 June 1990 implementing the Schengen Agreement of 14 June 1985 on the gradual abolition of checks at common borders.

2. Member States may continue to apply bilateral or multilateral agreements or arrangements in force when this Framework Decision is adopted in so far as such agreements or arrangements allow the objectives of this Framework Decision to be extended or enlarged and help to simplify or facilitate further the procedures for surrender of persons who are the subject of European arrest warrants.

   Member States may conclude bilateral or multilateral agreements or arrangements after this Framework Decision has come into force in so far as such agreements or arrangements allow the prescriptions of this Framework Decision to be extended or enlarged and help to simplify or facilitate further the procedures for surrender of persons who are the subject of European arrest warrants, in particular by fixing time limits shorter than those fixed in Article 17, by extending the list of offences laid down in Article 2(2), by further limiting the grounds for refusal set out in Articles 3 and 4, or by lowering the threshold provided for in Article 2(1) or (2).

The agreements and arrangements referred to in the second subparagraph may in no case affect relations with Member States which are not parties to them.

Member States shall, within three months from the entry into force of this Framework Decision, notify the Council and the Commission of the existing agreements and arrangements referred to in the first subparagraph which they wish to continue applying.

Member States shall also notify the Council and the Commission of any new agreement or arrangement as referred to in the second subparagraph, within three months of signing it.

3. Where the conventions or agreements referred to in paragraph 1 apply to the territories of Member States or to territories for whose external relations a Member State is responsible to which this Framework Decision does not apply, these instruments shall continue to govern the relations existing between those territories and the other Members States.

Article 32
Transitional provision

1. Extradition requests received before 1 January 2004 will continue to be governed by existing instruments relating to extradition. Requests received after that date will be governed by the rules adopted by Member States pursuant to this Framework Decision. However, any Member State may, at the time of the adoption of this Framework Decision by the Council, make a statement indicating that as executing Member State it will continue to deal with requests relating to acts committed before a date which it specifies in accordance with the extradition system applicable before 1 January 2004. The date in question may not be later than 7 August 2002. The said statement will be published in the Official Journal of the European Communities. It may be withdrawn at any time.

Article 33
Provisions concerning Austria and Gibraltar

1. As long as Austria has not modified Article 12(1) of the 'Auslieferungs- und Rechtshilfegesetz' and, at the latest, until 31 December 2008, it may allow its executing judicial authorities to refuse the enforcement of a European arrest warrant if the requested person is an Austrian citizen and if the act for which the European arrest warrant has been issued is not punishable under Austrian law.

2. This Framework Decision shall apply to Gibraltar.

Article 34
Implementation

1. Member States shall take the necessary measures to comply with the provisions of this Framework Decision by 31 December 2003.

2. Member States shall transmit to the General Secretariat of the Council and

to the Commission the text of the provisions transposing into their national law the obligations imposed on them under this Framework Decision. When doing so, each Member State may indicate that it will apply immediately this Framework Decision in its relations with those Member States which have given the same notification.

The General Secretariat of the Council shall communicate to the Member States and to the Commission the information received pursuant to Article 7(2), Article 8(2), Article 13(4) and Article 25(2). It shall also have the information published in the Official Journal of the European Communities.

3. On the basis of the information communicated by the General Secretariat of the Council, the Commission shall, by 31 December 2004 at the latest, submit a report to the European Parliament and to the Council on the operation of this Framework Decision, accompanied, where necessary, by legislative proposals.

4. The Council shall in the second half of 2003 conduct a review, in particular of the practical application, of the provisions of this Framework Decision by the Member States as well as the functioning of the Schengen Information System.

Article 35
Entry into force

This Framework Decision shall enter into force on the twentieth day following that of its publication in the Official Journal of the European Communities.

Done at Luxembourg, 13 June 2002.

For the Council

The President

M. Rajoy Brey

ANNEX
EUROPEAN ARREST WARRANT(1)

This warrant has been issued by a competent judicial authority. I request that the person mentioned below be arrested and surrendered for the purposes of conducting a criminal prosecution or executing a custodial sentence or detention order.

(1) This warrant must be written in, or translated into, one of the official languages of the executing Member State, when that State is known, or any other language accepted by that State.

Statements made by certain Member States on the adoption of the Framework Decision
Statements provided for in Article 32

Statement by France:
Pursuant to Article 32 of the framework decision on the European arrest warrant and the surrender procedures between Member States, France states that

as executing Member State it will continue to deal with requests relating to acts committed before 1 November 1993, the date of entry into force of the Treaty on European Union signed in Maastricht on 7 February 1992, in accordance with the extradition system applicable before 1 January 2004.

Statement by Italy:
Italy will continue to deal in accordance with the extradition rules in force with all requests relating to acts committed before the date of entry into force of the framework decision on the European arrest warrant, as provided for in Article 32 thereof.

Statement by Austria:
Pursuant to Article 32 of the framework decision on the European arrest warrant and the surrender procedures between Member States, Austria states that as executing Member State it will continue to deal with requests relating to punishable acts committed before the date of entry into force of the framework decision in accordance with the extradition system applicable before that date.

Statements provided for in Article 13(4)

Statement by Belgium:
The consent of the person concerned to his or her surrender may be revoked until the time of surrender.

Statement by Denmark:
Consent to surrender and express renunciation of entitlement to the speciality rule may be revoked in accordance with the relevant rules applicable at any time under Danish law.

Statement by Ireland:
In Ireland, consent to surrender and, where appropriate, express renunciation of the entitlement to the 'specialty' rule referred to in Article 27(2) may be revoked. Consent may be revoked in accordance with domestic law until surrender has been executed.

Statement by Finland:
In Finland, consent to surrender and, where appropriate, express renunciation of entitlement to the 'speciality rule' referred to in Article 27(2) may be revoked. Consent may be revoked in accordance with domestic law until surrender has been executed.

Statement by Sweden:
Consent or renunciation within the meaning of Article 13(1) may be revoked by the party whose surrender has been requested. Revocation must take place before the decision on surrender is executed.

Extradition Act 2003 ss1–25, 64, 65, 70–75, 137–138[1]

PART 1: EXTRADITION TO CATEGORY 1 TERRITORIES

Introduction

Extradition to category 1 territories

1 (1) This Part deals with extradition from the United Kingdom to the territories designated for the purposes of this Part by order made by the Secretary of State.

(2) In this Act references to category 1 territories are to the territories designated for the purposes of this Part.

(3) A territory may not be designated for the purposes of this Part if a person found guilty in the territory of a criminal offence may be sentenced to death for the offence under the general criminal law of the territory.

Part 1 warrant and certificate

2 (1) This section applies if the designated authority receives a Part 1 warrant in respect of a person.

(2) A Part 1 warrant is an arrest warrant which is issued by a judicial authority of a category 1 territory and which contains–

    (a) the statement referred to in subsection (3) and the information referred to in subsection (4), or

    (b) the statement referred to in subsection (5) and the information referred to in subsection (6).

(3) The statement is one that–

    (a) the person in respect of whom the Part 1 warrant is issued is accused in the category 1 territory of the commission of an offence specified in the warrant, and

    (b) the Part 1 warrant is issued with a view to his arrest and extradition to the category 1 territory for the purpose of being prosecuted for the offence.

(4) The information is–

    (a) particulars of the person's identity;

    (b) particulars of any other warrant issued in the category 1 territory for the person's arrest in respect of the offence;

    (c) particulars of the circumstances in which the person is alleged to have committed the offence, including the conduct alleged to constitute the offence, the time and place at which he is alleged to have committed the offence and any provision of the law of the category 1 territory under which the conduct is alleged to constitute an offence;

(d) particulars of the sentence which may be imposed under the law of the category 1 territory in respect of the offence if the person is convicted of it.

(5) The statement is one that–

(a) the person in respect of whom the Part 1 warrant is issued has been convicted of an offence specified in the warrant by a court in the category 1 territory, and

(b) the Part 1 warrant is issued with a view to his arrest and extradition to the category 1 territory for the purpose of being sentenced for the offence or of serving a sentence of imprisonment or another form of detention imposed in respect of the offence.

(6) The information is–

(a) particulars of the person's identity;

(b) particulars of the conviction;

(c) particulars of any other warrant issued in the category 1 territory for the person's arrest in respect of the offence;

(d) particulars of the sentence which may be imposed under the law of the category 1 territory in respect of the offence, if the person has not been sentenced for the offence;

(e) particulars of the sentence which has been imposed under the law of the category 1 territory in respect of the offence, if the person has been sentenced for the offence.

(7) The designated authority may issue a certificate under this section if it believes that the authority which issued the Part 1 warrant has the function of issuing arrest warrants in the category 1 territory.

(7A) But in the case of a Part 1 warrant containing the statement referred to in subsection (3), the designated authority must not issue a certificate under this section if it is clear to the designated authority that a judge proceeding under section 21A would be required to order the person's discharge on the basis that extradition would be disproportionate.

In deciding that question, the designated authority must apply any general guidance issued for the purposes of this subsection.

(7B) Any guidance under subsection (7A) may be revised, withdrawn or replaced.

(7C) The function of issuing guidance under subsection (7A), or of revising, withdrawing or replacing any such guidance, is exercisable by the Lord Chief Justice of England and Wales with the concurrence of–

(a) the Lord Justice General of Scotland, and

(b) the Lord Chief Justice of Northern Ireland.

(8) A certificate under this section must certify that the authority which issued the Part 1 warrant has the function of issuing arrest warrants in the category 1 territory.

(9) The designated authority is the authority designated for the purposes of this Part by order made by the Secretary of State.

(10) An order made under subsection (9) may–

(a) designate more than one authority;

(b) designate different authorities for different parts of the United Kingdom.

Arrest

Arrest under certified Part 1 warrant

3 (1) This section applies if a certificate is issued under section 2 in respect of a Part 1 warrant issued in respect of a person.

(2) The warrant may be executed by a constable or a customs officer in any part of the United Kingdom.

(3) The warrant may be executed by a service policeman anywhere, but only if the person is subject to service law or is a civilian subject to service discipline.

(5) The warrant may be executed even if neither the warrant nor a copy of it is in the possession of the person executing it at the time of the arrest.

Person arrested under Part 1 warrant

4 (1) This section applies if a person is arrested under a Part 1 warrant.

(2) A copy of the warrant must be given to the person as soon as practicable after his arrest.

(3) The person must be brought as soon as practicable before the appropriate judge.

(4) If subsection (2) is not complied with and the person applies to the judge to be discharged, the judge may order his discharge.

(5) If subsection (3) is not complied with and the person applies to the judge to be discharged, the judge must order his discharge.

(6) A person arrested under the warrant must be treated as continuing in legal custody until he is brought before the appropriate judge under subsection (3) or he is discharged under subsection (4) or (5).

Provisional arrest

5 (1) A constable, a customs officer or a service policeman may arrest a person without a warrant if he has reasonable grounds for believing–

    (a) that a Part 1 warrant has been or will be issued in respect of the person by an authority of a category 1 territory, and

    (b) that the authority has the function of issuing arrest warrants in the category 1 territory.

(2) A constable or a customs officer may arrest a person under subsection (1) in any part of the United Kingdom.

(3) A service policeman may arrest a person under subsection (1) only if the person is subject to service law or is a civilian subject to service discipline.

(4) If a service policeman has power to arrest a person under subsection (1) he may exercise the power anywhere.

Person arrested under section 5

6 (1) This section applies if a person is arrested under section 5.

(2) The person must be brought before the appropriate judge within 48 hours starting with the time when the person is arrested.

(2A) The documents specified in subsection (4) must be produced to the judge within 48 hours starting with the time when the person is arrested but this is subject to any extension under subsection (3B).

(2B) Subsection (3) applies if–

    (a) the person has been brought before the judge in compliance with subsection (2); but

   (b) documents have not been produced to the judge in compliance with subsection (2A).

  (3) The person must be brought before the judge when the documents are produced to the judge.

(3A) While the person is before the judge in pursuance of subsection (2), the authority of the category 1 territory may apply to the judge for an extension of the 48 hour period mentioned in subsection (2A) by a further 48 hours.

(3B) The judge may grant an extension if the judge decides that subsection (2A) could not reasonably be complied with within the initial 48 hour period.

(3C) The judge must decide whether that subsection could reasonably be so complied with on a balance of probabilities.

(3D) Notice of an application under subsection (3A) must be given in accordance with rules of court.

  (4) The documents are–
    (a) a Part 1 warrant in respect of the person;
    (b) a certificate under section 2 in respect of the warrant.

  (5) A copy of the warrant must be given to the person as soon as practicable after his arrest.

(5A) Subsection (5B) applies if–
    (a) the person is before the judge in pursuance of subsection (2); and
    (b) the documents specified in subsection (4) have not been produced to the judge.

(5B) The judge must remand the person in custody or on bail (subject to subsection (6)).

  (6) If subsection (2), (2A) or (3) is not complied with and the person applies to the judge to be discharged, the judge must order his discharge.

  (7) If subsection (5) is not complied with and the person applies to the judge to be discharged, the judge may order his discharge.

  (8) The person must be treated as continuing in legal custody until he is brought before the appropriate judge under subsection (2) or he is discharged under subsection (6) or (7).

(8A) In calculating a period of 48 hours for the purposes of this section no account is to be taken of–
    (a) any Saturday or Sunday;
    (b) Christmas Day;
    (c) Good Friday; or
    (d) any day falling within subsection (8B).

(8B) The following days fall within this subsection–
    (a) in Scotland, any day prescribed under section 8(2) of the Criminal Procedure (Scotland) Act 1995 as a court holiday in the court of the appropriate judge;
    (b) in any part of the United Kingdom, any day that is a bank holiday under the Banking and Financial Dealings Act 1971 in that part of the United Kingdom.

  (9) Subsection (10) applies if–
    (a) a person is arrested under section 5 on the basis of a belief that a Part 1 warrant has been or will be issued in respect of him;
    (b) the person is discharged under subsection (6) or (7).

(10) The person must not be arrested again under section 5 on the basis of a belief relating to the same Part 1 warrant.

The initial hearing

Identity of person arrested

7 (1) This section applies if–
   (a) a person arrested under a Part 1 warrant is brought before the appropriate judge under section 4(3), or
   (b) a person arrested under section 5 is brought before the appropriate judge under section 6 and section 6(2A) is complied with in relation to him.
  (2) The judge must decide whether the person brought before him is the person in respect of whom–
   (a) the warrant referred to in subsection (1)(a) was issued, or
   (b) the warrant referred to in section 6(4) was issued.
  (3) The judge must decide the question in subsection (2) on a balance of probabilities.
  (4) If the judge decides the question in subsection (2) in the negative he must order the person's discharge.
  (5) If the judge decides that question in the affirmative he must proceed under section 8.
  (6) In England and Wales, the judge has the same powers (as nearly as may be) as a magistrates' court would have if the proceedings were the summary trial of an information against the person.
  (7) In Scotland–
   (a) the judge has the same powers (as nearly as may be) as if the proceedings were summary proceedings in respect of an offence alleged to have been committed by the person; but
   (b) in his making any decision under subsection (2) evidence from a single source shall be sufficient.
  (8) In Northern Ireland, the judge has the same powers (as nearly as may be) as a magistrates' court would have if the proceedings were the hearing and determination of a complaint against the person.
  (9) If the judge exercises his power to adjourn the proceedings he must remand the person in custody or on bail.
 (10) If the person is remanded in custody, the appropriate judge may later grant bail.

Remand etc

8 (1) If the judge is required to proceed under this section he must–
   (a) fix a date on which the extradition hearing is to begin;
   (b) inform the person of the contents of the Part 1 warrant;
   (c) give the person the required information about consent;
   (d) remand the person in custody or on bail.
  (2) If the person is remanded in custody, the appropriate judge may later grant bail.
  (3) The required information about consent is–
   (a) that the person may consent to his extradition to the category 1 territory in which the Part 1 warrant was issued;

(b) an explanation of the effect of consent and the procedure that will apply if he gives consent;

(c) that consent must be given before the judge and is irrevocable.

(4) The date fixed under subsection (1) must not be later than the end of the permitted period, which is 21 days starting with the date of the arrest referred to in section 7(1)(a) or (b).

(4A) But if proceedings in respect of the extradition are adjourned under section 8A or 8B, the permitted period is extended by the number of days for which the proceedings are so adjourned.

(5) If before the date fixed under subsection (1) (or this subsection) a party to the proceedings applies to the judge for a later date to be fixed and the judge believes it to be in the interests of justice to do so, he may fix a later date; and this subsection may apply more than once.

(6) Subsections (7) and (8) apply if the extradition hearing does not begin on or before the date fixed under this section.

(7) If the person applies to the judge to be discharged the judge must order his discharge, unless reasonable cause is shown for the delay.

(8) If no application is made under subsection (7) the judge must order the person's discharge on the first occasion after the date fixed under this section when the person appears or is brought before the judge, unless reasonable cause is shown for the delay.

Person charged with offence in United Kingdom before extradition hearing

8A(1) This section applies if–

(a) a person has been brought before the appropriate judge under section 4(3) or 6(2) but the extradition hearing has not begun; and

(b) the judge is informed that the person is charged with an offence in the United Kingdom.

(2) The judge must order further proceedings in respect of the extradition to be adjourned until one of these occurs–

(a) the charge is disposed of;

(b) the charge is withdrawn;

(c) proceedings in respect of the charge are discontinued;

(d) an order is made for the charge to lie on the file, or in relation to Scotland, the diet is deserted *pro loco et tempore.*

(3) If a sentence of imprisonment or another form of detention is imposed in respect of the offence charged, the judge may order further proceedings in respect of the extradition to be adjourned until the person is released from detention pursuant to the sentence (whether on licence or otherwise).

Person serving sentence in United Kingdom before extradition hearing

8B(1) This section applies if–

(a) a person has been brought before the appropriate judge under section 4(3) or 6(2) but the extradition hearing has not begun; and

(b) the judge is informed that the person is in custody serving a sentence of imprisonment or another form of detention in the United Kingdom.

(2) The judge may order further proceedings in respect of the extradition to be adjourned until the person is released from detention pursuant to the sentence (whether on licence or otherwise).

(3) In a case where further proceedings in respect of the extradition are adjourned under subsection (2)–
  (a) section 131 of the Magistrates' Courts Act 1980 (remand of accused already in custody) has effect as if a reference to 28 clear days in subsection (1) or (2) of that section were a reference to six months;
  (b) Article 47(2) of the Magistrates' Courts (Northern Ireland) Order 1981 (period of remand in custody) has effect as if a reference to 28 days in–
    (i) sub-paragraph (a)(iii), or
    (ii) the words after sub-paragraph (b),
    were a reference to six months.

The extradition hearing

Judge's powers at extradition hearing

9 (1) In England and Wales, at the extradition hearing the appropriate judge has the same powers (as nearly as may be) as a magistrates' court would have if the proceedings were the summary trial of an information against the person in respect of whom the Part 1 warrant was issued.
  (2) In Scotland, at the extradition hearing the appropriate judge has the same powers (as nearly as may be) as if the proceedings were summary proceedings in respect of an offence alleged to have been committed by the person in respect of whom the Part 1 warrant was issued.
  (3) In Northern Ireland, at the extradition hearing the appropriate judge has the same powers (as nearly as may be) as a magistrates' court would have if the proceedings were the hearing and determination of a complaint against the person in respect of whom the Part 1 warrant was issued.
  (4) If the judge adjourns the extradition hearing he must remand the person in custody or on bail.
  (5) If the person is remanded in custody, the appropriate judge may later grant bail.

Initial stage of extradition hearing

10 (1) This section applies if a person in respect of whom a Part 1 warrant is issued appears or is brought before the appropriate judge for the extradition hearing.
  (2) The judge must decide whether the offence specified in the Part 1 warrant is an extradition offence.
  (3) If the judge decides the question in subsection (2) in the negative he must order the person's discharge.
  (4) If the judge decides that question in the affirmative he must proceed under section 11.

Bars to extradition

11 (1) If the judge is required to proceed under this section he must decide whether the person's extradition to the category 1 territory is barred by reason of–
  (a) the rule against double jeopardy;
  (aa) absence of prosecution decision;
  (b) extraneous considerations;
  (c) the passage of time;
  (d) the person's age;
  (e) [*Repealed*]

(f) speciality;

(g) the person's earlier extradition to the United Kingdom from another category 1 territory;

(h) the person's earlier extradition to the United Kingdom from a non-category 1 territory;

(i) the person's earlier transfer to the United Kingdom by the International Criminal Court;

(j) forum.

(1A) But the judge is to decide whether the person's extradition is barred by reason of–

(a) absence of prosecution decision, or

(b) forum,

only in a case where the Part 1 warrant contains the statement referred to in section 2(3) (warrant issued for purposes of prosecution for offence in category 1 territory).

(2) Sections 12 to 19F apply for the interpretation of subsection (1).

(3) If the judge decides any of the questions in subsection (1) in the affirmative he must order the person's discharge.

(4) If the judge decides those questions in the negative and the person is alleged to be unlawfully at large after conviction of the extradition offence, the judge must proceed under section 20.

(5) If the judge decides those questions in the negative and the person is accused of the commission of the extradition offence but is not alleged to be unlawfully at large after conviction of it, the judge must proceed under section 21A.

Rule against double jeopardy

12 A person's extradition to a category 1 territory is barred by reason of the rule against double jeopardy if (and only if) it appears that he would be entitled to be discharged under any rule of law relating to previous acquittal or conviction on the assumption–

(a) that the conduct constituting the extradition offence constituted an offence in the part of the United Kingdom where the judge exercises jurisdiction;

(b) that the person were charged with the extradition offence in that part of the United Kingdom.

Absence of prosecution decision

12A(1) A person's extradition to a category 1 territory is barred by reason of absence of prosecution decision if (and only if)–

(a) it appears to the appropriate judge that there are reasonable grounds for believing that–

(i) the competent authorities in the category 1 territory have not made a decision to charge or have not made a decision to try (or have made neither of those decisions), and

(ii) the person's absence from the category 1 territory is not the sole reason for that failure,

and

(b) those representing the category 1 territory do not prove that–

(i) the competent authorities in the category 1 territory have made a decision to charge and a decision to try, or

(ii) in a case where one of those decisions has not been made (or neither of them has been made), the person's absence from the category 1 territory is the sole reason for that failure.

(2) In this section 'to charge' and 'to try', in relation to a person and an extradition offence, mean–

(a) to charge the person with the offence in the category 1 territory, and

(b) to try the person for the offence in the category 1 territory.

Extraneous considerations

13 A person's extradition to a category 1 territory is barred by reason of extraneous considerations if (and only if) it appears that–

(a) the Part 1 warrant issued in respect of him (though purporting to be issued on account of the extradition offence) is in fact issued for the purpose of prosecuting or punishing him on account of his race, religion, nationality, gender, sexual orientation or political opinions, or

(b) if extradited he might be prejudiced at his trial or punished, detained or restricted in his personal liberty by reason of his race, religion, nationality, gender, sexual orientation or political opinions.

Passage of time

14 A person's extradition to a category 1 territory is barred by reason of the passage of time if (and only if) it appears that it would be unjust or oppressive to extradite him by reason of the passage of time since he is alleged to have–

(a) committed the extradition offence (where he is accused of its commission), or

(b) become unlawfully at large (where he is alleged to have been convicted of it).

Age

15 A person's extradition to a category 1 territory is barred by reason of his age if (and only if) it would be conclusively presumed because of his age that he could not be guilty of the extradition offence on the assumption–

(a) that the conduct constituting the extradition offence constituted an offence in the part of the United Kingdom where the judge exercises jurisdiction;

(b) that the person carried out the conduct when the extradition offence was committed (or alleged to be committed);

(c) that the person carried out the conduct in the part of the United Kingdom where the judge exercises jurisdiction.

16 [*repealed*]

Speciality

17 (1) A person's extradition to a category 1 territory is barred by reason of speciality if (and only if) there are no speciality arrangements with the category 1 territory.

(2) There are speciality arrangements with a category 1 territory if, under the law of that territory or arrangements made between it and the United Kingdom, a person who is extradited to the territory from the United Kingdom may be

dealt with in the territory for an offence committed before his extradition only if–
(a) the offence is one falling within subsection (3), or
(b) the condition in subsection (4) is satisfied.

(3) The offences are–
(a) the offence in respect of which the person is extradited;
(b) an extradition offence disclosed by the same facts as that offence;
(c) an extradition offence in respect of which the appropriate judge gives his consent under section 55 to the person being dealt with;
(d) an offence which is not punishable with imprisonment or another form of detention;
(e) an offence in respect of which the person will not be detained in connection with his trial, sentence or appeal;
(f) an offence in respect of which the person waives the right that he would have (but for this paragraph) not to be dealt with for the offence.

(4) The condition is that the person is given an opportunity to leave the category 1 territory and–
(a) he does not do so before the end of the permitted period, or
(b) if he does so before the end of the permitted period, he returns there.

(5) The permitted period is 45 days starting with the day on which the person arrives in the category 1 territory.

(6) Arrangements made with a category 1 territory which is a Commonwealth country or a British overseas territory may be made for a particular case or more generally.

(7) A certificate issued by or under the authority of the Secretary of State confirming the existence of arrangements with a category 1 territory which is a Commonwealth country or a British overseas territory and stating the terms of the arrangements is conclusive evidence of those matters.

Earlier extradition to United Kingdom from category 1 territory

18 A person's extradition to a category 1 territory is barred by reason of his earlier extradition to the United Kingdom from another category 1 territory if (and only if)–
(a) the person was extradited to the United Kingdom from another category 1 territory (the extraditing territory);
(b) under arrangements between the United Kingdom and the extraditing territory, that territory's consent is required to the person's extradition from the United Kingdom to the category 1 territory in respect of the extradition offence under consideration;
(c) that consent has not been given on behalf of the extraditing territory.

Earlier extradition to United Kingdom from non-category 1 territory

19 A person's extradition to a category 1 territory is barred by reason of his earlier extradition to the United Kingdom from a non-category 1 territory if (and only if)–
(a) the person was extradited to the United Kingdom from a territory that is not a category 1 territory (the extraditing territory);
(b) under arrangements between the United Kingdom and the extraditing territory, that territory's consent is required to the person's being dealt

with in the United Kingdom in respect of the extradition offence under consideration;

(c) consent has not been given on behalf of the extraditing territory to the person's extradition from the United Kingdom to the category 1 territory in respect of the extradition offence under consideration.

Earlier transfer to United Kingdom by International Criminal Court

19A(1) A person's extradition to a category 1 territory is barred by reason of his earlier transfer by the International Criminal Court if (and only if)–

(a) the person was transferred to the United Kingdom to serve a sentence imposed by the Court;

(b) under arrangements between the United Kingdom and the Court, the consent of the Presidency of the Court is required to the person's extradition from the United Kingdom to the category 1 territory in respect of the extradition offence under consideration;

(c) that consent has not been given.

(2) Subsection (1) does not apply if the person has served the sentence imposed by the Court and has subsequently–

(a) remained voluntarily in the United Kingdom for more than 30 days, or

(b) left the United Kingdom and returned to it.

Forum

19B(1) The extradition of a person ('D') to a category 1 territory is barred by reason of forum if the extradition would not be in the interests of justice.

(2) For the purposes of this section, the extradition would not be in the interests of justice if the judge–

(a) decides that a substantial measure of D's relevant activity was performed in the United Kingdom; and

(b) decides, having regard to the specified matters relating to the interests of justice (and only those matters), that the extradition should not take place.

(3) These are the specified matters relating to the interests of justice–

(a) the place where most of the loss or harm resulting from the extradition offence occurred or was intended to occur;

(b) the interests of any victims of the extradition offence;

(c) any belief of a prosecutor that the United Kingdom, or a particular part of the United Kingdom, is not the most appropriate jurisdiction in which to prosecute D in respect of the conduct constituting the extradition offence;

(d) were D to be prosecuted in a part of the United Kingdom for an offence that corresponds to the extradition offence, whether evidence necessary to prove the offence is or could be made available in the United Kingdom;

(e) any delay that might result from proceeding in one jurisdiction rather than another;

(f) the desirability and practicability of all prosecutions relating to the extradition offence taking place in one jurisdiction, having regard (in particular) to–

(i) the jurisdictions in which witnesses, co-defendants and other suspects are located, and

      (ii) the practicability of the evidence of such persons being given in the United Kingdom or in jurisdictions outside the United Kingdom;

    (g) D's connections with the United Kingdom.

(4) In deciding whether the extradition would not be in the interests of justice, the judge must have regard to the desirability of not requiring the disclosure of material which is subject to restrictions on disclosure in the category 1 territory concerned.

(5) If, on an application by a prosecutor, it appears to the judge that the prosecutor has considered the offences for which D could be prosecuted in the United Kingdom, or a part of the United Kingdom, in respect of the conduct constituting the extradition offence, the judge must make that prosecutor a party to the proceedings on the question of whether D's extradition is barred by reason of forum.

(6) In this section 'D's relevant activity' means activity which is material to the commission of the extradition offence and which is alleged to have been performed by D.

Effect of prosecutor's certificates on forum proceedings

19C(1) The judge hearing proceedings under section 19B (the 'forum proceedings') must decide that the extradition is not barred by reason of forum if (at a time when the judge has not yet decided the proceedings) the judge receives a prosecutor's certificate relating to the extradition.

(2) That duty to decide the forum proceedings in that way is subject to the determination of any question relating to the prosecutor's certificate raised in accordance with section 19E.

(3) A designated prosecutor may apply for the forum proceedings to be adjourned for the purpose of assisting that or any other designated prosecutor–

    (a) in considering whether to give a prosecutor's certificate relating to the extradition,

    (b) in giving such a certificate, or

    (c) in sending such a certificate to the judge.

(4) If such an application is made, the judge must–

    (a) adjourn the forum proceedings until the application is decided; and

    (b) continue the adjournment, for such period as appears to the judge to be reasonable, if the application is granted.

(5) But the judge must end the adjournment if the application is not granted.

Prosecutor's certificates

19D(1) A 'prosecutor's certificate' is a certificate given by a designated prosecutor which–

    (a) certifies both matter A and matter B, and

    (b) certifies either matter C or matter D.

(2) Matter A is that a responsible prosecutor has considered the offences for which D could be prosecuted in the United Kingdom, or a part of the United Kingdom, in respect of the conduct constituting the extradition offence.

(3) Matter B is that the responsible prosecutor has decided that there are one or more such offences that correspond to the extradition offence (the 'corresponding offences').

(4) Matter C is that–

(a) the responsible prosecutor has made a formal decision as to the prosecution of D for the corresponding offences,

(b) that decision is that D should not be prosecuted for the corresponding offences, and

(c) the reason for that decision is a belief that–

(i) there would be insufficient admissible evidence for the prosecution; or

(ii) the prosecution would not be in the public interest.

(5) Matter D is that the responsible prosecutor believes that D should not be prosecuted for the corresponding offences because there are concerns about the disclosure of sensitive material in–

(a) the prosecution of D for the corresponding offences, or

(b) any other proceedings.

(6) In relation to the extradition of any person to a category 1 territory, neither this section nor any other rule of law (whether or not contained in an enactment) may require a designated prosecutor–

(a) to consider any matter relevant to giving a prosecutor's certificate; or

(b) to consider whether to give a prosecutor's certificate.

(7) In this section 'sensitive material' means material which appears to the responsible prosecutor to be sensitive, including material appearing to be sensitive on grounds relating to–

(a) national security,

(b) international relations, or

(c) the prevention or detection of crime (including grounds relating to the identification or activities of witnesses, informants or any other persons supplying information to the police or any other law enforcement agency who may be in danger if their identities are revealed).

Questioning of prosecutor's certificate

19E(1) No decision of a designated prosecutor relating to a prosecutor's certificate in respect of D's extradition (a 'relevant certification decision') may be questioned except on an appeal under section 26 against an order for that extradition.

(2) In England and Wales, and Northern Ireland, for the purpose of–

(a) determining whether to give permission for a relevant certification decision to be questioned, and

(b) determining any such question (if that permission is given),

the High Court must apply the procedures and principles which would be applied by it on an application for judicial review.

(3) In Scotland, for the purpose of determining any questioning of a relevant certification decision, the High Court must apply the procedures and principles that would be applied by it on an application for judicial review.

(4) In a case where the High Court quashes a prosecutor's certificate, the High Court is to decide the question of whether or not the extradition is barred by reason of forum.

(5) Where the High Court is required to decide that question by virtue of subsection (4)–

(a) sections 19B to 19D and this section apply in relation to that decision (with the appropriate modifications) as they apply to a decision by a judge; and

(b) in particular–
  (i) a reference in this section to an appeal under section 26 has effect as a reference to an appeal under section 32 to the Supreme Court;
  (ii) a reference in this section to the High Court has effect as a reference to the Supreme Court.

Interpretation of sections 19B to 19E

19F (1) This section applies for the purposes of sections 19B to 19E (and this section).

(2) These expressions have the meanings given–
'D' has the meaning given in section 19B(1);
'designated prosecutor' means–
  (a) a member of the Crown Prosecution Service, or
  (b) any other person who–
    (i) is a prosecutor designated for the purposes of this section by order made by the Secretary of State, or
    (ii) is within a description of prosecutors so designated;
'extradition offence' means the offence specified in the Part 1 warrant (including the conduct that constitutes the extradition offence);
'forum proceedings' has the meaning given in section 19C(1);
'part of the United Kingdom' means–
  (a) England and Wales;
  (b) Scotland;
  (c) Northern Ireland;
'prosecutor' means a person who has responsibility for prosecuting offences in any part of the United Kingdom (whether or not the person also has other responsibilities);
'prosecutor's certificate' has the meaning given in section 19D(1);
'responsible prosecutor', in relation to a prosecutor's certificate, means–
  (a) the designated prosecutor giving the certificate, or
  (b) another designated prosecutor.

(3) In determining for any purpose whether an offence corresponds to the extradition offence, regard must be had, in particular, to the nature and seriousness of the two offences.

(4) A reference to a formal decision as to the prosecution of D for an offence is a reference to a decision (made after complying with, in particular, any applicable requirement concerning a code of practice) that D should, or should not, be prosecuted for the offence.

Case where person has been convicted

20 (1) If the judge is required to proceed under this section (by virtue of section 11) he must decide whether the person was convicted in his presence.

(2) If the judge decides the question in subsection (1) in the affirmative he must proceed under section 21.

(3) If the judge decides that question in the negative he must decide whether the person deliberately absented himself from his trial.

(4) If the judge decides the question in subsection (3) in the affirmative he must proceed under section 21.

(5) If the judge decides that question in the negative he must decide whether the person would be entitled to a retrial or (on appeal) to a review amounting to a retrial.

(6) If the judge decides the question in subsection (5) in the affirmative he must proceed under section 21.

(7) If the judge decides that question in the negative he must order the person's discharge.

(8) The judge must not decide the question in subsection (5) in the affirmative unless, in any proceedings that it is alleged would constitute a retrial or a review amounting to a retrial, the person would have these rights–

(a) the right to defend himself in person or through legal assistance of his own choosing or, if he had not sufficient means to pay for legal assistance, to be given it free when the interests of justice so required;

(b) the right to examine or have examined witnesses against him and to obtain the attendance and examination of witnesses on his behalf under the same conditions as witnesses against him.

Person unlawfully at large: human rights

21 (1) If the judge is required to proceed under this section (by virtue of section 20) he must decide whether the person's extradition would be compatible with the Convention rights within the meaning of the Human Rights Act 1998.

(2) If the judge decides the question in subsection (1) in the negative he must order the person's discharge.

(3) If the judge decides that question in the affirmative he must order the person to be extradited to the category 1 territory in which the warrant was issued.

(4) If the judge makes an order under subsection (3) he must remand the person in custody or on bail to wait for his extradition to the category 1 territory.

(5) If the person is remanded in custody, the appropriate judge may later grant bail.

Person not convicted: human rights and proportionality

21A(1) If the judge is required to proceed under this section (by virtue of section 11), the judge must decide both of the following questions in respect of the extradition of the person ('D')–

(a) whether the extradition would be compatible with the Convention rights within the meaning of the Human Rights Act 1998;

(b) whether the extradition would be disproportionate.

(2) In deciding whether the extradition would be disproportionate, the judge must take into account the specified matters relating to proportionality (so far as the judge thinks it appropriate to do so); but the judge must not take any other matters into account.

(3) These are the specified matters relating to proportionality–

(a) the seriousness of the conduct alleged to constitute the extradition offence;

(b) the likely penalty that would be imposed if D was found guilty of the extradition offence;

(c) the possibility of the relevant foreign authorities taking measures that would be less coercive than the extradition of D.

(4) The judge must order D's discharge if the judge makes one or both of these decisions–

(a) that the extradition would not be compatible with the Convention rights;

(b) that the extradition would be disproportionate.

(5) The judge must order D to be extradited to the category 1 territory in which the warrant was issued if the judge makes both of these decisions–

    (a) that the extradition would be compatible with the Convention rights;

    (b) that the extradition would not be disproportionate.

(6) If the judge makes an order under subsection (5) he must remand the person in custody or on bail to wait for extradition to the category 1 territory.

(7) If the person is remanded in custody, the appropriate judge may later grant bail.

(8) In this section 'relevant foreign authorities' means the authorities in the territory to which D would be extradited if the extradition went ahead.

Matters arising before end of extradition hearing

Request for temporary transfer etc

21B(1) This section applies if–

    (a) a Part 1 warrant is issued which contains the statement referred to in section 2(3) (warrant issued for purposes of prosecution for offence in category 1 territory), and

    (b) at any time before or in the extradition hearing, the appropriate judge is informed that a request under subsection (2) or (3) has been made.

(2) A request under this subsection is a request by a judicial authority of the category 1 territory in which the warrant is issued ('the requesting territory')–

    (a) that the person in respect of whom the warrant is issued be temporarily transferred to the requesting territory, or

    (b) that arrangements be made to enable the person to speak with representatives of an authority in the requesting territory responsible for investigating, prosecuting or trying the offence specified in the warrant.

(3) A request under this subsection is a request by the person in respect of whom the warrant is issued–

    (a) to be temporarily transferred to the requesting territory, or

    (b) that arrangements be made to enable the person to speak with representatives of an authority in the requesting territory responsible for investigating, prosecuting or trying the offence specified in the warrant.

(4) The judge must order further proceedings in respect of the extradition to be adjourned if the judge thinks it necessary to do so to enable the person (in the case of a request under subsection (2)) or the authority by which the warrant is issued (in the case of a request under subsection (3)) to consider whether to consent to the request.

An adjournment under this subsection must not be for more than 7 days.

(5) If the person or authority consents to the request, the judge must–

    (a) make whatever orders and directions seem appropriate for giving effect to the request;

    (b) order further proceedings in respect of the extradition to be adjourned for however long seems necessary to enable the orders and directions to be carried out.

(6) If the request, or consent to the request, is withdrawn before effect (or full effect) has been given to it–

    (a) no steps (or further steps) may be taken to give effect to the request;

(b) the judge may make whatever further orders and directions seem appropriate (including an order superseding one made under subsection (5)(b)).

(7) A person may not make a request under paragraph (a) or (b) of subsection (3) in respect of a warrant if the person has already given consent to a request under the corresponding paragraph of subsection (2) in respect of that warrant (even if that consent has been withdrawn).

(8) A person may not make a further request under paragraph (a) or (b) of subsection (3) in respect of a warrant if the person has already made a request under that paragraph in respect of that warrant (even if that request has been withdrawn).

(9) If–

(a) a request under subsection (2) or (3) is made before a date has been fixed on which the extradition hearing is to begin, and

(b) the proceedings are adjourned under this section,

the permitted period for the purposes of fixing that date (see section 8(4)) is extended by the number of days for which the proceedings are so adjourned.

Person charged with offence in United Kingdom

22 (1) This section applies if at any time in the extradition hearing the judge is informed that the person in respect of whom the Part 1 warrant is issued is charged with an offence in the United Kingdom.

(2) The judge must adjourn the extradition hearing until one of these occurs–

(a) the charge is disposed of;

(b) the charge is withdrawn;

(c) proceedings in respect of the charge are discontinued;

(d) an order is made for the charge to lie on the file, or in relation to Scotland, the diet is deserted *pro loco et tempore*.

(3) If a sentence of imprisonment or another form of detention is imposed in respect of the offence charged, the judge may adjourn the extradition hearing until the person is released from detention pursuant to the sentence (whether on licence or otherwise).

(4) If before he adjourns the extradition hearing under subsection (2) the judge has decided under section 11 whether the person's extradition is barred by reason of the rule against double jeopardy, the judge must decide that question again after the resumption of the hearing.

Person serving sentence in United Kingdom

23 (1) This section applies if at any time in the extradition hearing the judge is informed that the person in respect of whom the Part 1 warrant is issued is in custody serving a sentence of imprisonment or another form of detention in the United Kingdom.

(2) The judge may adjourn the extradition hearing until the person is released from detention pursuant to the sentence (whether on licence or otherwise).

(3) In a case where an extradition hearing is adjourned under subsection (2)–

(a) section 131 of the Magistrates' Courts Act 1980 (remand of accused already in custody) has effect as if a reference to 28 clear days in subsection (1) or (2) of that section were a reference to six months;

(b) Article 47(2) of the Magistrates' Courts (Northern Ireland) Order 1981 (SI

No 1675 (NI 26)) (period of remand in custody) has effect as if a reference to 28 days in–
(i) paragraph (a)(iii), or
(ii) the words after paragraph (b),
were a reference to six months.

Extradition request

24 (1) This section applies if at any time in the extradition hearing the judge is informed that–
(a) a certificate has been issued under section 70 in respect of a request for the person's extradition;
(b) the request has not been disposed of;
(c) an order has been made under section 179(2) for further proceedings on the warrant to be deferred until the request has been disposed of.
(2) The judge must remand the person in custody or on bail.
(3) If the person is remanded in custody, the appropriate judge may later grant bail.

Physical or mental condition

25 (1) This section applies if at any time in the extradition hearing it appears to the judge that the condition in subsection (2) is satisfied.
(2) The condition is that the physical or mental condition of the person in respect of whom the Part 1 warrant is issued is such that it would be unjust or oppressive to extradite him.
(3) The judge must–
(a) order the person's discharge, or
(b) adjourn the extradition hearing until it appears to him that the condition in subsection (2) is no longer satisfied.
...

Interpretation

Extradition offences: person not sentenced for offence

64 (1) This section sets out whether a person's conduct constitutes an 'extradition offence' for the purposes of this Part in a case where the person–
(a) is accused in a category 1 territory of an offence constituted by the conduct, or
(b) has been convicted in that territory of an offence constituted by the conduct but not sentenced for it.
(2) The conduct constitutes an extradition offence in relation to the category 1 territory if the conditions in subsection (3), (4) or (5) are satisfied.
(3) The conditions in this subsection are that–
(a) the conduct occurs in the category 1 territory;
(b) the conduct would constitute an offence under the law of the relevant part of the United Kingdom if it occurred in that part of the United Kingdom;
(c) the conduct is punishable under the law of the category 1 territory with imprisonment or another form of detention for a term of 12 months or a greater punishment.
(4) The conditions in this subsection are that–
(a) the conduct occurs outside the category 1 territory;

   (b) in corresponding circumstances equivalent conduct would constitute an extra-territorial offence under the law of the relevant part of the United Kingdom;
   (c) the conduct is punishable under the law of the category 1 territory with imprisonment or another form of detention for a term of 12 months or a greater punishment.
(5) The conditions in this subsection are that–
   (a) the conduct occurs in the category 1 territory;
   (b) no part of the conduct occurs in the United Kingdom;
   (c) a certificate issued by an appropriate authority of the category 1 territory shows that the conduct falls within the European framework list;
   (d) the certificate shows that the conduct is punishable under the law of the category 1 territory with imprisonment or another form of detention for a term of 3 years or a greater punishment.
(6) For the purposes of subsections (3)(b) and (4)(b)–
   (a) if the conduct relates to a tax or duty, it does not matter whether the law of the relevant part of the United Kingdom imposes the same kind of tax or duty or contains rules of the same kind as those of the law of the category 1 territory;
   (b) if the conduct relates to customs or exchange, it does not matter whether the law of the relevant part of the United Kingdom contains rules of the same kind as those of the law of the category 1 territory.

Extradition offences: person sentenced for offence

65 (1) This section sets out whether a person's conduct constitutes an 'extradition offence' for the purposes of this Part in a case where the person–
   (a) has been convicted in a category 1 territory of an offence constituted by the conduct, and
   (b) has been sentenced for the offence.
(2) The conduct constitutes an extradition offence in relation to the category 1 territory if the conditions in subsection (3), (4) or (5) are satisfied.
(3) The conditions in this subsection are that–
   (a) the conduct occurs in the category 1 territory;
   (b) the conduct would constitute an offence under the law of the relevant part of the United Kingdom if it occurred in that part of the United Kingdom;
   (c) a sentence of imprisonment or another form of detention for a term of 4 months or a greater punishment has been imposed in the category 1 territory in respect of the conduct.
(4) The conditions in this subsection are that–
   (a) the conduct occurs outside the category 1 territory;
   (b) in corresponding circumstances equivalent conduct would constitute an extra-territorial offence under the law of the relevant part of the United Kingdom;
   (c) a sentence of imprisonment or another form of detention for a term of 4 months or a greater punishment has been imposed in the category 1 territory in respect of the conduct.
(5) The conditions in this subsection are that–
   (a) the conduct occurs in the category 1 territory;

(b) no part of the conduct occurs in the United Kingdom;

(c) a certificate issued by an appropriate authority of the category 1 territory shows that the conduct falls within the European framework list;

(d) the certificate shows that a sentence of imprisonment or another form of detention for a term of 4 months or a greater punishment has been imposed in the category 1 territory in respect of the conduct.

(6) For the purposes of subsections (3)(b) and (4)(b)–

(a) if the conduct relates to a tax or duty, it does not matter whether the law of the relevant part of the United Kingdom imposes the same kind of tax or duty or contains rules of the same kind as those of the law of the category 1 territory;

(b) if the conduct relates to customs or exchange, it does not matter whether the law of the relevant part of the United Kingdom contains rules of the same kind as those of the law of the category 1 territory.

...

PART 2: EXTRADITION TO CATEGORY 2 TERRITORIES

Extradition request and certificate

70 (1) The Secretary of State must (subject to subsection (2)) issue a certificate under this section if he receives a valid request for the extradition of a person to a category 2 territory.

(2) The Secretary of State may refuse to issue a certificate under this section if–

(a) he has power under section 126 to order that proceedings on the request be deferred,

(b) the person whose extradition is requested has been recorded by the Secretary of State as a refugee within the meaning of the Refugee Convention, or

(c) the person whose extradition is requested has been granted leave to enter or remain in the United Kingdom on the ground that it would be a breach of Article 2 or 3 of the Human Rights Convention to remove him to the territory to which extradition is requested.

(3) A request for a person's extradition is valid if–

(a) it contains the statement referred to in subsection (4) or the statement referred to in subsection (4A), and

(b) it is made in the approved way.

(4) The statement is one that–

(a) the person is accused in the category 2 territory of the commission of an offence specified in the request, and

(b) the request is made with a view to his arrest and extradition to the category 2 territory for the purpose of being prosecuted for the offence.

(4A) The statement is one that–

(a) the person has been convicted of an offence specified in the request by a court in the category 2 territory, and

(b) the request is made with a view to his arrest and extradition to the category 2 territory for the purpose of being sentenced for the offence or of serving a sentence of imprisonment or another form of detention imposed in respect of the offence.

(5) A request for extradition to a category 2 territory which is a British overseas

territory is made in the approved way if it is made by or on behalf of the person administering the territory.

(6) A request for extradition to a category 2 territory which is the Hong Kong Special Administrative Region of the People's Republic of China is made in the approved way if it is made by or on behalf of the government of the Region.

(7) A request for extradition to any other category 2 territory is made in the approved way if it is made–
  (a) by an authority of the territory which the Secretary of State believes has the function of making requests for extradition in that territory, or
  (b) by a person recognised by the Secretary of State as a diplomatic or consular representative of the territory.

(8) A certificate under this section must–
  (a) certify that the request is made in the approved way, and
  (b) identify the order by which the territory in question is designated as a category 2 territory.

(9) If a certificate is issued under this section the Secretary of State must send the request and the certificate to the appropriate judge.

(10) Subsection (11) applies at all times after the Secretary of State issues a certificate under this section.

(11) The Secretary of State is not to consider whether the extradition would be compatible with the Convention rights within the meaning of the Human Rights Act 1998.

Arrest

Arrest warrant following extradition request

71 (1) This section applies if the Secretary of State sends documents to the appropriate judge under section 70.

(2) The judge may issue a warrant for the arrest of the person whose extradition is requested if the judge has reasonable grounds for believing that–
  (a) the offence in respect of which extradition is requested is an extradition offence, and
  (b) there is evidence falling within subsection (3).

(3) The evidence is–
  (a) evidence that would justify the issue of a warrant for the arrest of a person accused of the offence within the judge's jurisdiction, if the person whose extradition is requested is accused of the commission of the offence;
  (b) evidence that would justify the issue of a warrant for the arrest of a person unlawfully at large after conviction of the offence within the judge's jurisdiction, if the person whose extradition is requested is alleged to be unlawfully at large after conviction of the offence.

(4) But if the category 2 territory to which extradition is requested is designated for the purposes of this section by order made by the Secretary of State, subsections (2) and (3) have effect as if 'evidence' read 'information'.

(5) A warrant issued under this section may–
  (a) be executed by any person to whom it is directed or by any constable or customs officer;
  (b) be executed even if neither the warrant nor a copy of it is in the possession of the person executing it at the time of the arrest.

(6) If a warrant issued under this section—
  (a) is directed to a service policeman, and
  (b) is in respect of a person subject to service law or a civilian subject to service discipline,
  it may be executed anywhere.
(7) In any other case, a warrant issued under this section may be executed in any part of the United Kingdom.

Person arrested under section 71

72 (1) This section applies if a person is arrested under a warrant issued under section 71.
(2) A copy of the warrant must be given to the person as soon as practicable after his arrest.
(3) The person must be brought as soon as practicable before the appropriate judge.
(4) But subsection (3) does not apply if—
  (a) the person is granted bail by a constable following his arrest, or
  (b) the Secretary of State decides under section 126 that the request for the person's extradition is not to be proceeded with.
(5) If subsection (2) is not complied with and the person applies to the judge to be discharged, the judge may order his discharge.
(6) If subsection (3) is not complied with and the person applies to the judge to be discharged, the judge must order his discharge.
(7) When the person first appears or is brought before the appropriate judge, the judge must—
  (a) inform him of the contents of the request for his extradition;
  (b) give him the required information about consent;
  (c) remand him in custody or on bail.
(8) The required information about consent is—
  (a) that the person may consent to his extradition to the category 2 territory to which his extradition is requested;
  (b) an explanation of the effect of consent and the procedure that will apply if he gives consent;
  (c) that consent must be given in writing and is irrevocable.
(9) If the person is remanded in custody, the appropriate judge may later grant bail.
(10) Subsection (4)(a) applies to Scotland with the omission of the words 'by a constable'.

Provisional warrant

73 (1) This section applies if a justice of the peace is satisfied on information in writing and on oath that a person within subsection (2)—
  (a) is or is believed to be in the United Kingdom, or
  (b) is or is believed to be on his way to the United Kingdom.
(2) A person is within this subsection if—
  (a) he is accused in a category 2 territory of the commission of an offence, or
  (b) he is alleged to be unlawfully at large after conviction of an offence by a court in a category 2 territory.

(3) The justice may issue a warrant for the arrest of the person (a provisional warrant) if he has reasonable grounds for believing that–
    (a) the offence of which the person is accused or has been convicted is an extradition offence, and
    (b) there is written evidence falling within subsection (4).

(4) The evidence is–
    (a) evidence that would justify the issue of a warrant for the arrest of a person accused of the offence within the justice's jurisdiction, if the person in respect of whom the warrant is sought is accused of the commission of the offence;
    (b) evidence that would justify the issue of a warrant for the arrest of a person unlawfully at large after conviction of the offence within the justice's jurisdiction, if the person in respect of whom the warrant is sought is alleged to be unlawfully at large after conviction of the offence.

(5) But if the category 2 territory is designated for the purposes of this section by order made by the Secretary of State, subsections (3) and (4) have effect as if 'evidence' read 'information'.

(6) A provisional warrant may–
    (a) be executed by any person to whom it is directed or by any constable or customs officer;
    (b) be executed even if neither the warrant nor a copy of it is in the possession of the person executing it at the time of the arrest.

(7) If a warrant issued under this section–
    (a) is directed to a service policeman, and
    (b) is in respect of a person subject to service law or a civilian subject to service discipline,
it may be executed anywhere.

(8) In any other case, a warrant issued under this section may be executed in any part of the United Kingdom.

(9) ...

(10) The preceding provisions of this section apply to Scotland with these modifications–
    (a) in subsection (1) for 'justice of the peace is satisfied on information in writing and on oath' substitute 'sheriff is satisfied, on an application by a procurator fiscal,';
    (b) in subsection (3) for 'justice' substitute 'sheriff';
    (c) in subsection (4) for 'justice's', in paragraphs (a) and (b), substitute 'sheriff's'.

(11) Subsection (1) applies to Northern Ireland with the substitution of 'a complaint' for 'information'.

Person arrested under provisional warrant

74 (1) This section applies if a person is arrested under a provisional warrant.

(2) A copy of the warrant must be given to the person as soon as practicable after his arrest.

(3) The person must be brought as soon as practicable before the appropriate judge.

(4) But subsection (3) does not apply if–
    (a) the person is granted bail by a constable following his arrest, or

(b) in a case where the Secretary of State has received a valid request for the person's extradition, the Secretary of State decides under section 126 that the request is not to be proceeded with.

(5) If subsection (2) is not complied with and the person applies to the judge to be discharged, the judge may order his discharge.

(6) If subsection (3) is not complied with and the person applies to the judge to be discharged, the judge must order his discharge.

(7) When the person first appears or is brought before the appropriate judge, the judge must–

    (a) inform him that he is accused of the commission of an offence in a category 2 territory or that he is alleged to be unlawfully at large after conviction of an offence by a court in a category 2 territory;

    (b) give him the required information about consent;

    (c) remand him in custody or on bail.

(8) The required information about consent is–

    (a) that the person may consent to his extradition to the category 2 territory in which he is accused of the commission of an offence or is alleged to have been convicted of an offence;

    (b) an explanation of the effect of consent and the procedure that will apply if he gives consent;

    (c) that consent must be given in writing and is irrevocable.

(9) If the person is remanded in custody, the appropriate judge may later grant bail.

(10) The judge must order the person's discharge if the documents referred to in section 70(9) are not received by the judge within the required period.

(11) The required period is–

    (a) 45 days starting with the day on which the person was arrested, or

    (b) if the category 2 territory is designated by order made by the Secretary of State for the purposes of this section, any longer period permitted by the order.

(12) Subsection (4)(a) applies to Scotland with the omission of the words 'by a constable'.

The extradition hearing

Date of extradition hearing: arrest under section 71

75 (1) When a person arrested under a warrant issued under section 71 first appears or is brought before the appropriate judge, the judge must fix a date on which the extradition hearing is to begin.

(2) The date fixed under subsection (1) must not be later than the end of the permitted period, which is 2 months starting with the date on which the person first appears or is brought before the judge.

(3) If before the date fixed under subsection (1) (or this subsection) a party to the proceedings applies to the judge for a later date to be fixed and the judge believes it to be in the interests of justice to do so, he may fix a later date; and this subsection may apply more than once.

(4) If the extradition hearing does not begin on or before the date fixed under this section and the person applies to the judge to be discharged, the judge must order his discharge.

...

Interpretation

Extradition offences: person not sentenced for offence

137 (1) This section sets out whether a person's conduct constitutes an 'extradition offence' for the purposes of this Part in a case where the person–

(a) is accused in a category 2 territory of an offence constituted by the conduct, or

(b) has been convicted in that territory of an offence constituted by the conduct but not sentenced for it.

(2) The conduct constitutes an extradition offence in relation to the category 2 territory if the conditions in subsection (3), (4) or (5) are satisfied.

(3) The conditions in this subsection are that–

(a) the conduct occurs in the category 2 territory;

(b) the conduct would constitute an offence under the law of the relevant part of the United Kingdom punishable with imprisonment or another form of detention for a term of 12 months or a greater punishment if it occurred in that part of the United Kingdom;

(c) the conduct is so punishable under the law of the category 2 territory.

(4) The conditions in this subsection are that–

(a) the conduct occurs outside the category 2 territory;

(b) in corresponding circumstances equivalent conduct would constitute an extra-territorial offence under the law of the relevant part of the United Kingdom punishable with imprisonment or another form of detention for a term of 12 months or a greater punishment;

(c) the conduct is so punishable under the law of the category 2 territory.

(5) The conditions in this subsection are that–

(a) the conduct occurs outside the category 2 territory;

(b) no part of the conduct occurs in the United Kingdom;

(c) the conduct constitutes, or if committed in the United Kingdom would constitute, an offence mentioned in subsection (6);

(d) the conduct is punishable under the law of the category 2 territory with imprisonment or another form of detention for a term of 12 months or a greater punishment.

(6) The offences are–

(a) an offence under section 51 or 58 of the International Criminal Court Act 2001 (genocide, crimes against humanity and war crimes);

(b) an offence under section 52 or 59 of that Act (conduct ancillary to genocide etc committed outside the jurisdiction);

(c) an ancillary offence, as defined in section 55 or 62 of that Act, in relation to an offence falling within paragraph (a) or (b);

(d) an offence under section 1 of the International Criminal Court (Scotland) Act 2001 (asp 13) (genocide, crimes against humanity and war crimes);

(e) an offence under section 2 of that Act (conduct ancillary to genocide etc committed outside the jurisdiction);

(f) an ancillary offence, as defined in section 7 of that Act, in relation to an offence falling within paragraph (d) or (e).

(7) If the conduct constitutes an offence under the military law of the category 2 territory but does not constitute an offence under the general criminal law of

the relevant part of the United Kingdom it does not constitute an extradition offence; and subsections (1) to (6) have effect subject to this.

(7A) References in this section to 'conduct'(except in the expression 'equivalent conduct') are to the conduct specified in the request for the person's extradition.

(8) The relevant part of the United Kingdom is the part of the United Kingdom in which–

(a) the extradition hearing took place, if the question of whether conduct constitutes an extradition offence is to be decided by the Secretary of State;

(b) proceedings in which it is necessary to decide that question are taking place, in any other case.

Extradition offences: person sentenced for offence

138 (1) This section applies in relation to conduct of a person if–

(a) he is alleged to be unlawfully at large after conviction by a court in a category 2 territory of an offence constituted by the conduct, and

(b) he has been sentenced for the offence.

(2) The conduct constitutes an extradition offence in relation to the category 2 territory if these conditions are satisfied–

(a) the conduct occurs in the category 2 territory;

(b) the conduct would constitute an offence under the law of the relevant part of the United Kingdom punishable with imprisonment or another form of detention for a term of 12 months or a greater punishment if it occurred in that part of the United Kingdom;

(c) a sentence of imprisonment or another form of detention for a term of 4 months or a greater punishment has been imposed in the category 2 territory in respect of the conduct.

(3) The conduct also constitutes an extradition offence in relation to the category 2 territory if these conditions are satisfied–

(a) the conduct occurs outside the category 2 territory;

(b) a sentence of imprisonment or another form of detention for a term of 4 months or a greater punishment has been imposed in the category 2 territory in respect of the conduct;

(c) in corresponding circumstances equivalent conduct would constitute an extra-territorial offence under the law of the relevant part of the United Kingdom punishable with imprisonment or another form of detention for a term of 12 months or a greater punishment.

(4) The conduct also constitutes an extradition offence in relation to the category 2 territory if these conditions are satisfied–

(a) the conduct occurs outside the category 2 territory and no part of it occurs in the United Kingdom;

(b) the conduct would constitute an offence under the law of the relevant part of the United Kingdom punishable with imprisonment or another form of detention for a term of 12 months or a greater punishment if it occurred in that part of the United Kingdom;

(c) a sentence of imprisonment or another form of detention for a term of 4 months or a greater punishment has been imposed in the category 2 territory in respect of the conduct.

(5) The conduct also constitutes an extradition offence in relation to the category 2 territory if these conditions are satisfied–
  (a) the conduct occurs outside the category 2 territory and no part of it occurs in the United Kingdom;
  (b) a sentence of imprisonment or another form of detention for a term of 4 months or a greater punishment has been imposed in the category 2 territory in respect of the conduct;
  (c) the conduct constitutes or if committed in the United Kingdom would constitute an offence mentioned in subsection (6).

(6) The offences are–
  (a) an offence under section 51 or 58 of the International Criminal Court Act 2001 (genocide, crimes against humanity and war crimes);
  (b) an offence under section 52 or 59 of that Act (conduct ancillary to genocide etc committed outside the jurisdiction);
  (c) an ancillary offence, as defined in section 55 or 62 of that Act, in relation to an offence falling within paragraph (a) or (b);
  (d) an offence under section 1 of the International Criminal Court (Scotland) Act 2001 (genocide, crimes against humanity and war crimes);
  (e) an offence under section 2 of that Act (conduct ancillary to genocide etc committed outside the jurisdiction);
  (f) an ancillary offence, as defined in section 7 of that Act, in relation to an offence falling within paragraph (d) or (e).

(7) If the conduct constitutes an offence under the military law of the category 2 territory but does not constitute an offence under the general criminal law of the relevant part of the United Kingdom it does not constitute an extradition offence; and subsections (1) to (6) have effect subject to this.

(7A) References in this section to "conduct" (except in the expression 'equivalent conduct') are to the conduct specified in the request for the person's extradition.

(8) The relevant part of the United Kingdom is the part of the United Kingdom in which–
  (a) the extradition hearing took place, if the question of whether conduct constitutes an extradition offence is to be decided by the Secretary of State;
  (b) proceedings in which it is necessary to decide that question are taking place, in any other case.

EAW validity checklist

——————— v ———————

Date EAW issued	
Date EAW certified	
Is it an accusation or conviction warrant? [Box B] Is the warrant as a whole unclear?	
Date of offence [Box E]	
Place of offence [Box E]	
Description of offence [Box E] Is the description sufficiently particularised?	
Accusation: maximum sentence [Box C] **Conviction: sentence imposed [Box C]** Is the sentence sufficiently particularised?	
Extradition offences? [Box E] a) Would the conduct constitute an offence in the UK? If so, is it punishable in requesting state by at least 12 months (accusation) or did requested person receive sentence of at least 4 months (conviction)? b) If not an offence in UK, is it a framework offence? If so, is it punishable in requesting state by at least 3 years (accusation) or did requested person receive sentence of at least 12 months (conviction)?	
Conviction: Was the requested person present at trial? [Box D]	

FORM A – supplementary information – Article 26 SIS II Decision

EAW – European Arrest Warrant request

Form details

Date + time of message	001	
Message reference number	002	
Sending SIRENE	003	
Destination SIRENE	004	
Schengen reference number	005	
Important notice	311	
Important notice text		
Targeted to		

Extradition or surrender	239	
Sequence number of EAW	272	

Identity

Main record	316	
Identity alias number	310	
Family names	006	
First names	007	
Name at birth	008	
Previously used name(s)	266	
Date of birth	009	
Place of birth	010	
Gender	012	
Nationalities	013	
Alias	011	

Supplementary Information on identity

Last known address	061	
Spoken or understood languages	238	
Description of the wanted person	058	
Photos held on record	059	
Fingerprint held on record	060	
DNA held on record	237	
Other identity information	275	
Origin of identity document	050	
Identity document number	051	
Date of issue	052	
Place of issue	053	
Issuing authority	054	
Expiry date	055	
Father's name	056	
Mother's name	057	

Warrant/decision information

Arrest warrant or judicial decision having the same effect	240	
Date warrant was issued	032	
Magistrate or court issuing the decision	035	
Enforceable judgment	241	
Decision reference number	037	
Date of decision	036	
Maximum penalty	034	
Sentence imposed	038	
Remaining sentence to be served	039	

Service of summons, subject tried in person or decision rendered in absentia

Tried in person	294	
Date summons served in person	296	

Summons served by other means	297	
Defended in absence by counsellor	298	
Date decision served	300	
Decision not contested	301	
Timeframe for retrial or appeal lapsed	302	
Timeframe for retrial of appeal	303	
Relevant conditions	244	

Crime section

Total number of offences	245	
Date(s) or period(s) the offence(s) was/were committed	042	
Place(s) of offence(s)	043	
Description of the circumstances	044	
Degree of participation	045	
Legal classification	040	
EAW offences	247	
Legal description	041	

Additional information
Fill only if filled in EAW, do not copy text of laws

Other circumstances relevant the case	267	
Reason for seizure of property	249	
Description of property	250	
Life sentence and/or clemency	268	

Judicial authority: specific information

Official name of issuing authority	251	
Name of issuing authority representative	259	
Post held at issuing authority	252	
File reference	031	
Address of issuing authority	254	
Telephone number of using authority	255	
Fax number of issuing authority	256	
E-mail address of issuing authority	257	
Contact person for surrender	258	

Specific information of central authority concerning EAW
(Fill only in case the central authority is involved according to national legislation)

Name of central authority	260	
Address of central authority	293	
Contact person of central authority	261	
Telephone number of central authority	262	
Fax number of central authority	263	
E-mail address of central authority	264	

Specific information of judicial authority signing the EAW

Name of signatory	269	
Post held of signatory	270	
Date of signature	271	

Attachments

File type	401	
File name	402	

EAW first appearance checklist

Check identity	
Consider section 4: date and time of arrest; EAW provided?	
Has the requested person been given a copy of the EAW? If not, judge may discharge	
Has the requested person been brought as soon as practicable before the appropriate judge? If not, judge must discharge	
Explain extradition procedure – court not interested in whether/by whom offence was committed, but whether procedural requirements met; timescale	
Explain consent and specialty	
Is the requested person serving a sentence in the UK or subject to a domestic charge?	
Are there any issues to raise?	
Consider bars	
Conviction in absence?	
Human rights	
Physical/mental health	
Why does the requested person think s/he shouldn't be extradited?	
In appropriate cases, fill out the legal aid form	
Explain appeal process	

Bail checklist

Circumstances of arrest: where was the requested person arrested (ie home? work?) Does s/he accept any statements said to have been made by him/her?	
When did the requested person come to the UK and why?	
Has the requested person been back to the requesting state?	
Was the requested person aware of criminal proceedings and if so, was s/he present and why did s/he leave?	
Does the requested person have family? Where are the family based and what are their circumstances? Are they dependent?	
Is the requested person employed? If so, what are his or her hours of work? How far is the place of work from home?	
What is the requested person's housing situation?	
Does the requested person have community ties?	
Are details on police national computer print out correct? Is there any explanation for failing to attend on previous occasions?	
Has the requested person instructed lawyers in requesting state?	
What is his/her immigration status?	

Where are his/her identity documents? If not in the requested person's property, can someone else find them to surrender them to the court/police?	
Does the requested person know whether a surety or security may be available? If so, obtain telephone numbers.	
Where is the nearest police station to the requested person's home address located? Would a reporting condition at any particular time be problematic?	
If a curfew were imposed, what hours would be practicable for the requested person?	

Case management form

It is now a standard direction in extradition cases at Westminster Magistrates' Court that you provide the following details that may be relevant in these proceedings. The information you provide must be accurate as it may be checked, and it may be referred to at later hearings.

About you

Please print your full name and date of birth:

1. Are you the person requested in the warrant? **Y/N**

2. Have you any serious physical or mental health problems that may be relevant to these proceedings? **Y/N**
   If so, please describe them

3. Are you currently working? **Y/N**
   If so, please state whether employed or self employed

About your family

1. Please give names and dates of birth (or ages) of any family member dependent on you in the United Kingdom.

2. Do any of your UK dependants have serious physical or mental health problems relevant to these proceedings? **Y/N**
   If so, please describe them:

3. If your extradition is ordered will any other person be able to care for your dependant(s)? **Y/N**
   If not, why not?

Your connection with the United Kingdom

1. Do you live here? **Y/N**
   If so, since when?

Your connection with the Requesting State

1. Are you a citizen of the requesting state? **Y/N**

2. If not, have you been there? **Y/N**
   If so, when were you last there?

3. If you have now been arrested on a conviction warrant, were you present at the conviction hearing? **Y/N**

4. When did you first know of these proceedings?

5. Have you been granted asylum from the requesting state? **Y/N**
   If so, when?

6. What hardship do you believe you would suffer in the requesting state, if returned?

7. Is there any other good reason why you should not be extradited?

SIGNED BY REQUESTED PERSON ....

DATE ....

INFORMATION FROM LAWYER

Name ....
   (please print)

Name of firm of solicitors ....
   (please print)

Have you had sufficient time to advise your client on potential challenges? **Y/N**
If not, please explain:

What potential issues have been identified for these proceedings?

CPS internal process for dealing with forum bar cases

1. This process is to assist extradition and domestic prosecutors who have cause to apply the Guidelines on the Handling of Cases where the Jurisdiction to Prosecute is shared with Prosecuting Authorities Overseas ('the Guidelines') or where he/she is dealing with a case where there appears to be a forum issue.

2. The extradition and domestic units within CPS will share information unless it is inappropriate or unlawful to do so in accordance with general principles.

3. The Extradition Unit will inform requesting states or judicial authorities generally or on a case by case basis that this information will be shared in cases where forum may be an issue.

4. Decisions on forum will be taken by a domestic prosecutor as the Extradition Unit acts for the foreign state making the extradition request.

5. The Extradition Unit will provide advice on how forum might apply in extradition if requested by a domestic prosecutor.

6. Where a domestic prosecutor who is involved in a case where the guidelines are engaged, makes a decision on appropriate jurisdiction he or she will make a record of the decision using the template Record of a decision of Concurrent Jurisdiction. This record should include a note of the extent to which the prosecutor has been able to consider the specified matters set out in the forum bar and any relevant information regarding each. Where public interest or other considerations determine that sensitive information cannot be shared publically it should be recorded elsewhere.

7. If on the basis of information contained in the extradition request it is obvious that that forum will be in issue the Extradition Unit lawyer will check CMS to see if a domestic case has been registered involving the same defendant and conduct. It will also be necessary to contact directly the relevant Central Casework Division and Complex Casework Units to find out if a domestic prosecutor is or has been engaged in the case.

8. Four separate scenarios may be envisaged.

No domestic prosecutor is or has been engaged

9. If it appears that no prosecutor is or has been seized of the case but it appears to be a case where one might expect contact under the guidelines, the

Deputy Head of Division (Extradition) will notify the Head of Special Crime and Counter Terrorism Division to decide if any further action is required.

10. If forum is raised and there has been no domestic involvement, the Extradition Unit lawyer will inform the judge. The Extradition Unit lawyer will assist the court with the specified matters as far as is possible. If further information is requested by the court, a domestic prosecutor may need to confirm that the CPS is not engaged domestically and that they have no evidence to consider.

A decision to charge in this jurisdiction

11. Where a domestic prosecutor has decided that it is appropriate to charge requested person with corresponding offences, Section 8A or 76A of the Act applies the extradition proceedings must be adjourned.

A decision that England and Wales is not the most appropriate jurisdiction

12. Where a prosecutor has engaged the guidelines without making a formal Code Test decision and it has been decided that a prosecution should be conducted elsewhere he/she will inform the Extradition Unit and provide the template containing a record of that decision. If forum is raised in the subsequent extradition, the Extradition Unit lawyer will inform the court of the domestic prosecutor's decision and will assist on the specified matters using the template and any relevant material from the extradition papers.

13. In the event that the extradition court needs further information, the Extradition Unit lawyer will consider whether it is necessary to seek an adjournment so that the prosecutor who made the relevant decision may be made a party to the proceedings.

A decision to issue a prosecutor's certificate

14. A prosecutor can issue a certificate where he/she has made a decision whether or not to prosecute on the basis of the Full Code Test or where it is appropriate to do so because of concerns about the disclosure of sensitive material. A prosecutor considering the issuance of a certificate must consider in doing so, his/her ability to protect that material during any appeal proceedings under s19E.

15. If it appears to the prosecutor with conduct of the domestic prosecution that it may be appropriate to issue a certificate, he/she will draft a briefing note outlining why a certificate is appropriate together with a draft certificate using the template Forum Bar Prosecutor's Certificate. This should be sent in the first instance, via the CCP, to the Head of Special Crime and Counter Terrorism Division (SCCTD) (or in her absence the Head of Central Fraud Division (CFD)). The prosecutor's certificate will be considered, authorised and given under the signature of the Head of SCCTD, the Head of CFD or the Principal Legal Advisor in consultation with the Director of Public Prosecutions.

16. If authorisation is given, the prosecutor will provide the signed certificate to the Extradition Unit lawyer to enable him/her to provide a copy to the court and to serve it on other parties as appropriate.

17. Any appeal against a 'relevant certification decision' should be conducted by the domestic unit which is dealing or has been dealing with the case.

Role of the Extradition Unit lawyer in the forum hearing

18. Where the fugitive provides sufficient information for the court to determine that the forum bar is engaged,[1] the court may require the Extradition Unit lawyer to provide further information to assist in deciding whether a substantial measure of the relevant activity[2] occurred within the United Kingdom and/or information about any of the specified matters listed at ss (3). If the Extradition Unit lawyer is unable to assist from the information contained in the extradition request or the template provided by a domestic prosecutor (if engaged), further enquiries should be made of the requesting state or the relevant prosecutor.

19. Where appeal proceedings are being conducted by a prosecutor following the issuing of a prosecutor's certificate, the Extradition Unit lawyer should assist by providing the records of any extradition hearing and any relevant advice about law and procedure.

1 In the absence of judicial guidance, the CPS believes that the provisions in the Act require the fugitive to produce sufficient information to engage the forum bar before further information is sought from the requesting state.
2 This is not currently defined. We are advised that it is intended to be the definition determined by Wallace Duncan and adopted in Sheppard and Whittle however this is likely to be the subject of legal argument in due course.

APPENDIX I

Application for permission to appeal

Appellant's notice

Application for permission to appeal under sections 26, 28, 103, 105, 108 and 110 of the Extradition Act 2003

Notes for guidance are available which will help you complete this form. Please read them carefully before you complete each section.

In the High Court of Justice
Administrative Court
For Court use only
Case Ref. No.

SECTION 1 Details of the parties

Name(s) of the appellant
Address (including postcode) If in custody please include the Prison Number and date of birth
Tel No:
Email:

Name of the 1st respondent
Address (including postcode) If in custody please include the Prison Index Number
Tel No:
Email:

Name of the 2nd respondent (if any)
Address (including postcode)
Tel No:
Email:

SECTION 2 Details of the decision

What is the decision you wish to appeal?

What is the date of the decision you wish to appeal?

SECTION 3 Legal Representation

Are you legally represented?

Yes

No

Your solicitor's name

Your solicitor's address

Tel No

Email

DX

Ref

SECTION 4 Other Information required for the appeal

Appeals made pursuant to Sections 26 and 28: Have you lodged this notice with the Court within 7 days of the date on which the decision you wish to appeal was made? Yes/No

Appeals made pursuant to Sections 103, 105 and 108: Have you lodged this notice with the Court within 14 days starting with the day on which the Secretary of State's order was made? Yes/No

The grounds of appeal must be attached to this notice of application (See Criminal Procedure Rules r.17.20)

The grounds of appeal must:

   (i)   Specify the date of arrest

   (ii)   Specify whether the appellant is in custody

   (iii) Specify the issues raised in the Court below

   (iv) If the appellant is raising an issue not raised at the extradition hearing or evidence which was not available at the extradition hearing an explanation must be provided for its omission

   (v)   Identify each ground of appeal on which the appellant relies, numbering them consecutively (if there is more than one) and concisely outlining each argument in support

(vi) Summarise the relevant facts

(vii) Identify any relevant authorities

(viii) Identify any other document or thing that the appellant thinks the Court will need to decide the permission to appeal and the appeal, if the Court grants permission (please note that any report relied upon must be attached to this application form)

(ix) Include or attach a list of those on whom the appellant has served the notice of appeal and the date of service

(x) Where an appellant is in custody, include any application for:

    a.   Bail pending appeal

    b.   A direction that an unrepresented appellant be produced for the hearing of the appeal

(xi) Where grounds have been settled by counsel they must be signed by counsel with the name of counsel printed underneath;

SECTION 5 Service

A copy of this form of application was served on the respondent(s) as follows:

Respondent 1

☐ by fax machine to   time sent

Fax no.	time

☐ by handing to or leaving it with

name

☐ by e-mail to

e-mail address

Date served

Date

Respondent 2

☐ by fax machine to   time sent

Fax no.	time

☐ by handing to or leaving it with

name

☐ by e-mail to

e-mail address

Date served

Date

I confirm that all relevant facts have been disclosed in this application

Name of appellant's advocate

name

Appellant (appellant's advocate)

Signed

If an extension of time is needed for service of the appeal notice, the detailed reasons for the delay must be attached to the grounds of appeal, preferably under a separate heading explaining what the defendant did to ensure that it was served in time.

EXN161

Application notice

EX244 - APPLICATION NOTICE

(PURSUANT TO THE EXTRADITION ACT 2003)

ADMINISTRATIVE COURT

Application notices must comply with Part 17 of Criminal Procedure Rules 2014 and 17D of the Criminal Practice Directions and must be served on all parties

SECTION 1
I/We (1)
the [Solicitor on behalf of the] (2)
Apply for an order, a draft of which is attached, for (3)
(please note that all applications will initially be dealt with on the papers unless a judge orders that there be an oral hearing)

(1) State full name of Appellant or his/her Solicitor
(2) State title of party e.g. Appellant, Respondent etc.
(3) State briefly the nature of the order sought and the reason it is sought including the material facts relied on and identifying any rule or statutory provision.

1

SECTION 2

I/We wish to rely on

[*] the attached Witness Statement

[*] my statement of case

[*] the evidence in Section 3

*tick as appropriate

Dated --------------------------

Signed ------------------------------ (name)---------------------------------

position or office held --

*(Appellant)(Respondent)(Litigation friend)(Appellant's/Respondent's Solicitor)(Signing on behalf of firm or company)*delete as appropriate

SECTION 3

Evidence:

Statement of Truth (to be signed when Section 3 is completed)
*(I believe)(The Appellant / Respondent believes) that the facts stated in this application notice are true.
*I am duly authorised by the Appellant / Respondent to sign this statement
Full name

Name of Appellant's/Respondent's Solicitor's firm

Signed ---------------------------- (name) -------------------------------

Position/office held ---
*(Appellant)(Respondent)(Litigation friend)(Appellant's / Respondent's Solicitor)(Signing on behalf of firm or company)
*delete as appropriate

To: Respondent/Respondents Solicitor's address, DX or e-mail	To: Appellant / Appellant's Solicitor's address, DX or e-mail
Ref No. Tel No. Fax No.	Ref No. Tel No. Fax No.

3

Respondent's notice

Respondent's notice
To an application for permission to appeal under sections 26, 28, 103, 105, 108 and 110 of the Extradition Act 2003

Notes for guidance are available which will help you complete this form. Please read them carefully before you complete each section.

In the High Court of Justice

Administrative Court

For Court use only

Case Ref. No.

SECTION 1 Details of the Respondent

Case Reference:

Name of appellant

In the lower court, were you the:

Defendant ☐   Judicial Authority ☐   Secretary of State for the Home Department ☐

Your (respondent's) name and address (including postcode) If in custody please include the Prison Number and date of birth

Address (including postcode):

Tel No:

E mail:

SECTION 2 Legal Representation

Are you legally represented?

Yes ☐

No ☐

Your solicitor's name

Your solicitor's address (including postcode)

Tel No

Email

DX

Ref

SECTION 3 Other Information required

Have you lodged this notice with the Court within 5 business days of the date on which you were served with the
Application for Permission to Appeal? Yes/No

In accordance with Crim PR 17.21(4) you must:

(i)   Give the date on which the respondent was served with, as appropriate
　　　(a) the appeal notice
　　　(b) the appellant's notice renewing the application for permission to appeal
　　　(c) a direction to serve a respondent's notice

(ii)   identify any other document or thing that the appellant thinks the Court will need to decide the permission to
　　　appeal and the appeal, if the Court grants permission (please note that any report relied upon must be
　　　attached to this application form);

(iii)   Identify each ground of opposition on which the respondent relies, and identify the ground of appeal to which
　　　each relates

(iv)   Identify any relevant authorities

(v)   Where the respondent is in custody, include any application for: (a) Bail pending appeal (b) directions that an
　　　unrepresented respondent be produced for the hearing of the appeal

(vi)   Where grounds have been settled by counsel they must be signed by counsel with the name of counsel printed
　　　underneath

SECTION 4 Service

A copy of this respondent's notice was served on the appellant(s) as follows:

Appellant 1   Appellant 2

☐ by fax machine to   time sent   ☐ by fax machine to   time sent

Fax no.	time		Fax no.	time

☐ by handing to or leaving it with   ☐ by handing to or leaving it with

name		name

☐ by e-mail to   ☐ by e-mail to

e-mail address		e-mail address

Date served   Date served

Date		Date

I confirm that all relevant facts have been disclosed in this notice

Name of respondent (if acting in person) or
respondent's advocate

Name		Signed
		Date

If an extension of time is needed for service of the respondent's notice, the detailed reasons for the delay must be attached to the notice, preferably under a separate heading explaining what the respondent did to ensure that it was served in time.

Form EXN162

Directive 2010/64/EU on the right to interpretation and translation in criminal proceedings

Directive 2010/64/EU of the European Parliament and of the Council of 20 October 2010 on the right to interpretation and translation in criminal proceedings

THE EUROPEAN PARLIAMENT AND THE COUNCIL OF THE EUROPEAN UNION,

Having regard to the Treaty on the Functioning of the European Union, and in particular point (b) of the second subparagraph of Article 82(2) thereof,

Having regard to the initiative of the Kingdom of Belgium, the Federal Republic of Germany, the Republic of Estonia, the Kingdom of Spain, the French Republic, the Italian Republic, the Grand-Duchy of Luxembourg, the Republic of Hungary, the Republic of Austria, the Portuguese Republic, Romania, the Republic of Finland and the Kingdom of Sweden,

After transmission of the draft legislative act to the national parliaments,

Acting in accordance with the ordinary legislative procedure,

Whereas:

(1) The Union has set itself the objective of maintaining and developing an area of freedom, security and justice. According to the Presidency Conclusions of the European Council in Tampere of 15 and 16 October 1999, and in particular point 33 thereof, the principle of mutual recognition of judgments and other decisions of judicial authorities should become the cornerstone of judicial cooperation in civil and criminal matters within the Union because enhanced mutual recognition and the necessary approximation of legislation would facilitate cooperation between competent authorities and the judicial protection of individual rights.

(2) On 29 November 2000, the Council, in accordance with the Tampere Conclusions, adopted a programme of measures to implement the principle of mutual recognition of decisions in criminal matters. The introduction to the programme states that mutual recognition is 'designed to strengthen cooperation between Member States but also to enhance the protection of individual rights'.

(3) The implementation of the principle of mutual recognition of decisions in criminal matters presupposes that Member States have trust in each other's criminal justice systems. The extent of mutual recognition is very much dependent on a number of parameters, which include mechanisms for safeguarding the rights of suspected or accused persons and common minimum standards necessary to facilitate the application of the principle of mutual recognition.

(4) Mutual recognition of decisions in criminal matters can operate effectively only in a spirit of trust in which not only judicial authorities but all actors in the criminal process consider decisions of the judicial authorities of other Member States as equivalent to their own, implying not only trust in the adequacy of other Member States' rules, but also trust that those rules are correctly applied.

(5) Article 6 of the European Convention for the Protection of Human Rights and Fundamental Freedoms (hereinafter the ECHR) and Article 47 of the Charter of Fundamental Rights of the European Union (hereinafter the Charter) enshrine the right to a fair trial. Article 48(2) of the Charter guarantees respect for the right of defence. This Directive respects those rights and should be implemented accordingly.

(6) Although all the Member States are party to the ECHR, experience has shown that that alone does not always provide a sufficient degree of trust in the criminal justice systems of other Member States.

(7) Strengthening mutual trust requires a more consistent implementation of the rights and guarantees set out in Article 6 of the ECHR. It also requires, by means of this Directive and other measures, further development within the Union of the minimum standards set out in the ECHR and the Charter.

(8) Article 82(2) of the Treaty on the Functioning of the European Union provides for the establishment of minimum rules applicable in the Member States so as to facilitate mutual recognition of judgments and judicial decisions and police and judicial cooperation in criminal matters having a cross-border dimension. Point (b) of the second subparagraph of Article 82(2) refers to 'the rights of individuals in criminal procedure' as one of the areas in which minimum rules may be established.

(9) Common minimum rules should lead to increased confidence in the criminal justice systems of all Member States, which, in turn, should lead to more efficient judicial cooperation in a climate of mutual trust. Such common minimum rules should be established in the fields of interpretation and translation in criminal proceedings.

(10) On 30 November 2009, the Council adopted a resolution on a Roadmap for strengthening procedural rights of suspected or accused persons in criminal proceedings (4). Taking a step-by-step approach, the Roadmap called for the adoption of measures regarding the right to translation and interpretation (measure A), the right to information on rights and information about the charges (measure B), the right to legal advice and legal aid (measure C), the right to communication with relatives, employers and consular authorities

(measure D), and special safeguards for suspected or accused persons who are vulnerable (measure E).

(11) In the Stockholm programme, adopted on 10 December 2009, the European Council welcomed the Roadmap and made it part of the Stockholm programme (point 2.4). The European Council underlined the non-exhaustive character of the Roadmap, by inviting the Commission to examine further elements of minimum procedural rights for suspected and accused persons, and to assess whether other issues, for instance the presumption of innocence, need to be addressed, in order to promote better cooperation in that area.

(12) This Directive relates to measure A of the Roadmap. It lays down common minimum rules to be applied in the fields of interpretation and translation in criminal proceedings with a view to enhancing mutual trust among Member States.

(13) This Directive draws on the Commission proposal for a Council Framework Decision on the right to interpretation and to translation in criminal proceedings of 8 July 2009, and on the Commission proposal for a Directive of the European Parliament and of the Council on the right to interpretation and translation in criminal proceedings of 9 March 2010.

(14) The right to interpretation and translation for those who do not speak or understand the language of the proceedings is enshrined in Article 6 of the ECHR, as interpreted in the case-law of the European Court of Human Rights. This Directive facilitates the application of that right in practice. To that end, the aim of this Directive is to ensure the right of suspected or accused persons to interpretation and translation in criminal proceedings with a view to ensuring their right to a fair trial.

(15) The rights provided for in this Directive should also apply, as necessary accompanying measures, to the execution of a European arrest warrant within the limits provided for by this Directive. Executing Members States should provide, and bear the costs of, interpretation and translation for the benefit of the requested persons who do not speak or understand the language of the proceedings.

(16) In some Member States an authority other than a court having jurisdiction in criminal matters has competence for imposing sanctions in relation to relatively minor offences. That may be the case, for example, in relation to traffic offences which are committed on a large scale and which might be established following a traffic control. In such situations, it would be unreasonable to require that the competent authority ensure all the rights under this Directive. Where the law of a Member State provides for the imposition of a sanction regarding minor offences by such an authority and there is a right of appeal to a court having jurisdiction in criminal matters, this Directive should therefore apply only to the proceedings before that court following such an appeal.

(17) This Directive should ensure that there is free and adequate linguistic assistance, allowing suspected or accused persons who do not speak or understand

the language of the criminal proceedings fully to exercise their right of defence and safeguarding the fairness of the proceedings.

(18) Interpretation for the benefit of the suspected or accused persons should be provided without delay. However, where a certain period of time elapses before interpretation is provided, that should not constitute an infringement of the requirement that interpretation be provided without delay, as long as that period of time is reasonable in the circumstances.

(19) Communication between suspected or accused persons and their legal counsel should be interpreted in accordance with this Directive. Suspected or accused persons should be able, inter alia, to explain their version of the events to their legal counsel, point out any statements with which they disagree and make their legal counsel aware of any facts that should be put forward in their defence.

(20) For the purposes of the preparation of the defence, communication between suspected or accused persons and their legal counsel in direct connection with any questioning or hearing during the proceedings, or with the lodging of an appeal or other procedural applications, such as an application for bail, should be interpreted where necessary in order to safeguard the fairness of the proceedings.

(21) Member States should ensure that there is a procedure or mechanism in place to ascertain whether suspected or accused persons speak and understand the language of the criminal proceedings and whether they need the assistance of an interpreter. Such procedure or mechanism implies that competent authorities verify in any appropriate manner, including by consulting the suspected or accused persons concerned, whether they speak and understand the language of the criminal proceedings and whether they need the assistance of an interpreter.

(22) Interpretation and translation under this Directive should be provided in the native language of the suspected or accused persons or in any other language that they speak or understand in order to allow them fully to exercise their right of defence, and in order to safeguard the fairness of the proceedings.

(23) The respect for the right to interpretation and translation contained in this Directive should not compromise any other procedural right provided under national law.

(24) Member States should ensure that control can be exercised over the adequacy of the interpretation and translation provided when the competent authorities have been put on notice in a given case.

(25) The suspected or accused persons or the persons subject to proceedings for the execution of a European arrest warrant should have the right to challenge the finding that there is no need for interpretation, in accordance with procedures in national law. That right does not entail the obligation for Member States to provide for a separate mechanism or complaint procedure in which such finding may be challenged and should not prejudice the time limits applicable to the execution of a European arrest warrant.

(26) When the quality of the interpretation is considered insufficient to ensure

the right to a fair trial, the competent authorities should be able to replace the appointed interpreter.

(27) The duty of care towards suspected or accused persons who are in a potentially weak position, in particular because of any physical impairments which affect their ability to communicate effectively, underpins a fair administration of justice. The prosecution, law enforcement and judicial authorities should therefore ensure that such persons are able to exercise effectively the rights provided for in this Directive, for example by taking into account any potential vulnerability that affects their ability to follow the proceedings and to make themselves understood, and by taking appropriate steps to ensure those rights are guaranteed.

(28) When using videoconferencing for the purpose of remote interpretation, the competent authorities should be able to rely on the tools that are being developed in the context of European e-Justice (eg information on courts with videoconferencing equipment or manuals).

(29) This Directive should be evaluated in the light of the practical experience gained. If appropriate, it should be amended so as to improve the safeguards which it lays down.

(30) Safeguarding the fairness of the proceedings requires that essential documents, or at least the relevant passages of such documents, be translated for the benefit of suspected or accused persons in accordance with this Directive. Certain documents should always be considered essential for that purpose and should therefore be translated, such as any decision depriving a person of his liberty, any charge or indictment, and any judgment. It is for the competent authorities of the Member States to decide, on their own motion or upon a request of suspected or accused persons or of their legal counsel, which other documents are essential to safeguard the fairness of the proceedings and should therefore be translated as well.

(31) Member States should facilitate access to national databases of legal translators and interpreters where such databases exist. In that context, particular attention should be paid to the aim of providing access to existing databases through the e-Justice portal, as planned in the multiannual European e-Justice action plan 2009-2013 of 27 November 2008.

(32) This Directive should set minimum rules. Member States should be able to extend the rights set out in this Directive in order to provide a higher level of protection also in situations not explicitly dealt with in this Directive. The level of protection should never fall below the standards provided by the ECHR or the Charter as interpreted in the case-law of the European Court of Human Rights or the Court of Justice of the European Union.

(33) The provisions of this Directive that correspond to rights guaranteed by the ECHR or the Charter should be interpreted and implemented consistently with those rights, as interpreted in the relevant case-law of the European Court of Human Rights and the Court of Justice of the European Union.

(34) Since the objective of this Directive, namely establishing common minimum rules, cannot be sufficiently achieved by the Member States and can therefore, by reason of its scale and effects, be better achieved at Union level, the Union

may adopt measures in accordance with the principle of subsidiarity as set out in Article 5 of the Treaty on European Union. In accordance with the principle of proportionality, as set out in that Article, this Directive does not go beyond what is necessary in order to achieve that objective.

(35) In accordance with Article 3 of the Protocol (No 21) on the position of the United Kingdom and Ireland in respect of the Area of Freedom, Security and Justice, annexed to the Treaty on European Union and to the Treaty on the Functioning of the European Union, those Member States have notified their wish to take part in the adoption and application of this Directive.

(36) In accordance with Articles 1 and 2 of the Protocol (No 22) on the position of Denmark, annexed to the Treaty on European Union and to the Treaty on the Functioning of the European Union, Denmark is not taking part in the adoption of this Directive and is not bound by it or subject to its application,

HAVE ADOPTED THIS DIRECTIVE:

Article 1: Subject matter and scope

1. This Directive lays down rules concerning the right to interpretation and translation in criminal proceedings and proceedings for the execution of a European arrest warrant.

2. The right referred to in paragraph 1 shall apply to persons from the time that they are made aware by the competent authorities of a Member State, by official notification or otherwise, that they are suspected or accused of having committed a criminal offence until the conclusion of the proceedings, which is understood to mean the final determination of the question whether they have committed the offence, including, where applicable, sentencing and the resolution of any appeal.

3. Where the law of a Member State provides for the imposition of a sanction regarding minor offences by an authority other than a court having jurisdiction in criminal matters, and the imposition of such a sanction may be appealed to such a court, this Directive shall apply only to the proceedings before that court following such an appeal.

4. This Directive does not affect national law concerning the presence of legal counsel during any stage of the criminal proceedings, nor does it affect national law concerning the right of access of a suspected or accused person to documents in criminal proceedings.

Article 2: Right to interpretation

1. Member States shall ensure that suspected or accused persons who do not speak or understand the language of the criminal proceedings concerned are provided, without delay, with interpretation during criminal proceedings before investigative and judicial authorities, including during police questioning, all court hearings and any necessary interim hearings.

2. Member States shall ensure that, where necessary for the purpose of safeguarding the fairness of the proceedings, interpretation is available for communication between suspected or accused persons and their legal counsel in direct connection with any questioning or hearing during the proceedings or with the lodging of an appeal or other procedural applications.

3. The right to interpretation under paragraphs 1 and 2 includes appropriate assistance for persons with hearing or speech impediments.

4. Member States shall ensure that a procedure or mechanism is in place to ascertain whether suspected or accused persons speak and understand the language of the criminal proceedings and whether they need the assistance of an interpreter.

5. Member States shall ensure that, in accordance with procedures in national law, suspected or accused persons have the right to challenge a decision finding that there is no need for interpretation and, when interpretation has been provided, the possibility to complain that the quality of the interpretation is not sufficient to safeguard the fairness of the proceedings.

6. Where appropriate, communication technology such as videoconferencing, telephone or the Internet may be used, unless the physical presence of the interpreter is required in order to safeguard the fairness of the proceedings.

7. In proceedings for the execution of a European arrest warrant, the executing Member State shall ensure that its competent authorities provide persons subject to such proceedings who do not speak or understand the language of the proceedings with interpretation in accordance with this Article.

8. Interpretation provided under this Article shall be of a quality sufficient to safeguard the fairness of the proceedings, in particular by ensuring that suspected or accused persons have knowledge of the case against them and are able to exercise their right of defence.

Article 3: Right to translation of essential documents

1. Member States shall ensure that suspected or accused persons who do not understand the language of the criminal proceedings concerned are, within a reasonable period of time, provided with a written translation of all documents which are essential to ensure that they are able to exercise their right of defence and to safeguard the fairness of the proceedings.

2. Essential documents shall include any decision depriving a person of his liberty, any charge or indictment, and any judgment.

3. The competent authorities shall, in any given case, decide whether any other document is essential. Suspected or accused persons or their legal counsel may submit a reasoned request to that effect.

4. There shall be no requirement to translate passages of essential documents which are not relevant for the purposes of enabling suspected or accused persons to have knowledge of the case against them.

5. Member States shall ensure that, in accordance with procedures in national law, suspected or accused persons have the right to challenge a decision finding that there is no need for the translation of documents or passages thereof and, when a translation has been provided, the possibility to complain that the quality of the translation is not sufficient to safeguard the fairness of the proceedings.

6. In proceedings for the execution of a European arrest warrant, the executing Member State shall ensure that its competent authorities provide any person subject to such proceedings who does not understand the language in which

the European arrest warrant is drawn up, or into which it has been translated by the issuing Member State, with a written translation of that document.

7. As an exception to the general rules established in paragraphs 1, 2, 3 and 6, an oral translation or oral summary of essential documents may be provided instead of a written translation on condition that such oral translation or oral summary does not prejudice the fairness of the proceedings.

8. Any waiver of the right to translation of documents referred to in this Article shall be subject to the requirements that suspected or accused persons have received prior legal advice or have otherwise obtained full knowledge of the consequences of such a waiver, and that the waiver was unequivocal and given voluntarily.

9. Translation provided under this Article shall be of a quality sufficient to safeguard the fairness of the proceedings, in particular by ensuring that suspected or accused persons have knowledge of the case against them and are able to exercise their right of defence.

Article 4: Costs of interpretation and translation

Member States shall meet the costs of interpretation and translation resulting from the application of Articles 2 and 3, irrespective of the outcome of the proceedings.

Article 5: Quality of the interpretation and translation

1. Member States shall take concrete measures to ensure that the interpretation and translation provided meets the quality required under Article 2(8) and Article 3(9).

2. In order to promote the adequacy of interpretation and translation and efficient access thereto, Member States shall endeavour to establish a register or registers of independent translators and interpreters who are appropriately qualified. Once established, such register or registers shall, where appropriate, be made available to legal counsel and relevant authorities.

3. Member States shall ensure that interpreters and translators be required to observe confidentiality regarding interpretation and translation provided under this Directive.

Article 6: Training

Without prejudice to judicial independence and differences in the organisation of the judiciary across the Union, Member States shall request those responsible for the training of judges, prosecutors and judicial staff involved in criminal proceedings to pay special attention to the particularities of communicating with the assistance of an interpreter so as to ensure efficient and effective communication.

Article 7: Record-keeping

Member States shall ensure that when a suspected or accused person has been subject to questioning or hearings by an investigative or judicial authority with the assistance of an interpreter pursuant to Article 2, when an oral translation or oral summary of essential documents has been provided in the presence of such an authority pursuant to Article 3(7), or when a person has waived the right to translation pursuant to Article 3(8), it will be noted that these events have occurred, using the recording procedure in accordance with the law of the Member State concerned.

Article 8: Non-regression

Nothing in this Directive shall be construed as limiting or derogating from any of the rights and procedural safeguards that are ensured under the European Convention for the Protection of Human Rights and Fundamental Freedoms, the Charter of Fundamental Rights of the European Union, other relevant provisions of international law or the law of any Member State which provides a higher level of protection.

Article 9: Transposition

1. Member States shall bring into force the laws, regulations and administrative provisions necessary to comply with this Directive by 27 October 2013.

2. Member States shall transmit the text of those measures to the Commission.

3. When Member States adopt those measures, they shall contain a reference to this Directive or be accompanied by such a reference on the occasion of their official publication. The methods of making such reference shall be laid down by the Member States.

Article 10: Report

The Commission shall, by 27 October 2014, submit a report to the European Parliament and to the Council, assessing the extent to which the Member States have taken the necessary measures in order to comply with this Directive, accompanied, if necessary, by legislative proposals.

Article 11: Entry into force

This Directive shall enter into force on the 20th day following its publication in the Official Journal of the European Union.

Article 12: Addressees

This Directive is addressed to the Member States in accordance with the Treaties.

Done at Strasbourg, 20 October 2010.

For the European Parliament
The President
J. Buzek

For the Council
The President
O. Chastel

Directive 2012/13/EU on the right to information in criminal proceedings

Directive 2012/13/EU of the European Parliament and of the Council of 22 May 2012 on the right to information in criminal proceedings

THE EUROPEAN PARLIAMENT AND THE COUNCIL OF THE EUROPEAN UNION,

Having regard to the Treaty on the Functioning of the European Union, and in particular Article 82(2) thereof,

Having regard to the proposal from the European Commission,

After transmission of the draft legislative act to the national parliaments,

Having regard to the opinion of the European Economic and Social Committee,

After consulting the Committee of the Regions,

Acting in accordance with the ordinary legislative procedure,

Whereas:

(1) The Union has set itself the objective of maintaining and developing an area of freedom, security and justice. According to the Presidency Conclusions of the European Council in Tampere of 15 and 16 October 1999, and in particular point 33 thereof, the principle of mutual recognition of judgments and other decisions of judicial authorities should become the cornerstone of judicial cooperation in both civil and criminal matters within the Union because enhanced mutual recognition and the necessary approximation of legislation would facilitate cooperation between competent authorities and the judicial protection of individual rights.

(2) On 29 November 2000, the Council, in accordance with the Tampere conclusions, adopted a programme of measures to implement the principle of mutual recognition of decisions in criminal matters. The introduction to the programme states that mutual recognition is 'designed to strengthen cooperation between Member States but also to enhance the protection of individual rights'.

(3) The implementation of the principle of mutual recognition of decisions in criminal matters presupposes that Member States trust in each other's criminal justice systems. The extent of mutual recognition is very much dependent

on a number of parameters, which include mechanisms for safeguarding the rights of suspects or accused persons and common minimum standards necessary to facilitate the application of the principle of mutual recognition.

(4) Mutual recognition of decisions in criminal matters can operate effectively only in a spirit of trust in which not only judicial authorities but all actors in the criminal process consider decisions of the judicial authorities of other Member States as equivalent to their own, implying not only trust in the adequacy of other Member States' rules, but also trust that those rules are correctly applied.

(5) Article 47 of the Charter of Fundamental Rights of the European Union (hereinafter 'the Charter') and Article 6 of the European Convention for the Protection of Human Rights and Fundamental Freedoms (hereinafter 'the ECHR') enshrine the right to a fair trial. Article 48(2) of the Charter guarantees respect for the rights of the defence.

(6) Article 6 of the Charter and Article 5 ECHR enshrine the right to liberty and security of person. Any restrictions on that right must not exceed those permitted in accordance with Article 5 ECHR and inferred from the case-law of the European Court of Human Rights.

(7) Although all the Member States are party to the ECHR, experience has shown that that alone does not always provide a sufficient degree of trust in the criminal justice systems of other Member States.

(8) Strengthening mutual trust requires detailed rules on the protection of the procedural rights and guarantees arising from the Charter and from the ECHR.

(9) Article 82(2) of the Treaty on the Functioning of the European Union provides for the establishment of minimum rules applicable in the Member States so as to facilitate mutual recognition of judgments and judicial decisions and police and judicial cooperation in criminal matters having a cross-border dimension. That Article refers to 'the rights of individuals in criminal procedure' as one of the areas in which minimum rules may be established.

(10) Common minimum rules should lead to increased confidence in the criminal justice systems of all Member States, which, in turn, should lead to more efficient judicial cooperation in a climate of mutual trust. Such common minimum rules should be established in the field of information in criminal proceedings.

(11) On 30 November 2009, the Council adopted a resolution on a Roadmap for strengthening procedural rights of suspected or accused persons in criminal proceedings (hereinafter 'the Roadmap'). Taking a step-by-step approach, the Roadmap called for the adoption of measures regarding the right to translation and interpretation (measure A), the right to information on rights and information about the charges (measure B), the right to legal advice and legal aid (measure C), the right to communication with relatives, employers and consular authorities (measure D), and special safeguards for suspects or accused persons who are vulnerable (measure E). The Roadmap emphasises that the order of the rights is only indicative and thus implies that it may be changed in accordance with priorities. The Roadmap is designed to operate

as a whole; only when all its component parts have been implemented will its benefits be felt in full.

(12) On 11 December 2009, the European Council welcomed the Roadmap and made it part of the Stockholm Programme — An open and secure Europe serving and protecting citizens (point 2.4). The European Council underlined the non-exhaustive character of the Roadmap, by inviting the Commission to examine further elements of minimum procedural rights for suspects and accused persons, and to assess whether other issues, for instance the presumption of innocence, need to be addressed, in order to promote better cooperation in that area.

(13) The first measure adopted pursuant to the Roadmap, measure A, was Directive 2010/64/EU of the European Parliament and of the Council of 20 October 2010 on the right to interpretation and translation in criminal proceedings.

(14) This Directive relates to measure B of the Roadmap. It lays down common minimum standards to be applied in the field of information about rights and about the accusation to be given to persons suspected or accused of having committed a criminal offence, with a view to enhancing mutual trust among Member States. This Directive builds on the rights laid down in the Charter, and in particular Articles 6, 47 and 48 thereof, by building upon Articles 5 and 6 ECHR as interpreted by the European Court of Human Rights. In this Directive, the term 'accusation' is used to describe the same concept as the term 'charge' used in Article 6(1) ECHR.

(15) In its Communication of 20 April 2010 entitled 'Delivering an area of freedom, security and justice for Europe's citizens — Action Plan Implementing the Stockholm Programme', the Commission announced that it would present a proposal on the right to information on rights and information about charges in 2010.

(16) This Directive should apply to suspects and accused persons regardless of their legal status, citizenship or nationality.

(17) In some Member States an authority other than a court having jurisdiction in criminal matters has competence for imposing sanctions in relation to relatively minor offences. That may be the case, for example, in relation to traffic offences which are committed on a large scale and which might be established following a traffic control. In such situations, it would be unreasonable to require that the competent authority ensure all the rights under this Directive. Where the law of a Member State provides for the imposition of a sanction regarding minor offences by such an authority and there is either a right of appeal or the possibility for the case to be otherwise referred to a court having jurisdiction in criminal matters, this Directive should therefore apply only to the proceedings before that court following such an appeal or referral.

(18) The right to information about procedural rights, which is inferred from the case-law of the European Court of Human Rights, should be explicitly established by this Directive.

(19) The competent authorities should inform suspects or accused persons promptly of those rights, as they apply under national law, which are essential to safeguarding the fairness of the proceedings, either orally or in writing,

as provided for by this Directive. In order to allow the practical and effective exercise of those rights, the information should be provided promptly in the course of the proceedings and at the latest before the first official interview of the suspect or accused person by the police or by another competent authority.

(20) This Directive lays down minimum rules with respect to the information on rights of suspects or accused persons. This is without prejudice to information to be given on other procedural rights arising out of the Charter, the ECHR, national law and applicable Union law as interpreted by the relevant courts and tribunals. Once the information about a particular right has been provided, the competent authorities should not be required to reiterate it, unless the specific circumstances of the case or the specific rules laid down in national law so require.

(21) References in this Directive to suspects or accused persons who are arrested or detained should be understood to refer to any situation where, in the course of criminal proceedings, suspects or accused persons are deprived of liberty within the meaning of Article 5(1)(c) ECHR, as interpreted by the case-law of the European Court of Human Rights.

(22) Where suspects or accused persons are arrested or detained, information about applicable procedural rights should be given by means of a written Letter of Rights drafted in an easily comprehensible manner so as to assist those persons in understanding their rights. Such a Letter of Rights should be provided promptly to each arrested person when deprived of liberty by the intervention of law enforcement authorities in the context of criminal proceedings. It should include basic information concerning any possibility to challenge the lawfulness of the arrest, obtaining a review of the detention, or requesting provisional release where, and to the extent that, such a right exists in national law. To help Member States draw up such a Letter of Rights, a model is provided in Annex I. That model is indicative and may be subject to review in the context of the Commission's report on the implementation of this Directive and also once all the Roadmap measures have entered into force. The Letter of Rights may include other relevant procedural rights that apply in Member States.

(23) Specific conditions and rules relating to the right of suspects or accused persons to have another person informed about their arrest or detention are to be determined by the Member States in their national law. As set out in the Roadmap, the exercise of that right should not prejudice the due course of the criminal proceedings.

(24) This Directive is without prejudice to the provisions of national law concerning safety of persons remaining in detention facilities.

(25) Member States should ensure that, when providing information in accordance with this Directive, suspects or accused persons are provided, where necessary, with translations or interpretation into a language that they understand, in accordance with the standards set out in Directive 2010/64/EU.

(26) When providing suspects or accused persons with information in accordance with this Directive, competent authorities should pay particular attention to

persons who cannot understand the content or meaning of the information, for example because of their youth or their mental or physical condition.

(27) Persons accused of having committed a criminal offence should be given all the information on the accusation necessary to enable them to prepare their defence and to safeguard the fairness of the proceedings.

(28) The information provided to suspects or accused persons about the criminal act they are suspected or accused of having committed should be given promptly, and at the latest before their first official interview by the police or another competent authority, and without prejudicing the course of ongoing investigations. A description of the facts, including, where known, time and place, relating to the criminal act that the persons are suspected or accused of having committed and the possible legal classification of the alleged offence should be given in sufficient detail, taking into account the stage of the criminal proceedings when such a description is given, to safeguard the fairness of the proceedings and allow for an effective exercise of the rights of the defence.

(29) Where, in the course of the criminal proceedings, the details of the accusation change to the extent that the position of suspects or accused persons is substantially affected, this should be communicated to them where necessary to safeguard the fairness of the proceedings and in due time to allow for an effective exercise of the rights of the defence.

(30) Documents and, where appropriate, photographs, audio and video recordings, which are essential to challenging effectively the lawfulness of an arrest or detention of suspects or accused persons in accordance with national law, should be made available to suspects or accused persons or to their lawyers at the latest before a competent judicial authority is called to decide upon the lawfulness of the arrest or detention in accordance with Article 5(4) ECHR, and in due time to allow the effective exercise of the right to challenge the lawfulness of the arrest or detention.

(31) For the purpose of this Directive, access to the material evidence, as defined in national law, whether for or against the suspect or accused person, which is in the possession of the competent authorities in relation to the specific criminal case, should include access to materials such as documents, and where appropriate photographs and audio and video recordings. Such materials may be contained in a case file or otherwise held by competent authorities in any appropriate way in accordance with national law.

(32) Access to the material evidence in the possession of the competent authorities, whether for or against the suspect or accused person, as provided for under this Directive, may be refused, in accordance with national law, where such access may lead to a serious threat to the life or fundamental rights of another person or where refusal of such access is strictly necessary to safeguard an important public interest. Any refusal of such access must be weighed against the rights of the defence of the suspect or accused person, taking into account the different stages of the criminal proceedings. Restrictions on such access should be interpreted strictly and in accordance with the principle of the right to a fair trial under the ECHR and as interpreted by the case-law of the European Court of Human Rights.

(33) The right of access to the materials of a case should be without prejudice to the provisions of national law on the protection of personal data and the whereabouts of protected witnesses.

(34) Access to the materials of the case, as provided for by this Directive, should be provided free of charge, without prejudice to provisions of national law providing for fees to be paid for documents to be copied from the case file or for sending materials to the persons concerned or to their lawyer.

(35) Where information is provided in accordance with this Directive, the competent authorities should take note of this in accordance with existing recording procedures under national law and should not be subject to any additional obligation to introduce new mechanisms or to any additional administrative burden.

(36) Suspects or accused persons or their lawyers should have the right to challenge, in accordance with national law, the possible failure or refusal of the competent authorities to provide information or to disclose certain materials of the case in accordance with this Directive. That right does not entail the obligation for Member States to provide for a specific appeal procedure, a separate mechanism, or a complaint procedure in which such failure or refusal may be challenged.

(37) Without prejudice to judicial independence and to differences in the organisation of the judiciary across the Union, Member States should provide or encourage the provision of adequate training with respect to the objectives of this Directive to the relevant officials in Member States.

(38) Member States should undertake all the necessary action to comply with this Directive. A practical and effective implementation of some of the provisions such as the obligation to provide suspects or accused persons with information about their rights in simple and accessible language could be achieved by different means including non-legislative measures such as appropriate training for the competent authorities or by a Letter of Rights drafted in simple and non-technical language so as to be easily understood by a lay person without any knowledge of criminal procedural law.

(39) The right to written information about rights on arrest provided for in this Directive should also apply, mutatis mutandis, to persons arrested for the purpose of the execution of a European Arrest Warrant under Council Framework Decision 2002/584/JHA of 13 June 2002 on the European arrest warrant and the surrender procedures between Member States. To help Member States draw up a Letter of Rights for such persons, a model is provided in Annex II. That model is indicative and may be subject to review in the context of the Commission's report on implementation of this Directive and also once all the Roadmap measures have come into force.

(40) This Directive sets minimum rules. Member States may extend the rights set out in this Directive in order to provide a higher level of protection also in situations not explicitly dealt with in this Directive. The level of protection should never fall below the standards provided by the ECHR as interpreted in the case-law of the European Court of Human Rights.

(41) This Directive respects fundamental rights and observes the principles recognised by the Charter. In particular, this Directive seeks to promote the right

to liberty, the right to a fair trial and the rights of the defence. It should be implemented accordingly.

(42) The provisions of this Directive that correspond to rights guaranteed by the ECHR should be interpreted and implemented consistently with those rights, as interpreted in the case-law of the European Court of Human Rights.

(43) Since the objective of this Directive, namely establishing common minimum standards relating to the right to information in criminal proceedings, cannot be achieved by Member States acting unilaterally, at national, regional or local level, and can therefore, by reason of its scale and effects, be better achieved at Union level, the Union may adopt measures in accordance with the principle of subsidiarity as set out in Article 5 of the Treaty on European Union. In accordance with the principle of proportionality, as set out in that Article, this Directive does not go beyond what is necessary in order to achieve that objective.

(44) In accordance with Article 3 of the Protocol (No 21) on the position of the United Kingdom and Ireland in respect of the Area of Freedom, Security and Justice, annexed to the Treaty on European Union and to the Treaty on the Functioning of the European Union, those Member States have notified their wish to take part in the adoption and application of this Directive.

(45) In accordance with Articles 1 and 2 of the Protocol (No 22) on the position of Denmark, annexed to the Treaty on European Union and to the Treaty on the Functioning of the European Union, Denmark is not taking part in the adoption of this Directive and is not bound by it or subject to its application,

HAVE ADOPTED THIS DIRECTIVE:

Article 1: Subject matter

This Directive lays down rules concerning the right to information of suspects or accused persons, relating to their rights in criminal proceedings and to the accusation against them. It also lays down rules concerning the right to information of persons subject to a European Arrest Warrant relating to their rights.

Article 2: Scope

1. This Directive applies from the time persons are made aware by the competent authorities of a Member State that they are suspected or accused of having committed a criminal offence until the conclusion of the proceedings, which is understood to mean the final determination of the question whether the suspect or accused person has committed the criminal offence, including, where applicable, sentencing and the resolution of any appeal.

2. Where the law of a Member State provides for the imposition of a sanction regarding minor offences by an authority other than a court having jurisdiction in criminal matters, and the imposition of such a sanction may be appealed to such a court, this Directive shall apply only to the proceedings before that court, following such an appeal.

Article 3: Right to information about rights

1. Member States shall ensure that suspects or accused persons are provided

promptly with information concerning at least the following procedural rights, as they apply under national law, in order to allow for those rights to be exercised effectively:

(a) the right of access to a lawyer;
(b) any entitlement to free legal advice and the conditions for obtaining such advice;
(c) the right to be informed of the accusation, in accordance with Article 6;
(d) the right to interpretation and translation;
(e) the right to remain silent.

2. Member States shall ensure that the information provided for under paragraph 1 shall be given orally or in writing, in simple and accessible language, taking into account any particular needs of vulnerable suspects or vulnerable accused persons.

Article 4: Letter of Rights on arrest

1. Member States shall ensure that suspects or accused persons who are arrested or detained are provided promptly with a written Letter of Rights. They shall be given an opportunity to read the Letter of Rights and shall be allowed to keep it in their possession throughout the time that they are deprived of liberty.

2. In addition to the information set out in Article 3, the Letter of Rights referred to in paragraph 1 of this Article shall contain information about the following rights as they apply under national law:
(a) the right of access to the materials of the case;
(b) the right to have consular authorities and one person informed;
(c) the right of access to urgent medical assistance; and
(d) the maximum number of hours or days suspects or accused persons may be deprived of liberty before being brought before a judicial authority.

3. The Letter of Rights shall also contain basic information about any possibility, under national law, of challenging the lawfulness of the arrest; obtaining a review of the detention; or making a request for provisional release.

4. The Letter of Rights shall be drafted in simple and accessible language. An indicative model Letter of Rights is set out in Annex I.

5. Member States shall ensure that suspects or accused persons receive the Letter of Rights written in a language that they understand. Where a Letter of Rights is not available in the appropriate language, suspects or accused persons shall be informed of their rights orally in a language that they understand. A Letter of Rights in a language that they understand shall then be given to them without undue delay.

Article 5: Letter of Rights in European Arrest Warrant proceedings

1. Member States shall ensure that persons who are arrested for the purpose of the execution of a European Arrest Warrant are provided promptly with an appropriate Letter of Rights containing information on their rights according to the law implementing Framework Decision 2002/584/JHA in the executing Member State.

2. The Letter of Rights shall be drafted in simple and accessible language. An indicative model Letter of Rights is set out in Annex II.

Article 6: Right to information about the accusation

1. Member States shall ensure that suspects or accused persons are provided with information about the criminal act they are suspected or accused of having committed. That information shall be provided promptly and in such detail as is necessary to safeguard the fairness of the proceedings and the effective exercise of the rights of the defence.

2. Member States shall ensure that suspects or accused persons who are arrested or detained are informed of the reasons for their arrest or detention, including the criminal act they are suspected or accused of having committed.

3. Member States shall ensure that, at the latest on submission of the merits of the accusation to a court, detailed information is provided on the accusation, including the nature and legal classification of the criminal offence, as well as the nature of participation by the accused person.

4. Member States shall ensure that suspects or accused persons are informed promptly of any changes in the information given in accordance with this Article where this is necessary to safeguard the fairness of the proceedings.

Article 7: Right of access to the materials of the case

1. Where a person is arrested and detained at any stage of the criminal proceedings, Member States shall ensure that documents related to the specific case in the possession of the competent authorities which are essential to challenging effectively, in accordance with national law, the lawfulness of the arrest or detention, are made available to arrested persons or to their lawyers.

2. Member States shall ensure that access is granted at least to all material evidence in the possession of the competent authorities, whether for or against suspects or accused persons, to those persons or their lawyers in order to safeguard the fairness of the proceedings and to prepare the defence.

3. Without prejudice to paragraph 1, access to the materials referred to in paragraph 2 shall be granted in due time to allow the effective exercise of the rights of the defence and at the latest upon submission of the merits of the accusation to the judgment of a court. Where further material evidence comes into the possession of the competent authorities, access shall be granted to it in due time to allow for it to be considered.

4. By way of derogation from paragraphs 2 and 3, provided that this does not prejudice the right to a fair trial, access to certain materials may be refused if such access may lead to a serious threat to the life or the fundamental rights of another person or if such refusal is strictly necessary to safeguard an important public interest, such as in cases where access could prejudice an ongoing investigation or seriously harm the national security of the Member State in which the criminal proceedings are instituted. Member States shall ensure that, in accordance with procedures in national law, a decision to refuse access to certain materials in accordance with this paragraph is taken by a judicial authority or is at least subject to judicial review.

5. Access, as referred to in this Article, shall be provided free of charge.

Article 8: Verification and remedies

1. Member States shall ensure that when information is provided to suspects or accused persons in accordance with Articles 3 to 6 this is noted using the recording procedure specified in the law of the Member State concerned.

2. Member States shall ensure that suspects or accused persons or their lawyers have the right to challenge, in accordance with procedures in national law, the possible failure or refusal of the competent authorities to provide information in accordance with this Directive.

Article 9: Training

Without prejudice to judicial independence and differences in the organisation of the judiciary across the Union, Member States shall request those responsible for the training of judges, prosecutors, police and judicial staff involved in criminal proceedings to provide appropriate training with respect to the objectives of this Directive.

Article 10: Non-regression

Nothing in this Directive shall be construed as limiting or derogating from any of the rights or procedural safeguards that are ensured under the Charter, the ECHR, other relevant provisions of international law or the law of any Member State which provides a higher level of protection.

Article 11: Transposition

1. Member States shall bring into force the laws, regulations and administrative provisions necessary to comply with this Directive by 2 June 2014.

2. Member States shall transmit the text of those measures to the Commission.

3. When Member States adopt those measures they shall contain a reference to this Directive or be accompanied by such a reference on the occasion of their official publication. The methods of making such reference shall be laid down by the Member States.

Article 12: Report

The Commission shall, by 2 June 2015, submit a report to the European Parliament and to the Council, assessing the extent to which the Member States have taken the necessary measures in order to comply with this Directive, accompanied, if necessary, by legislative proposals.

Article 13: Entry into force

This Directive shall enter into force on the twentieth day following that of its publication in the Official Journal of the European Union.

Article 14: Addressees

This Directive is addressed to the Member States in accordance with the Treaties.

Done at Strasbourg, 22 May 2012.

For the European Parliament

The President

M. Schulz

For the Council

The President

N. Wammen

ANNEX I

Indicative model Letter of Rights

The sole purpose of this model is to assist national authorities in drawing up their Letter of Rights at national level. Member States are not bound to use this model. When preparing their Letter of Rights, Member States may amend this model in order to align it with their national rules and add further useful information. The Member State's Letter of Rights must be given upon arrest or detention. This however does not prevent Member States from providing suspects or accused persons with written information in other situations during criminal proceedings.

A. ASSISTANCE OF A LAWYER/ENTITLEMENT TO LEGAL AID

You have the right to speak confidentially to a lawyer. A lawyer is independent from the police. Ask the police if you need help to get in contact with a lawyer, the police shall help you. In certain cases the assistance may be free of charge. Ask the police for more information.

B. INFORMATION ABOUT THE ACCUSATION

You have the right to know why you have been arrested or detained and what you are suspected or accused of having done.

C. INTERPRETATION AND TRANSLATION

If you do not speak or understand the language spoken by the police or other competent authorities, you have the right to be assisted by an interpreter, free of charge. The interpreter may help you to talk to your lawyer and must keep the content of that communication confidential. You have the right to translation of at least the relevant passages of essential documents, including any order by a judge allowing your arrest or keeping you in custody, any charge or indictment and any judgment. You may in some circumstances be provided with an oral translation or summary.

D. RIGHT TO REMAIN SILENT

While questioned by the police or other competent authorities, you do not have to answer questions about the alleged offence. Your lawyer can help you to decide on that.

E. TO DOCUMENTS

When you are arrested and detained, you (or your lawyer) have the right to access essential documents you need to challenge the arrest or detention. If your case goes to court, you (or your lawyer) have the right to access the material evidence for or against you.

F. INFORMING SOMEONE ELSE ABOUT YOUR ARREST OR DETENTION/INFORMING YOUR CONSULATE OR EMBASSY

When you are arrested or detained, you should tell the police if you want someone to be informed of your detention, for example a family member or your employer. In certain cases the right to inform another person of your detention may be temporarily restricted. In such cases the police will inform you of this.

If you are a foreigner, tell the police if you want your consular authority or embassy to be informed of your detention. Please also tell the police if you want to contact an official of your consular authority or embassy.

G. URGENT MEDICAL ASSISTANCE

When you are arrested or detained, you have the right to urgent medical assistance. Please let the police know if you are in need of such assistance.

H. PERIOD OF DEPRIVATION OF LIBERTY

After your arrest you may be deprived of liberty or detained for a maximum period of ... [fill in applicable number of hours/days]. At the end of that period you must either be released or be heard by a judge who will decide on your further detention. Ask your lawyer or the judge for information about the possibility to challenge your arrest, to review the detention or to ask for provisional release.

ANNEX II

Indicative model Letter of Rights for persons arrested on the basis of a European Arrest Warrant

The sole purpose of this model is to assist national authorities in drawing up their Letter of Rights at national level. Member States are not bound to use this model. When preparing their Letter of Rights, Member States may amend this model in order to align it with their national rules and add further useful information.

A. INFORMATION ABOUT THE EUROPEAN ARREST WARRANT

You have the right to be informed about the content of the European Arrest Warrant on the basis of which you have been arrested.

B. ASSISTANCE OF A LAWYER

You have the right to speak confidentially to a lawyer. A lawyer is independent from the police. Ask the police if you need help to get in contact with a lawyer, the police shall help you. In certain cases the assistance may be free of charge. Ask the police for more information.

C. INTERPRETATION AND TRANSLATION

If you do not speak or understand the language spoken by the police or other competent authorities, you have the right to be assisted by an interpreter, free of charge. The interpreter may help you to talk to your lawyer and must keep the content of that communication confidential. You have the right to a translation of the European Arrest Warrant in a language you understand. You may in some circumstances be provided with an oral translation or summary.

D. POSSIBILITY TO CONSENT

You may consent or not consent to being surrendered to the State seeking you. Your consent would speed up the proceedings. [Possible addition of certain Member States: It may be difficult or even impossible to change this decision at a later stage.] Ask the authorities or your lawyer for more information.

E. HEARING

If you do not consent to your surrender, you have the right to be heard by a judicial authority.

Framework Decision on the European Supervision Order

2009/829/JHA: Council Framework Decision of 23 October 2009 on the application, between Member States of the European Union, of the principle of mutual recognition to decisions on supervision measures as an alternative to provisional detention.

THE COUNCIL OF THE EUROPEAN UNION,

Having regard to the Treaty on European Union, and in particular Article 31(1)(a) and (c) and Article 34(2)(b) thereof,

Having regard to the proposal from the Commission,

Having regard to the opinion of the European Parliament,

Whereas:

(1) The European Union has set itself the objective of maintaining and developing an area of freedom, security and justice.

(2) According to the Conclusions of the European Council meeting in Tampere on 15 and 16 October 1999, and in particular point 36 thereof, the principle of mutual recognition should apply to pre-trial orders. The programme of measures to implement the principle of mutual recognition in criminal matters addresses mutual recognition of supervision measures in its measure 10.

(3) The measures provided for in this Framework Decision should aim at enhancing the protection of the general public through enabling a person resident in one Member State, but subject to criminal proceedings in a second Member State, to be supervised by the authorities in the State in which he or she is resident whilst awaiting trial. As a consequence, the present Framework Decision has as its objective the monitoring of a defendants' movements in the light of the overriding objective of protecting the general public and the risk posed to the public by the existing regime, which provides only two alternatives: provisional detention or unsupervised movement. The measures will therefore give further effect to the right of law-abiding citizens to live in safety and security.

(4) The measures provided for in this Framework Decision should also aim at enhancing the right to liberty and the presumption of innocence in the European Union and at ensuring cooperation between Member States when a person is subject to obligations or supervision pending a court decision. As a consequence, the present Framework Decision has as its objective the promotion, where appropriate, of the use of non-custodial measures as an alternative to

provisional detention, even where, according to the law of the Member State concerned, a provisional detention could not be imposed ab initio.

(5) As regards the detention of persons subject to criminal proceedings, there is a risk of different treatment between those who are resident in the trial state and those who are not: a non-resident risks being remanded in custody pending trial even where, in similar circumstances, a resident would not. In a common European area of justice without internal borders, it is necessary to take action to ensure that a person subject to criminal proceedings who is not resident in the trial state is not treated any differently from a person subject to criminal proceedings who is so resident.

(6) The certificate, which should be forwarded together with the decision on supervision measures to the competent authority of the executing State, should specify the address where the person concerned will stay in the executing State, as well as any other relevant information which might facilitate the monitoring of the supervision measures in the executing State.

(7) The competent authority in the executing State should inform the competent authority in the issuing State of the maximum length of time, if any, during which the supervision measures could be monitored in the executing State. In Member States in which the supervision measures have to be periodically renewed, this maximum length of time has to be understood as the total length of time after which it is legally not possible anymore to renew the supervision measures.

(8) Any request by the competent authority in the executing State for confirmation of the necessity to prolong the monitoring of supervision measures should be without prejudice to the law of the issuing State, which applies to the decision on renewal, review and withdrawal of the decision on supervision measures. Such a request for confirmation should not oblige the competent authority in the issuing State to take a new decision to prolong the monitoring of supervision measures.

(9) The competent authority in the issuing State should have jurisdiction to take all subsequent decisions relating to a decision on supervision measures, including ordering a provisional detention. Such provisional detention might, in particular, be ordered following a breach of the supervision measures or a failure to comply with a summons to attend any hearing or trial in the course of criminal proceedings.

(10) In order to avoid unnecessary costs and difficulties in relation to the transfer of a person subject to criminal proceedings for the purposes of a hearing or a trial, Member States should be allowed to use telephone- and videoconferences.

(11) Where appropriate, electronic monitoring could be used for monitoring supervision measures in accordance with national law and procedures.

(12) This Framework Decision should make it possible that supervision measures imposed on the person concerned are monitored in the executing State, while ensuring the due course of justice and, in particular, that the person concerned will be available to stand trial. In case the person concerned does not return to the issuing State voluntarily, he or she may be surrendered to the issuing State in accordance with Council Framework Decision 2002/584/JHA

of 13 June 2002 on the European Arrest Warrant and the surrender procedures between Member States (2) (hereinafter referred to as the 'Framework Decision on the European Arrest Warrant').

(13) While this Framework Decision covers all crimes and is not restricted to particular types or levels of crime, supervision measures should generally be applied in case of less serious offences. Therefore all the provisions of the Framework Decision on the European Arrest Warrant, except Article 2(1) thereof, should apply in the situation when the competent authority in the executing State has to decide on the surrender of the person concerned. As a consequence, also Article 5(2) and (3) of the Framework Decision on the European Arrest Warrant should apply in that situation.

(14) Costs relating to the travel of the person concerned between the executing and issuing States in connection with the monitoring of supervision measures or for the purpose of attending any hearing are not regulated by this Framework Decision. The possibility, in particular for the issuing State, to bear all or part of such costs is a matter governed by national law.

(15) Since the objective of this Framework Decision, namely the mutual recognition of decisions on supervision measures in the course of criminal proceedings, cannot be sufficiently achieved by the Member States acting unilaterally and can therefore, by reason of its scale and effects, be better achieved at Union level, the Union may adopt measures, in accordance with the principle of subsidiarity as set out in Article 2 of the Treaty on European Union and Article 5 of the Treaty establishing the European Community. In accordance with the principle of proportionality, as set out in that Article, this Framework Decision does not go beyond what is necessary in order to achieve that objective.

(16) This Framework Decision respects fundamental rights and observes the principles recognised, in particular, by Article 6 of the Treaty on European Union and reflected by the Charter of Fundamental Rights of the European Union. Nothing in this Framework Decision should be interpreted as prohibiting refusal to recognise a decision on supervision measures if there are objective indications that it was imposed to punish a person because of his or her sex, race, religion, ethnic origin, nationality, language, political convictions or sexual orientation or that this person might be disadvantaged for one of these reasons.

(17) This Framework Decision should not prevent any Member State from applying its constitutional rules relating to entitlement to due process, freedom of association, freedom of the press, freedom of expression in other media and freedom of religion.

(18) The provisions of this Framework Decision should be applied in conformity with the right of the Union's citizens to move and reside freely within the territory of the Member States, pursuant to Article 18 of the Treaty establishing the European Community.

(19) Personal data processed when implementing this Framework Decision should be protected in accordance with Council Framework Decision 2008/977/JHA of 27 November 2008 on the protection of personal data processed in the

framework of police and judicial cooperation in criminal matters (3) and in accordance with the principles laid down in the Council of Europe Convention of 28 January 1981 for the Protection of Individuals with regard to Automatic Processing of Personal Data, which all Member States have ratified,

HAS ADOPTED THIS FRAMEWORK DECISION:

Article 1: Subject matter

This Framework Decision lays down rules according to which one Member State recognises a decision on supervision measures issued in another Member State as an alternative to provisional detention, monitors the supervision measures imposed on a natural person and surrenders the person concerned to the issuing State in case of breach of these measures.

Article 2: Objectives

1. The objectives of this Framework Decision are:
   (a) to ensure the due course of justice and, in particular, that the person concerned will be available to stand trial;
   (b) to promote, where appropriate, the use, in the course of criminal proceedings, of non-custodial measures for persons who are not resident in the Member State where the proceedings are taking place;
   (c) to improve the protection of victims and of the general public.
2. This Framework Decision does not confer any right on a person to the use, in the course of criminal proceedings, of a non-custodial measure as an alternative to custody. This is a matter governed by the law and procedures of the Member State where the criminal proceedings are taking place.

Article 3: Protection of law and order and the safeguarding of internal security

This Framework Decision is without prejudice to the exercise of the responsibilities incumbent upon Member States with regard to the protection of victims, the general public and the safeguarding of internal security, in accordance with Article 33 of the Treaty on European Union.

Article 4: Definitions

For the purposes of this Framework Decision:
   (a) 'decision on supervision measures' means an enforceable decision taken in the course of criminal proceedings by a competent authority of the issuing State in accordance with its national law and procedures and imposing on a natural person, as an alternative to provisional detention, one or more supervision measures;
   (b) 'supervision measures' means obligations and instructions imposed on a natural person, in accordance with the national law and procedures of the issuing State;
   (c) 'issuing State' means the Member State in which a decision on supervision measures has been issued;
   (d) 'executing State' means the Member State in which the supervision measures are monitored.

Article 5: Fundamental rights

This Framework Decision shall not have the effect of modifying the obligation to respect fundamental rights and fundamental legal principles as enshrined in Article 6 of the Treaty on European Union.

Article 6: Designation of competent authorities

1. Each Member State shall inform the General Secretariat of the Council which judicial authority or authorities under its national law are competent to act according to this Framework Decision in the situation where that Member State is the issuing State or the executing State.

2. As an exception to paragraph 1 and without prejudice to paragraph 3, Member States may designate non-judicial authorities as the competent authorities for taking decisions under this Framework Decision, provided that such authorities have competence for taking decisions of a similar nature under their national law and procedures.

3. Decisions referred to under Article 18(1)(c) shall be taken by a competent judicial authority.

4. The General Secretariat of the Council shall make the information received available to all Member States and to the Commission.

Article 7: Recourse to a central authority

1. Each Member State may designate a central authority or, where its legal system so provides, more than one central authority to assist its competent authorities.

2. A Member State may, if it is necessary as a result of the organisation of its internal judicial system, make its central authority(ies) responsible for the administrative transmission and reception of decisions on supervision measures, together with the certificates referred to in Article 10, as well as for all other official correspondence relating thereto. As a consequence, all communications, consultations, exchanges of information, enquiries and notifications between competent authorities may be dealt with, where appropriate, with the assistance of the central authority(ies) of the Member State concerned.

3. Member States wishing to make use of the possibilities referred to in this Article shall communicate to the General Secretariat of the Council information relating to the designated central authority or central authorities. These indications shall be binding upon all the authorities of the issuing Member State.

Article 8: Types of supervision measures

1. This Framework Decision shall apply to the following supervision measures:
   (a) an obligation for the person to inform the competent authority in the executing State of any change of residence, in particular for the purpose of receiving a summons to attend a hearing or a trial in the course of criminal proceedings;
   (b) an obligation not to enter certain localities, places or defined areas in the issuing or executing State;

(c) an obligation to remain at a specified place, where applicable during specified times;

(d) an obligation containing limitations on leaving the territory of the executing State;

(e) an obligation to report at specified times to a specific authority;

(f) an obligation to avoid contact with specific persons in relation with the
offence(s) allegedly committed.

2. Each Member State shall notify the General Secretariat of the Council, when
transposing this Framework Decision or at a later stage, which supervision
measures, apart from those referred to in paragraph 1, it is prepared to monitor. These measures may include in particular:

(a) an obligation not to engage in specified activities in relation with the
offence(s) allegedly committed, which may include involvement in a
specified profession or field of employment;

(b) an obligation not to drive a vehicle;

(c) an obligation to deposit a certain sum of money or to give another type of
guarantee, which may either be provided through a specified number of
instalments or entirely at once;

(d) an obligation to undergo therapeutic treatment or treatment for
addiction;

(e) an obligation to avoid contact with specific objects in relation with the
offence(s) allegedly committed.

3. The General Secretariat of the Council shall make the information received
under this Article available to all Member States and to the Commission.

Article 9: Criteria relating to the Member State to which the decision on supervision measures may be forwarded

1. A decision on supervision measures may be forwarded to the competent
authority of the Member State in which the person is lawfully and ordinarily
residing, in cases where the person, having been informed about the measures concerned, consents to return to that State.

2. The competent authority in the issuing State may, upon request of the person,
forward the decision on supervision measures to the competent authority of
a Member State other than the Member State in which the person is lawfully
and ordinarily residing, on condition that the latter authority has consented to
such forwarding.

3. When implementing this Framework Decision, Member States shall determine under which conditions their competent authorities may consent to the
forwarding of a decision on supervision measures in cases pursuant to paragraph 2.

4. Each Member State shall make a statement to the General Secretariat of the
Council of the determination made under paragraph 3. Member States may
modify such a statement at any time. The General Secretariat shall make the
information received available to all Member States and to the Commission.

Article 10: Procedure for forwarding a decision on supervision measures together with the certificate

1. When, in application of Article 9(1) or (2), the competent authority of the issuing State forwards a decision on supervision measures to another Member State, it shall ensure that it is accompanied by a certificate, the standard form of which is set out in Annex I.

2. The decision on supervision measures or a certified copy of it, together with the certificate, shall be forwarded by the competent authority in the issuing State directly to the competent authority in the executing State by any means which leaves a written record under conditions allowing the executing State to establish their authenticity. The original of the decision on supervision measures, or a certified copy of it, and the original of the certificate, shall be sent to the executing State if it so requires. All official communications shall also be made directly between the said competent authorities.

3. The certificate shall be signed, and its content certified as accurate, by the competent authority in the issuing State.

4. The certificate referred to in paragraph 1 of this Article shall include, apart from the measures referred to in Article 8(1), only such measures as notified by the executing State in accordance with Article 8(2).

5. The competent authority in the issuing State shall specify:
   (a) where applicable, the length of time to which the decision on supervision measures applies and whether a renewal of this decision is possible; and
   (b) on an indicative basis, the provisional length of time for which the monitoring of the supervision measures is likely to be needed, taking into account all the circumstances of the case that are known when the decision on supervision measures is forwarded.

6. The competent authority in the issuing State shall forward the decision on supervision measures together with the certificate only to one executing State at any one time.

7. If the competent authority in the executing State is not known to the competent authority in the issuing State, the latter shall make all necessary inquiries, including via the contact points of the European Judicial Network set up by Council Joint Action 98/428/JHA of 29 June 1998 on the creation of a European Judicial Network (4), in order to obtain the information from the executing State.

8. When an authority in the executing State which receives a decision on supervision measures together with a certificate has no competence to recognise that decision, this authority shall, ex officio, forward the decision together with the certificate to the competent authority.

Article 11: Competence over the monitoring of the supervision measures

1. As long as the competent authority of the executing State has not recognised the decision on supervision measures forwarded to it and has not informed the competent authority of the issuing State of such recognition, the competent

authority of the issuing State shall remain competent in relation to the monitoring of the supervision measures imposed.

2. If competence for monitoring the supervision measures has been transferred to the competent authority of the executing State, such competence shall revert back to the competent authority of the issuing State:
   (a) where the person concerned has established his/her lawful and ordinary residence in a State other than the executing State;
   (b) as soon as the competent authority in the issuing State has notified withdrawal of the certificate referred to in Article 10(1), pursuant to Article 13(3), to the competent authority of the executing State;
   (c) where the competent authority in the issuing State has modified the supervision measures and the competent authority in the executing State, in application of Article 18(4)(b), has refused to monitor the modified supervision measures because they do not fall within the types of supervision measures referred to in Article 8(1) and/or within those notified by the executing State concerned in accordance with Article 8(2);
   (d) when the period of time referred to in Article 20(2)(b) has elapsed;
   (e) where the competent authority in the executing State has decided to stop monitoring the supervision measures and has informed the competent authority in the issuing State thereof, in application of Article 23.

3. In cases referred to in paragraph 2, the competent authorities of the issuing and executing States shall consult each other so as to avoid, as far as possible, any discontinuance in the monitoring of the supervision measures.

Article 12: Decision in the executing State

1. The competent authority in the executing State shall, as soon as possible and in any case within 20 working days of receipt of the decision on supervision measures and certificate, recognise the decision on supervision measures forwarded in accordance with Article 9 and following the procedure laid down in Article 10 and without delay take all necessary measures for monitoring the supervision measures, unless it decides to invoke one of the grounds for non-recognition referred to in Article 15.

2. If a legal remedy has been introduced against the decision referred to in paragraph 1, the time limit for recognition of the decision on supervision measures shall be extended by another 20 working days.

3. If it is not possible, in exceptional circumstances, for the competent authority in the executing State to comply with the time limits laid down in paragraphs 1 and 2, it shall immediately inform the competent authority in the issuing State, by any means of its choosing, giving reasons for the delay and indicating how long it expects to take to issue a final decision.

4. The competent authority may postpone the decision on recognition of the decision on supervision measures where the certificate provided for in Article 10 is incomplete or obviously does not correspond to the decision on supervision measures, until such reasonable time limit set for the certificate to be completed or corrected.

Article 13: Adaptation of the supervision measures

1. If the nature of the supervision measures is incompatible with the law of the executing State, the competent authority in that Member State may adapt them in line with the types of supervision measures which apply, under the law of the executing State, to equivalent offences. The adapted supervision measure shall correspond as far as possible to that imposed in the issuing State.

2. The adapted supervision measure shall not be more severe than the supervision measure which was originally imposed.

3. Following receipt of information referred to in Article 20(2)(b) or (f), the competent authority in the issuing State may decide to withdraw the certificate as long as monitoring in the executing State has not yet begun. In any case, such a decision shall be taken and communicated as soon as possible and within ten days of the receipt of the relevant notification at the latest.

Article 14: Double criminality

1. The following offences, if they are punishable in the issuing State by a custodial sentence or a measure involving deprivation of liberty for a maximum period of at least three years, and as they are defined by the law of the issuing State, shall, under the terms of this Framework Decision and without verification of the double criminality of the act, give rise to recognition of the decision on supervision measures:
   - participation in a criminal organisation,
   - terrorism,
   - trafficking in human beings,
   - sexual exploitation of children and child pornography,
   - illicit trafficking in narcotic drugs and psychotropic substances,
   - illicit trafficking in weapons, munitions and explosives,
   - corruption,
   - fraud, including that affecting the financial interests of the European Communities within the meaning of the Convention of 26 July 1995 on the protection of the European Communities' financial interests (5),
   - laundering of the proceeds of crime,
   - counterfeiting currency, including of the euro,
   - computer-related crime,
   - environmental crime, including illicit trafficking in endangered animal species and in endangered plant species and varieties,
   - facilitation of unauthorised entry and residence,
   - murder, grievous bodily injury,
   - illicit trade in human organs and tissue,
   - kidnapping, illegal restraint and hostage-taking,
   - racism and xenophobia,
   - organised or armed robbery,
   - illicit trafficking in cultural goods, including antiques and works of art,
   - swindling,
   - racketeering and extortion,
   - counterfeiting and piracy of products,
   - forgery of administrative documents and trafficking therein,

- forgery of means of payment,
- illicit trafficking in hormonal substances and other growth promoters,
- illicit trafficking in nuclear or radioactive materials,
- trafficking in stolen vehicles,
- rape,
- arson,
- crimes within the jurisdiction of the International Criminal Court,
- unlawful seizure of aircraft/ships,
- sabotage.

2. The Council may decide to add other categories of offences to the list in paragraph 1 at any time, acting unanimously after consultation of the European Parliament under the conditions laid down in Article 39(1) of the Treaty on European Union. The Council shall examine, in the light of the report submitted to it pursuant to Article 27 of this Framework Decision, whether the list should be extended or amended.

3. For offences other than those covered by paragraph 1, the executing State may make the recognition of the decision on supervision measures subject to the condition that the decision relates to acts which also constitute an offence under the law of the executing State, whatever the constituent elements or however it is described.

4. Member States may, for constitutional reasons, on the adoption of this Framework Decision, by a declaration notified to the General Secretariat of the Council, declare that they will not apply paragraph 1 in respect of some or all of the offences referred to in that paragraph. Any such declaration may be withdrawn at any time. Such declarations or withdrawals of declarations shall be published in the Official Journal of the European Union.

Article 15: Grounds for non-recognition

1. The competent authority in the executing State may refuse to recognise the decision on supervision measures if:
   (a) the certificate referred to in Article 10 is incomplete or obviously does not correspond to the decision on supervision measures and is not completed or corrected within a reasonable period set by the competent authority in the executing State;
   (b) the criteria laid down in Article 9(1), 9(2) or 10(4) are not met;
   (c) recognition of the decision on supervision measures would contravene the ne bis in idem principle;
   (d) the decision on supervision measures relates, in the cases referred to in Article 14(3) and, where the executing State has made a declaration under Article 14(4), in the cases referred to in Article 14(1), to an act which would not constitute an offence under the law of the executing State; in tax, customs and currency matters, however, execution of the decision may not be refused on the grounds that the law of the executing State does not prescribe any taxes of the same kind or does not contain any tax, customs or currency provisions of the same kind as the law of the issuing State;
   (e) the criminal prosecution is statute-barred under the law of the executing

State and relates to an act which falls within the competence of the executing State under its national law;

(f) there is immunity under the law of the executing State, which makes it impossible to monitor supervision measures;

(g) under the law of the executing State, the person cannot, because of his age, be held criminally responsible for the act on which the decision on supervision measures is based;

(h) it would, in case of breach of the supervision measures, have to refuse to surrender the person concerned in accordance with Council Framework Decision 2002/584/JHA of 13 June 2002 on the European arrest warrant and the surrender procedures between Member States (6) (hereinafter referred to as the 'Framework Decision on the European Arrest Warrant').

2. In the cases referred to in paragraph 1(a), (b) and (c), before deciding not to recognise the decision on supervision measures, the competent authority in the executing State shall communicate, by appropriate means, with the competent authority in the issuing State and, as necessary, request the latter to supply without delay all additional information required.

3. Where the competent authority in the executing State is of the opinion that the recognition of a decision on supervision measures could be refused on the basis of paragraph 1 under (h), but it is nevertheless willing to recognise the decision on supervision measures and monitor the supervision measures contained therein, it shall inform the competent authority in the issuing State thereof providing the reasons for the possible refusal. In such a case, the competent authority in the issuing State may decide to withdraw the certificate in accordance with the second sentence of Article 13(3). If the competent authority in the issuing State does not withdraw the certificate, the competent authority in the executing State may recognise the decision on supervision measures and monitor the supervision measures contained therein, it being understood that the person concerned might not be surrendered on the basis of a European Arrest Warrant.

Article 16: Law governing supervision

The monitoring of supervision measures shall be governed by the law of the executing State.

Article 17: Continuation of the monitoring of supervision measures

Where the time period referred to in Article 20(2)(b) is due to expire and the supervision measures are still needed, the competent authority in the issuing State may request the competent authority in the executing State to extend the monitoring of the supervision measures, in view of the circumstances of the case at hand and the foreseeable consequences for the person if Article 11(2)(d) would apply. The competent authority in the issuing State shall indicate the period of time for which such an extension is likely to be needed.

The competent authority in the executing State shall decide on this request in accordance with its national law, indicating, where appropriate, the maximum duration of the extension. In these cases, Article 18(3) may apply.

Article 18: Competence to take all subsequent decisions and governing law

1. Without prejudice to Article 3, the competent authority in the issuing State shall have jurisdiction to take all subsequent decisions relating to a decision on supervision measures. Such subsequent decisions include notably:
   (a) renewal, review and withdrawal of the decision on supervision measures;
   (b) modification of the supervision measures;
   (c) issuing an arrest warrant or any other enforceable judicial decision having the same effect.

2. The law of the issuing State shall apply to decisions taken pursuant to paragraph 1.

3. Where required by its national law, a competent authority in the executing State may decide to use the procedure of recognition set out in this Framework Decision in order to give effect to decisions referred to in paragraph 1(a) and (b) in its national legal system. Such a recognition shall not lead to a new examination of the grounds of non-recognition.

4. If the competent authority in the issuing State has modified the supervision measures in accordance with paragraph 1(b), the competent authority in the executing State may:
   (a) adapt these modified measures in application of Article 13, in case the nature of the modified supervision measures is incompatible with the law of the executing State;
   or
   (b) refuse to monitor the modified supervision measures if these measures do not fall within the types of supervision measures referred to in Article 8(1) and/or within those notified by the executing State concerned in accordance with Article 8(2).

5. The jurisdiction of the competent authority in the issuing State pursuant to paragraph 1 is without prejudice to proceedings that may be initiated in the executing State against the person concerned in relation with criminal offences committed by him/her other than those on which the decision on supervision measures is based.

Article 19: Obligations of the authorities involved

1. At any time during the monitoring of the supervision measures, the competent authority in the executing State may invite the competent authority in the issuing State to provide information as to whether the monitoring of the measures is still needed in the circumstances of the particular case at hand. The competent authority in the issuing State shall, without delay, reply to such an invitation, where appropriate by taking a subsequent decision referred to in Article 18(1).

2. Before the expiry of the period referred to in Article 10(5), the competent authority in the issuing State shall specify, ex officio or at the request of the competent authority in the executing State, for which additional period, if any, it expects that the monitoring of the measures is still needed.

3. The competent authority in the executing State shall immediately notify the

competent authority in the issuing State of any breach of a supervision measure, and any other finding which could result in taking any subsequent decision referred to in Article 18(1). Notice shall be given using the standard form set out in Annex II.

4. With a view to hearing the person concerned, the procedure and conditions contained in instruments of international and European Union law that provide for the possibility of using telephone- and videoconferences for hearing persons may be used mutatis mutandis, in particular where the legislation of the issuing State provides that a judicial hearing must be held before a decision referred to in Article 18(1) is taken.

5. The competent authority in the issuing State shall immediately inform the competent authority in the executing State of any decision referred to in Article 18(1) and of the fact that a legal remedy has been introduced against a decision on supervision measures.

6. If the certificate relating to the decision on supervision measures has been withdrawn, the competent authority of the executing State shall end the measures ordered as soon as it has been duly notified by the competent authority of the issuing State.

Article 20: Information from the executing State

1. The authority in the executing State which has received a decision on supervision measures, which it has no competence to recognise, together with a certificate, shall inform the competent authority in the issuing State to which authority it has forwarded this decision, together with the certificate, in accordance with Article 10(8).

2. The competent authority in the executing State shall, without delay, inform the competent authority in the issuing State by any means which leaves a written record:

   (a) of any change of residence of the person concerned;
   (b) of the maximum length of time during which the supervision measures can be monitored in the executing State, in case the law of the executing State provides such a maximum;
   (c) of the fact that it is in practice impossible to monitor the supervision measures for the reason that, after transmission of the decision on supervision measures and the certificate to the executing State, the person cannot be found in the territory of the executing State, in which case there shall be no obligation of the executing State to monitor the supervision measures;
   (d) of the fact that a legal remedy has been introduced against a decision to recognise a decision on supervision measures;
   (e) of the final decision to recognise the decision on supervision measures and take all necessary measures for the monitoring of the supervision measures;
   (f) of any decision to adapt the supervision measures in accordance with Article 13;
   (g) of any decision not to recognise the decision on supervision measures

and to assume responsibility for monitoring of the supervision measures in accordance with Article 15, together with the reasons for the decision.

Article 21: Surrender of the person

1. If the competent authority of the issuing State has issued an arrest warrant or any other enforceable judicial decision having the same effect, the person shall be surrendered in accordance with the Framework Decision on the European Arrest Warrant.

2. In this context, Article 2(1) of the Framework Decision on the European Arrest Warrant may not be invoked by the competent authority of the executing State to refuse to surrender the person.

3. Each Member State may notify the General Secretariat of the Council, when transposing this Framework Decision or at a later stage, that it will also apply Article 2(1) of the Framework Decision on the European Arrest Warrant in deciding on the surrender of the person concerned to the issuing State.

4. The General Secretariat of the Council shall make the information received under paragraph 3 available to all Member States and to the Commission.

Article 22: Consultations

1. Unless impracticable, the competent authorities of the issuing State and of the executing State shall consult each other:
   (a) during the preparation, or, at least, before forwarding a decision on supervision measures together with the certificate referred to in Article 10;
   (b) to facilitate the smooth and efficient monitoring of the supervision measures;
   (c) where the person has committed a serious breach of the supervision measures imposed.

2. The competent authority in the issuing State shall take due account of any indications communicated by the competent authority of the executing State on the risk that the person concerned might pose to victims and to the general public.

3. In application of paragraph 1, the competent authorities of the issuing State and of the executing State shall exchange all useful information, including:
   (a) information allowing verification of the identity and place of residence of the person concerned;
   (b) relevant information extracted from criminal records in accordance with applicable legislative instruments.

Article 23: Unanswered notices

1. Where the competent authority in the executing State has transmitted several notices referred to in Article 19(3) in respect of the same person to the competent authority in the issuing State, without this latter authority having taken any subsequent decision referred to in Article 18(1), the competent authority in the executing State may invite the competent authority in the issuing State to take such a decision, giving it a reasonable time limit to do so.

2. If the competent authority in the issuing State does not act within the time limit indicated by the competent authority in the executing State, the latter

authority may decide to stop monitoring the supervision measures. In such case, it shall inform the competent authority in the issuing State of its decision, and the competence for the monitoring of the supervision measures shall revert back to the competent authority in the issuing State in application of Article 11(2).

3. Where the law of the executing State requires a periodic confirmation of the necessity to prolong the monitoring of the supervision measures, the competent authority in the executing State may request the competent authority in the issuing State to provide such confirmation, giving it a reasonable time limit to reply to such a request. In case the competent authority in the issuing State does not answer within the time limit concerned, the competent authority in the executing State may send a new request to the competent authority in the issuing State, giving it a reasonable time limit to reply to such a request and indicating that it may decide to stop monitoring the supervision measures if no reply is received within that time limit. Where the competent authority in the executing State does not receive a reply to such a new request within the time limit set, it may act in accordance with paragraph 2.

Article 24: Languages

Certificates shall be translated into the official language or one of the official languages of the executing State. Any Member State may, either when this Framework Decision is adopted or at a later date, state in a declaration deposited with the General Secretariat of the Council that it will accept a translation in one or more other official languages of the Institutions of the European Union.

Article 25: Costs

Costs resulting from the application of this Framework Decision shall be borne by the executing State, except for costs arising exclusively within the territory of the issuing State.

Article 26: Relation to other agreements and arrangements

1. In so far as such agreements or arrangements allow the objectives of this Framework Decision to be extended or enlarged and help to simplify or facilitate further the mutual recognition of decisions on supervision measures, Member States may:
   (a) continue to apply bilateral or multilateral agreements or arrangements in force when this Framework Decision enters into force;
   (b) conclude bilateral or multilateral agreements or arrangements after this Framework Decision has entered into force.

2. The agreements and arrangements referred to in paragraph 1 shall in no case affect relations with Member States which are not parties to them.

3. Member States shall, by 1 March 2010, notify the Commission and the Council of the existing agreements and arrangements referred to in paragraph 1(a) which they wish to continue applying.

4. Member States shall also notify the Commission and the Council of any new agreement or arrangement as referred to in paragraph 1(b), within three months of signing any such arrangement or agreement.

Article 27: Implementation

1. Member States shall take the necessary measures to comply with the provisions of this Framework Decision by 1 December 2012.

2. By the same date Member States shall transmit to the Council and to the Commission the text of the provisions transposing into their national law the obligations imposed on them under this Framework Decision.

Article 28: Report

1. By 1 December 2013 the Commission shall draw up a report on the basis of the information received from Member States under Article 27(2).

2. On the basis of this report, the Council shall assess:
   (a) the extent to which the Member States have taken the necessary measures in order to comply with this Framework Decision; and
   (b) the application of this Framework Decision.

3. The report shall be accompanied, if necessary, by legislative proposals.

Article 29: Entry into force

This Framework Decision shall enter into force on the 20th day following its publication in the Official Journal of the European Union.

Done at Luxembourg, 23 October 2009.

For the Council

The President

T. Billström

ANNEX I: CERTIFICATE

referred to in Article 10 of Council Framework Decision 2009/829/JHA of 23 October 2009 on the application, between Member States of the European Union, of the principle of mutual recognition to decisions on supervision measures as an alternative to provisional detention

(a) Issuing State:

Executing State:

(b) Authority which issued the decision on supervision measures:

Official name:
Please indicate whether any additional information concerning the decision on supervision measures is to be obtained from:
   _ the authority specified above
   _ the central authority; if you ticked this box, please provide the official name of this central authority:
   _ another competent authority; if you ticked this box, please provide the official name of this authority:

Contact details of the issuing authority/central authority/other competent authority
Address:
Tel. No: (country code) (area/city code)
Fax No: (country code) (area/city code)
Details of the person(s) to be contacted
Surname:
Forename(s):
Position (title/grade):
Tel. No: (country code) (area/city code)
Fax No: (country code) (area/city code)
E-mail (if any):
Languages that may be used for communication:

(c) Please indicate which authority is to be contacted if any additional information is to be obtained for the purposes of monitoring the supervision measures:
 _ the authority referred to in point (b)
 _ another authority; if you ticked this box, please provide the official name of this authority:

Contact details of the authority, if this information has not yet been provided under point (b)
Address:
Tel. No: (country code) (area/city code)
Fax No: (country code) (area/city code)
Details of the person(s) to be contacted
Surname:
Forename(s):
Position (title/grade):
Tel. No: (country code) (area/city code)
Fax No: (country code) (area/city code)
E-mail (if any):
Languages that may be used for communication:

(d) Information regarding the natural person in respect of whom the decision on supervision measures has been issued:
Surname:
Forename(s):
Maiden name, where applicable:
Aliases, where applicable:
Sex:
Nationality:
Identity number or social security number (if any):
Date of birth:
Place of birth:
Addresses/residences:
 – in the issuing State:
 – in the executing State:
 – elsewhere:
Language(s) understood (if known):

If available, please provide the following information:
- Type and number of the identity document(s) of the person (ID card, passport):
- Type and number of the residence permit of the person in the executing State:

(e) Information regarding the Member State to which the decision on supervision measures, together with the certificate are being forwarded
The decision on supervision measures, together with the certificate are being forwarded to the executing State indicated in point (a) for the following reason:
- the person concerned has his/her lawful and ordinary residence in the executing State and, having been informed about the measures concerned, consents to return to that State
- the person concerned has requested to forward the decision on supervision measures to the Member State other than that in which the person is lawfully and ordinarily residing, for the following reason(s):

(f) Indications regarding the decision on supervision measures:
The decision was issued on (date: DD-MM-YYYY):
The decision became enforceable on (date: DD-MM-YYYY):
If, at the time of transmission of this certificate, a legal remedy has been introduced against the decision on supervision measures, please tick this box ... _
File reference of the decision (if available):
The person concerned was in provisional detention during the following period (where applicable):
1. The decision covers in total: ... alleged offences.
   Summary of the facts and description of the circumstances in which the alleged offence(s) was (were) committed, including the time and place, and the nature of the involvement of the person concerned:
   Nature and legal classification of the alleged offence(s) and applicable statutory provisions on the basis of which the decision was issued:
2. If the alleged offence(s) referred to in point 1 constitute(s) one or more of the following offences, as defined in the law of the issuing State which are punishable in the issuing State by a custodial sentence or measure involving deprivation of liberty of a maximum of at least three years, please confirm by ticking the relevant box(es):
   - participation in a criminal organisation
   - terrorism
   - trafficking in human beings
   - sexual exploitation of children and child pornography
   - illicit trafficking in narcotic drugs and psychotropic substances
   - illicit trafficking in weapons, munitions and explosives
   - corruption
   - fraud, including that affecting the financial interests of the European Communities within the meaning of the Convention of 26 July 1995 on the protection of the European Communities' financial interests
   - laundering of the proceeds of crime
   - counterfeiting of currency, including the euro
   - computer-related crime

- environmental crime, including illicit trafficking in endangered animal species and in endangered plant species and varieties
- facilitation of unauthorised entry and residence
- murder, grievous bodily injury
- illicit trade in human organs and tissue
- kidnapping, illegal restraint and hostage-taking
- racism and xenophobia
- organised or armed robbery
- illicit trafficking in cultural goods, including antiques and works of art
- swindling
- racketeering and extortion
- counterfeiting and piracy of products
- forgery of administrative documents and trafficking therein
- forgery of means of payment
- illicit trafficking in hormonal substances and other growth promoters
- illicit trafficking in nuclear or radioactive materials
- trafficking in stolen vehicles
- rape
- arson
- crimes within the jurisdiction of the International Criminal Court
- unlawful seizure of aircraft/ships
- sabotage

3. To the extent that the alleged offence(s) identified under point 1 is (are) not covered by point 2 or if the decision, as well as the certificate are forwarded to a Member State, which has declared that it will verify the double criminality (Article 14(4) of the Framework Decision), please give a full description of the alleged offence(s) concerned:

(g) Indications regarding the duration and nature of the supervision measure(s)

1. Length of time to which the decision on supervision measures applies and whether a renewal of this decision is possible (where applicable):

2. Provisional length of time for which the monitoring of the supervision measures is likely to be needed, taking into account all the circumstances of the case that are known when the decision on supervision measures is forwarded (indicative information)

3. Nature of the supervision measure(s)(it is possible to tick multiple boxes):
   - an obligation for the person to inform the competent authority in the executing State of any change of residence, in particular for the purpose of receiving a summons to attend a hearing or a trial in the course of criminal proceedings;
   - an obligation not to enter certain localities, places or defined areas in the issuing or executing State;
   - an obligation to remain at a specified place, where applicable during specified times;
   - an obligation containing limitations on leaving the territory of the executing State;

- an obligation to report at specified times to a specific authority;
- an obligation to avoid contact with specific persons in relation with the offence(s) allegedly committed;
- other measures that the executing State is prepared to supervise in accordance with a notification under Article 8(2) of the Framework Decision:

If you ticked the box regarding 'other measures', please specify which measure is concerned by ticking the appropriate box(es):

- an obligation not to engage in specified activities in relation with the offence(s) allegedly committed, which may include involvement in a specified profession or field of employment;
- an obligation not to drive a vehicle;
- an obligation to deposit a certain sum of money or to give another type of guarantee, which may either be provided through a specified number of instalments or entirely at once;
- an obligation to undergo therapeutic treatment or treatment for addiction;
- an obligation to avoid contact with specific objects in relation with the offence(s) allegedly committed;
- other measure (please specify):

4. Please provide a detailed description of the supervision measure(s) indicated under 3:

(h) Other circumstances relevant to the case, including specific reasons for the imposition of the supervision measure(s) (optional information):
The text of the decision is attached to the certificate.
Signature of the authority issuing the certificate and/or of its representative to confirm the accuracy of the content of the certificate:
Name:
Position (title/grade):
Date:
File reference (if any):
(Where appropriate) Official stamp:

ANNEX II: FORM

referred to in Article 19 of Council Framework Decision 2009/829/JHA of 23 October 2009 on the application, between Member States of the European Union, of the principle of mutual recognition to decisions on supervision measures as an alternative to provisional detention

REPORT OF A BREACH OF A SUPERVISION MEASURE AND/OR ANY OTHER FINDINGS WHICH COULD RESULT IN TAKING ANY SUBSEQUENT DECISION

(a) Details of the identity of the person subject to supervision:
Surname:
Forename(s):
Maiden name, where applicable:
Aliases, where applicable:
Sex:

Nationality:
Identity number or social security number (if any):
Date of birth:
Place of birth:
Address:
Language(s) understood (if known):

(b) Details of the decision on supervision measure(s):
Decision issued on:
File reference (if any):
Authority which issued the decision
Official name:
Address:
Certificate issued on:
Authority which issued the certificate:
File reference (if any):

(c) Details of the authority responsible for monitoring the supervision measure(s):
Official name of the authority:
Name of the person to be contacted:
Position (title/grade):
Address:
Tel. (country code) (area code)
Fax (country code) (area code)
E-mail:
Languages that may be used for communication:

(d) Breach of supervision measure(s) and/or other findings which could result in taking any subsequent decision:

The person referred to in (a) is in breach of the following supervision measure(s):
- an obligation for the person to inform the competent authority in the executing State of any change of residence, in particular for the purpose of receiving a summons to attend a hearing or a trial in the course of criminal proceedings;
- an obligation not to enter certain localities, places or defined areas in the issuing or executing State;
- an obligation to remain at a specified place, where applicable during specified times;
- an obligation containing limitations on leaving the territory of the executing State;
- an obligation to report at specified times to a specific authority;
- an obligation to avoid contact with specific persons in relation with the offence(s) allegedly committed.
- other measures (please specify):

Description of the breach(es) (place, date and specific circumstances):
- other findings which could result in taking any subsequent decision

Description of the findings:

(e) Details of the person to be contacted if additional information is to be obtained concerning the breach:

> Surname:
> Forename(s):
> Address:
> Tel. No: (country code) (area/city code)
> Fax No: (country code) (area/city code)
> E-mail:
> Languages that may be used for communication:
> Signature of the authority issuing the form and/or its representative, to confirm that the contents of the form are correct:
> Name:
> Position (title/grade):
> Date:
> Official stamp (where applicable):

DECLARATION BY GERMANY:

'The Federal Republic of Germany hereby gives notification, pursuant to Article 14(4) of the Council Framework Decision on the application of the principle of mutual recognition to decisions on supervision measures as an alternative to provisional detention, that it will not apply Article 14(1) in respect of all of the offences referred to in that paragraph.'

This declaration will be published in the Official Journal of the European Union.

DECLARATION BY POLAND:

'Pursuant to Article 14(4) of the EU Council Framework Decision on the application, between Member States of the European Union, of the principle of mutual recognition to decisions on supervision measures as an alternative to provisional detention, the Republic of Poland declares that it will not apply paragraph (1) of the aforementioned Article 14 in respect of all of the offences referred to in that paragraph.'

This declaration will be published in the Official Journal of the European Union.

DECLARATION BY HUNGARY:

'Pursuant to Article 14(4) of the EU Council Framework Decision on the application, between Member States of the European Union, of the principle of mutual recognition to decisions on supervision measures as an alternative to provisional detention, the Republic of Hungary declares that it will not apply paragraph (1) of Article 14 of the above Framework Decision in respect of the offences referred to in that paragraph.'

This declaration will be published in the Official Journal of the European Union.

Referring to the 'constitutional reasons' mentioned in Article 14(4), Hungary provided the following explanation:

'Following the ratification of the Lisbon Treaty, Hungary amended its Constitution in order to comply with the obligations referred to therein, including the necessity not to apply the double criminality condition in criminal matters. This constitutional provision will enter into force at the same time as the Lisbon Treaty. Nevertheless, until the entry into force of the Treaty, double criminality remains an important constitutional issue and – as a constitutional principle enshrined by Article 57 of the Constitution – cannot be, shall not be disregarded. Therefore, Article 14(1) of the Framework Decision shall not be applied to any of the offences listed (or as formulated by the relevant article: shall not be applied "in respect of all of the offences").'

DECLARATION BY LITHUANIA:

'Pursuant to Article 14(4) of the Council Framework Decision on the application, between Member States of the European Union, of the principle of mutual recognition to decisions on supervision measures as an alternative to provisional detention, the Republic of Lithuania declares that for constitutional reasons it will not apply Article 14(1) in respect of any of the offences referred to therein.'

This declaration will be published in the Official Journal of the European Union.